Bernie Schotte
Headquarters
The Christian and Missionary Alliance
New York, New York
D1459958
THE CHRISTIAN AND
MISSIONARY ALLIANCE

ALL FOR JESUS

Dr. and Mrs. Albert B. Simpson in the midyears of their ministry

The inscription "All for Jesus" under Dr. Simpson in the original photo was too faded for reproduction.

All for Jesus

How can my heart the world refuse,
Content my earthly all to lose,
That I the better part may choose?
  I do it all for Jesus.

How can I meekly suffer wrong,
With patience sweet, and courage strong,
Repeating still my happy song?
  I do it all for Jesus.

How can I seek and save the lost,
The souls forlorn and tempest-tossed,
Regarding not the hardest cost?
  I do it all for Jesus.

—Albert B. Simpson
from *Millennium Times,* 1894

ALL FOR JESUS

God at Work in The Christian and Missionary Alliance Over One Hundred Years

ROBERT L. NIKLAUS

JOHN S. SAWIN

SAMUEL J. STOESZ

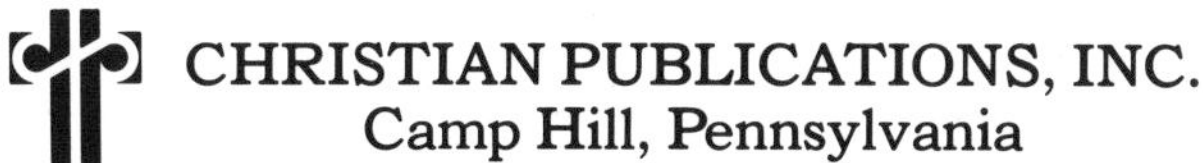
CHRISTIAN PUBLICATIONS, INC.
Camp Hill, Pennsylvania

Unless otherwise noted, Scripture quotations are from the New International Version.

ISBN 0-87509-383-3

LOC Catalog Card Number 86-72007

Printed in the United States of America.

Preface

History has a long record of being helpful. We are, in part, the product of our history. Understanding our past helps us to understand ourselves. Knowing where we came from helps us to know where we are going.

Joshua, successor to Moses and leader of Israel, appreciated the value of history. On one occasion he chose twelve men, one from each of the tribes, and had them take up twelve stones from the Jordan River to erect a rustic monument.

Joshua then explained, "In the future when your descendants ask their fathers, 'What do these stones mean?' tell them, 'Israel crossed the Jordan on dry ground. For the Lord your God dried up the Jordan before you until you had crossed over. The Lord your God did to the Jordan just what he had done to the Red Sea when he dried it up before us until we had crossed over. He did this so that all the peoples of the earth might know that the hand of the Lord is powerful and so that you might always fear the Lord your God'" (Joshua 4:21-24).

Even profit-conscious corporations in today's highly competitive business world, like AT&T and General Motors, finance expensive studies of their origins because they appreciate the value of corporate history. "The present is a moment in the past's trajectory into the future," they say. By knowing their company's past, managers can plan better for the future, employees can cope better with the present, and everyone can relate better to one another and work within the corporation.

The Christian and Missionary Alliance needs to look at its religious heritage in the same positive manner. The centennial celebration of the Alliance in 1987 provides a natural vantage point for looking back, so we can look ahead with clearer vision.

Reviewing the past 100 years will accomplish something else pleasing to the Lord: It will encourage a spirit of gratitude and appreciation for what He has done. The psalmist speaks for us all: "The boundary lines have fallen for me in pleasant places; surely I have a delightful inheritance" (Psalm 16:6).

Some people merit special recognition for making possible this historical narrative of the Alliance. Rev. John S. Sawin, who researched and wrote the first draft for the period 1843-1919, brings to his record of the movement's early period a wide range of service as an evangelist, pastor and missionary for forty years. For the last six years before retirement in 1981, he served as archivist and librarian of the A. B. Simpson Historical Library in Nyack, New York.

Dr. Samuel J. Stoesz, who researched and wrote drafts for the period 1920-1987, is currently professor of pastoral studies at Canadian Theological Seminary in Regina, Saskatchewan, Canada. In addition to serving Alliance pastorates in the Midwest and East, he was managing editor of Christian Publications, Inc., for five years. He authored *Understanding My Church,* a broad history of the Christian church with specific reference to the C&MA.

Rev. Robert L. Niklaus, coordinator and principal writer of the book, has been involved in writing and editing since 1958, when he was an Alliance missionary in Zaire and later involved with various publications in the United States, including *The Alliance Witness* for eight years. He supervised the preparation of all material for the history, did additional research and then rewrote both sections with consummate literary skill in order to integrate them into one cohesive narrative.

Woneta Sawin and Wanda Stoesz performed valuable service in this project by helping to research material, typing the several thousand pages of manuscripts and notes, and otherwise encouraging their husbands in this difficult assignment.

Carolyn Bush and Sharon McLean compiled material for "The Founder's Team."

Credit goes to Anne Moore for the excellent cover design and layout of photographs throughout the book.

We are also grateful to members of the review committee who spent many hours in reading and discussing the various drafts of this book. They are: Dr. Paul F. Bubna, Rev. Richard Bush, Rev. James A. Davey, Dr. Frank E. Farrell, Dr. David K. Huttar, Rev. Ronald H. Julian and Dr. Harold P. Shelly.

In addition, members of a larger committee read the material and contributed comments in writing. They are: Anita Bailey and June Smith, Dr. Gordon M. Cathey, Rev. H. Robert Cowles, Merlin C. Feather, Dr. Gilbert H. Johnson, Dr. Bill Lanpher, Dr. Gerald E. McGraw, June Moline, Lindsay Reynolds, Rev. Arni Shareski and Rev. Joseph M. Tewinkel.

The following provided valuable research assistance: Dr. Ernest G. Wilson, Shirley Woods, Michael Jaarsma and Janis Keys.

Louis L. King, President
The Christian and Missionary Alliance

Contents

Redirection 1912—1936

Acceleration 1936—1987

Appendices

Introduction

Movement or Memory?

One man's work becomes a movement that goes far beyond his worthy efforts and grows unchecked by his passing from the scene.

Another man's accomplishments of equal worth do not long outlive his days, shrinking to a brief mention in the footnotes of history.

What makes the difference between a movement and a memory?

One man, for example, was a sensitive leader compelled by compassion and vision in great measure. He saw crowds of pathetic invalids beyond the skill of medical science. He brought to them both hope and deliverance by proclaiming a gospel of healing, by opening a retreat center where the sick could quietly ponder the greatness of God and experience His renewing power, by compiling testimonies of divine healing so others could also believe and be healed by God's power.

He was a godly man who knew many of God's children did not live up to their spiritual potential. So he conducted summer camps and winter conventions focused on the deeper life of faith. He initiated among some largehearted, like-minded believers a fellowship that eventually became a local church.

He was a dynamic innovator who could not live quietly in a world impoverished through ignorance concerning the will and ways of God. Seeing that traditional denominations showed little concern, he founded the nation's first Bible school to train laymen for ministry. He then sent them off to the mission field. The same compulsion gave birth to missions for blacks in the South and for Chinese in California.

Who was this remarkable man? Dr. Charles Cullis, a medical doctor and Episcopalian layman in Boston.

Dr. Cullis was a contemporary of Dr. Albert B. Simpson. He lived in the same social, political and religious time frame of the late nineteenth century. His achievements paralleled in remarkable detail what Dr. Simpson did and saw materialize into The Christian and Missionary Alliance, a movement that after one century still has more to look forward to than back on.

Yet the church, retreat center, Bible school and missions Cullis founded have long disappeared. His work lies recorded in the yellowing pages of a book few people read. He himself moved to the land where God rewards His own though all others forget.

The Lasting Difference

What made the lasting difference between the ongoing movement of Dr. Simpson and the fading memory of Dr. Cullis? Was it a difference in the choice of coworkers, enlisted more wisely by one man than the other? Was it a difference in time span, since one lived longer than the other and therefore had more time in which to insure continuity? Was it a difference in message, whereby one centered his teaching more fully on the eternal Christ?

Comparisons are oftentimes as unfair as they are odious, especially when they concern the legacy of godly men and women. It is far better simply to say that when all else has been considered, there still remains the mystery of sovereignty as God allows one man's work to make history and another man's work to become history.

The comparison, however, does allow a fundamental lesson for the spiritual heirs of Dr. Simpson: God in sovereign pleasure brought the Alliance into being for a purpose that has continuing validity.

The work that began in one man's heart has grown into one of the more significant missionary forces of modern church history, while in North America its impact grows by the year.

Statement of Purpose

This history attempts to show how God used many people to make the Alliance what it is. Yet one man towers above all others. Dr. Harry M. Shuman, fourth president of the C&MA, accurately noted, "To Dr. A. B. Simpson must go the chief honor, for he was the instrument used of God to bring into evidence this missionary movement through which have flowed streams of blessing to the whole world."

The first three chapters of the account therefore concentrate on the life and ministry of Dr. Simpson—in that order of priority. The remaining chapters deal with the global impact of the movement he founded.

Dr. Simpson was totally committed to the principle that the quality of spiritual life must be the first priority of the believer. Jesus Christ became the source from which the Alliance founder's ministry flowed freely and effectively.

Christians, however, were not to mature and minister independently of one another. He viewed the church as essential in God's plan, both for the individual and the world. In a published sermon titled "The New Testament Pattern of Missions," Dr. Simpson recognized that the church of Jesus Christ has a definite pattern discernible in the New Testament.

"This house has a divine pattern," he wrote. "Just as the tabernacle of old was to be constructed strictly according to the pattern that was shown to Moses on the Mount, so the Church of Christ has a divine plan, and should be in every particular constructed accordingly.

"The failure to do this has been the cause of all apostasies, declensions and mistakes of the past eighteen centuries, and is the reason that the heathen world is still lying in darkness and crying to God against the unfaithfulness of His people."

Dr. Simpson had hoped initially to be a catalyst used of God to move the already existing churches back toward that divine plan. When his deeper-life and missions conferences fell short of widespread response, he found himself the reluctant founder not only of a missionary movement but also of a fellowship of Christians that has increasingly assumed the patterns evident in New Testament churches.

Therefore the common thread running through this history is how The Christian and Missionary Alliance was providentially led to become a dynamic body of New Testament-type churches giving preeminence to Jesus Christ in personal experience and universal witness, especially in neglected areas and among unreached peoples.

Recognizing this common thread throughout their history will help Alliance people better perceive who they are, why they are here and where they are going. Moreover, that understanding by Alliance people ought to be well seasoned with humility, for the future will be as promising as the measure of their faithfulness to the calling given by God.

That measure of faithfulness may be succinctly summed up in the simple phrase that characterized the life of Albert B. Simpson and summarized his prayer for the Alliance: All for Jesus.

PART ONE

FORMULATION

1873—1881

CHAPTER 1

The Louisville Experience

Ideals that mock us can, with God's help, become realities.

1873—1879

Context of the Times

The American Civil War was now a memory, but still a fresh one. Over 2.5 million men marched off to fight for the ideals of the North or South. One in every four did not come home.

Reconstruction of the defeated South, dictated in the harsh terms of the victors, reinforced the tragic maxim of history: Wars are more easily won than peace. The Union's generous president was assassinated, and into the vacuum of leadership stepped self-appointed executors of divine vengeance. The Confederacy's hero, General Robert E. Lee, was still honored by the majority of southerners, but some chose to follow another of their heroes: General Nathan Bedford Forrest, Grand Wizard of the Ku Klux Klan.

Religion should have made a difference. Between 100,000 and 200,000 soldiers of the grey or blue turned wholeheartedly to God on the sobering terrain of the battlefront; countless others were deeply affected. But while the foot soldiers prayed, some of their religious leaders deepened the wound of a nation divided through their sanctimonious and unforgiving rhetoric.

Yet while men persisted in their anger, God proved more enduring in His grace.

The Laymen's Revival, which began in a noon prayer meeting for New York businessmen, began shortly before the civil strife and continued through the war years to permeate and vitalize many churches.

William E. Boardman's book on sanctification, *The Higher Christian*

Life, appeared in numerous and large editions. (One publisher reported 60,000 copies sold by 1875.)

And in an unpublicized event of 1873, two little-known men quietly embarked for England: Dwight L. Moody and Ira Sankey. Before the year was out, the Moody/Sankey team had sparked something of a national revival in Scotland. During their two years in the British Isles, they preached and sang to over 3 million people. Returning home in 1875, they became national heroes and launched mass evangelistic campaigns that became a hallmark of religion in the latter years of the century.

The revival of evangelism for the masses and holiness for the believers thus answered the hollow echoes of the Civil War.

* * *

In those days a young Canadian pastor crossed the border enroute to a parish in Kentucky. He had no idea of the large role he would soon play in this movement of spiritual awakening.

THE YOUTHFUL CANADIAN MINISTER heading south to an American pastorate in the wintery close of 1873 seemed to have everything going for him.

In appearance he was a winner: his movements decisive, yet graceful; his pale but strong features and sensitive dark eyes denoted a maturity beyond his years. He was a man people instinctively trusted.

That trust was not misplaced. Although only age thirty, Albert Benjamin Simpson had already accomplished the difficult task of successful ministry in his home province of Ontario, Canada—the rare prophet who did find honor in his own country.

Fresh out of seminary in 1865, he had accepted the call to pastor Knox Church in Hamilton, a congregation with the dubious distinction of owning the second largest Presbyterian church building in Canada and only filling one-quarter of it.

But eight and one-half years later, when Simpson boarded the train for Louisville, Kentucky, to pastor his second church, he treasured vivid memories of his farewell service at Hamilton: a crowded sanctuary and an estimated 500 people turned away; a congregation whose membership listed 750 new people; and an admiring local press that reported "he was second to none in point of eloquence and ability and success in his ministry."[1]

The young pastor carried with him to Louisville another asset to a successful ministry: a lively, attractive family. Margaret Henry

Simpson, as energetic as she was petite (4′11″), had happily supported his ministry in Hamilton and agreed with his choice of Louisville for their next pastorate. Their two boys, Albert Henry and James Gordon Hamilton, and one-year-old daughter Mabel Jane enlivened the long train ride southward.

The prospects before Simpson in the gracious southern city of Louisville in December of 1873 appeared as promising as Hamilton had proven successful.

Members of the prosperous Chestnut Street Presbyterian Church had heard him preach when both he and they were visiting New York City just two months earlier. They had returned home greatly impressed and urged their church, in need of a pastor at the time, to offer him the position.

Investigation by the presbyters revealed that Simpson was an impressive pastor as well as pulpiteer. Perhaps they also had in mind another attractive asset he possessed by birth: his nationality. A neutral Canadian pastor at Chestnut Street Presbyterian, a member church of the Northern Presbyterian denomination, might help ease tensions between their congregation and others in Louisville. The city was still bitterly divided over the recently ended Civil War.

A request by the Louisville church for Simpson's services joined a similar letter of invitation presented to the Hamilton Presbytery when it convened on December 3, 1873. Although the other church was Canadian and may have stirred sentiments of national loyalty, Simpson indicated interest in the Louisville invitation. The presbyters reluctantly released him from his duties in Hamilton.

Had Simpson visited the southern city with its internal conflicts before deciding, he may have had second thoughts, but events would soon confirm the rightness of his choice.

Hidden Liabilities

All the known factors at Louisville indicated the possibility of an even greater ministry than the young pastor had previously known. But while others held great hopes for him, the introspective and sensitive Simpson struggled with personal problems that at times threatened to overwhelm him.

Simpson did not in fact go to Louisville in search of a larger ministry. Poor health dictated that he seek a smaller church that would require less pastoral activity and provide more opportunity for rest. Changing pastorates would also ease his arduous study schedule by permitting the use of previously prepared sermons over which he had labored many hours.

Aware of his physical limitations, the Louisville congregation had agreed to excuse him from all pastoral visitation except for situations of critical need, and to give him two full months of vacation each summer. The promise of an annual income of $5,000 in Louisville—almost twice his salary in Hamilton—could in its own way prove beneficial to his well-being.

The problem of poor health did not begin when Simpson entered the pastorate. While still in high school, he had pursued his studies so relentlessly that his health broke and he was ordered by his physician not to open a book for a whole year.

Later at Knox Church he gave himself so vigorously to the ministry that several times he came close to nervous collapse. Twice the church urged him to take an extended vacation. His physical frame seemed no match for the intensity of his nature and the deep depressions that overtook him.

But of even more serious consequence was Simpson's view of himself as a "blundering and ambitious young preacher."[2] His spiritual life he characterized as a long and vain struggle "with his intense nature, his strong self-will, his peculiar temptations,"[3] a state of the soul that subjected him to constant humiliation and gave a hollow ring to his lofty sermons on holy living.

Reflecting on this period of his life, Simpson later admitted, "I am always ashamed to say it, but it is true that in the years I did not know Christ as an indwelling Spirit in my heart...I seldom had a Christian come to me and say, 'Dear pastor, I want you to tell me how to enter into a deeper Christian life.' I had sinners come because I knew something about forgiveness, so I could preach to them."[4]

This dogged sense of inadequacy pushed him constantly to search for a deeper, more fulfilling spiritual life. But Simpson, though an intelligent and educated clergyman, had some strange ideas that generated a fearful attitude toward holiness. He admitted to regarding sanctification as "the very last thing God did for the soul...and then took it right home"— and he feared to ask for sanctification, lest he die soon after.[5]

Even after accepting sanctification as a totally positive experience of being made holy by God's Spirit, he failed to understand what he was seeking. On one occasion he felt something special in his spirit and remembered, "I held on with a desperate grip for fear I should lose it, and kept awake the whole night fearing it would go."[6]

The feeling, of course, evaporated with the next mood, and he was back in search of something better in his spiritual life. This inner struggle continued through his Hamilton ministry and became part of the spiritual baggage he carried south to Louisville.

The situation Simpson encountered upon arrival in the Bluegrass State's largest city did little to encourage his spirits. Civil War guns had fallen silent, but not the tongues of bitter protagonists on both sides. Churches were torn within themselves and separated one from another. Some ministers had not spoken to each other for ten years.

One writer observed that while the rest of the nation was getting back to normal, the congregations were still fighting the war: "The bitterness between the churches—even churches of the same denomination, distinguished only by that pugnacious countersign, 'North' or 'South'—was chilling the religious life of those cities lying near the line of Mason and Dixon, and freezing every sporadic attempt at revival put forth by any of them. Louisville was a northern city in a southern state, or a southern city in a northern state...and the smouldering animosity between the churches was particularly marked there."[7]

A New Secret

Between his inner struggles and the city's unresolved conflicts, Simpson found himself in the most discouraging situation yet in his ministry. Pressured by this double dilemma, he turned for greater resources to God, who promised to be found by those who sought Him with all their heart.

The search drew him one morning in 1874 to an old, musty book he discovered in his library. Poring over W. E. Boardman's *The Higher Christian Life,*[8] he saw the Lord Jesus in a new light, a living and all-sufficient presence.

"He who had justified us was waiting to sanctify us," Simpson testified, "to enter into our spirit and substitute His strength, His holiness, His joy, His love, His faith, His power, for all our worthlessness, helplessness and nothingness, and make it an actual living fact."[9]

Throwing himself at the feet of that glorious Master, he claimed the promise, "I will dwell in you and walk in you" (2 Corinthians 6:16). Across the threshold of his spirit passed a Person as real as the Christ who came to the Apostle John on the island of Patmos.

From that moment on, he said, a new secret became the charm and glory and strength of his life: "I can do all things through Christ who strengtheneth me" (Philippians 4:13).

During the next forty-plus years of ministry, Simpson would repeatedly refer back to that moment of surrender to Christ as his Sanctifier, the One who alone could make him holy. It was the decisive turning point of his ministry in much the same way as the Apostle Paul looked back upon his conversion experience on the road to Damascus.

He later commented, "I dare not say that every Christian has this Holy Ghost personally welcomed and dominant in his heart. I dare not say that I was not a Christian many years before I knew this, and that I [did not] preach the Gospel for at least ten years before I knew what it was to have a personal Divine Presence living and manifesting His reality in my brain, my affections, my will, my body, my thought, my work—the indwelling Holy Spirit.

"And I am sure He never came to me in that way, as the occupant of my house, until I gave Him the house and became no longer the owner of the house, but a lodger in it, and He the proprietor taking care of me and using me."[10]

The new secret Simpson learned that day did not end his search for spiritual excellence; it merely marked the end of the beginning. He constantly maintained that "sanctification is divine holiness, not human self improvement, nor perfection. It is the inflow into man's being of the life and purity of His own perfection and the working out of His own will."

For this reason he spoke of sanctification being "complete, but not completed; perfect, but not perfected."

Sanctification to Simpson was a heart attitude of ceaseless growth, not instant attainment: "He is the Author and Finisher of our faith, and the true attitude of the consecrated heart is that of a constant yielding and constant receiving. This...gives boundless scope to our spiritual progress. It is here that the gradual phase of sanctification comes in."[11]

This attitude was demonstrated on one occasion shortly after his surrender to the Holy Spirit. He traveled to Chicago to attend one of D. L. Moody's conventions for ministers. He entered a preliminary meeting before Moody was scheduled to speak.

He noted that "one plain, earnest preacher got up with his face all shining. He said, 'I came up here expecting Mr. Moody to help me. But last night I saw Jesus, and I got such a look at Jesus that I am never going to need anything again as long as I live.'

"Something smote my heart," Simpson recalled. "All you need is Jesus; you go to Him."

The young pastor from Louisville did not stay to hear Moody. He took the next train home and went to his office in the church vestry. "I waited there on my face at His blessed feet until He came, and thank God, He enabled me in some measure to say,

I have seen Jesus, and my heart is dead to all beside;
I have seen Jesus, and my wants are all supplied;
I have seen Jesus, and my heart is satisfied,
Satisfied with Jesus."[12]

A City Stirred

Simpson's receiving "the new light of the indwelling Christ and the baptism of the Holy Spirit" soon impacted on Louisville in a measure he had never seen in his earlier ministry. That new light became like a fire in his bones that kept him awake at night, crying out to God for a great revival in the tragically divided city.

The opportunity to do more than pray came when he was invited to preach in various pulpits across the city. His neutrality as a Canadian no doubt opened church doors otherwise barricaded by prejudice. His message to them all: Pray for the coming of the Holy Spirit. Only as reconciliation came to the pastors and revival to their parishoners would the unchurched of Louisville take the Gospel seriously.

The young pastor of Chestnut Street Presbyterian then gathered his fellow clergymen together to pray and discuss the possibility of revival services. It was undoubtedly Simpson who suggested the names of Major D. W. Whittle, evangelist, and Philip P. Bliss, soloist and song leader. He served as link between the evangelistic team and the local churches.

The next step was to organize union mass meetings to pray for revival. The first scheduled series took place on the first week of January, 1875, and may have been helped along by an appeal from the London-based Evangelical Alliance. For several years that international fellowship of evangelicals had encouraged Christians around the world to dedicate the opening week of the new year to prayer.

The Louisville pastors demonstrated a measure of faith by choosing the Walnut Street Baptist Church for the union prayer meetings. It contained the city's largest sanctuary. Even so, they were amazed at the large attendance in the morning and evening meetings, and they decided to add a mass rally on Sunday afternoon.

As often happens, the Spirit of God had already been at work among individual believers, preparing their hearts for reconciliation and renewal. They were waiting for their religious leaders to wake up and show them the way.

A second series of prayer meetings was called for the last week of January and then extended indefinitely because of the popular response. A whole year would pass before they ended.

Great Expectations

By Sunday evening, February 7, 1875, when the evangelistic meetings were to begin, revival had already begun among the churches, and the whole city was stirred. Whittle and Bliss did not arrive in time for the service, so several local pastors, including Simpson, preached to the large crowd that filled the auditorium and gallery of the Public Library Hall.

The problem of space remained throughout the campaign, as every public hall rented could not contain the capacity crowds. Inclement weather—rain, sleet, snow and ice—could not dampen the public's enthusiasm. The meetings had an opposite effect on attendance in bars and amusement places. Businessmen invited Whittle to their offices for counseling. Trains brought crowds of curious visitors and serious seekers as word spread of happenings in Louisville.

The sympathetic local press described progress of the campaign with phrases like "immense congregation...hundreds of seatless listeners...unprecedented attendance...building taxed to the uttermost."

One newspaper reported, "The Gospel tide seems to be rolling on with resistless force and bids fair to spread over this and other states."[13]

Toward the end of the campaign's third week, Whittle was summoned back to Chicago, where his father was dying. Various pastors supporting the meetings took their turn substituting for the evangelist. On Sunday evening Simpson preached to the capacity audience from Luke 14:17, "Come, for all things are ready."

The Monday paper reported, "This discourse, the finest yet delivered in these meetings, produced an effect that partook of the wonderful, as was evident by the rising of three or four hundred persons who desired the prayers of Christian people in their behalf."

The coverage concluded, "It is doubtful if such a marked result as was exhibited last night ever followed a discourse delivered in this city."[14]

The startling response of the audience must have been a deeply moving and novel experience for the young pastor who, until this campaign, by preference had largely restricted himself to his own people and pulpit.

The following Sunday, March 7, people crowded into every church or hall where the Gospel was being preached. In the morning each pastor preached in his own full sanctuary. In the afternoon a mass meeting was held for black people in Glover's Rink and white working-class people filled Liederkranz Hall. Only young men were given tickets to attend the service in the Public Library Hall, but men of all ages crowded in. The service in Macauley Theatre was open to everyone.

Friday, March 12, ended the union meetings with the two evangelists. Prayer meetings took place the entire day as one newspaper reported "ten thousand people at prayer; unprecedented religious enthusiasm."[15] Two mass meetings climaxed the campaign. At the 6:30 service only new converts were to attend, but when the doors were opened for the second service at 7:30, "the surge upstairs carried everybody upwards only to find every seat already occupied. Three thousand souls crowded together in a hopeless tangle and another three thousand were forced to retire."[16]

Following the sermon by Whittle the massive audience rose to sing "All Hail the Power of Jesus' Name." Bliss asked all the pastors identified with the meetings to join hands, and the line extended across the entire stage.

The Christians of Louisville were once again united under the sign of the Cross.

The Afterglow

The elated and enthusiastic pastor of Chestnut Street Presbyterian had no intention of letting the citywide movement toward God lurch to a halt after the campaign finale.

On the concluding night of the campaign he announced that the Sunday-evening mass meetings would continue. His church had already leased the Public Library Hall for this purpose. He may have hoped that other churches would continue in a cooperative effort, but they decided to carry on their efforts individually.

The local press reported on the move to continue public meetings "in view of the widespread desire among the people to hear the Gospel and who do not attend regular churches."[17] Simpson's concern for the unchurched masses, the thousands who felt themselves alienated from the formal church but not from the Lord, was beginning to assert itself—even if it meant acting alone.

The newspaper commented on another move by Simpson that was to prove one of his greatest strengths: "We are glad to know that the object of these services is not denominational and sectarian, but evangelical and catholic; and that the cooperation of all evangelical pastors and churches will be cordially welcomed."[18]

Another event in the week following the Whittle/Bliss campaign may have seemed minor at the time, but it marked a major change in Simpson's ministry. Pastors in Lexington, Kentucky, invited Simpson to conclude a series of evangelistic meetings. Several years earlier in Hamilton he had received a similar invitation from a fellow Presbyterian pastor, but he had refused with some stiff dignity: "I believe in the regular work of the ministry."[19]

In the afterglow of the Louisville campaign, however, and no doubt extremely weary after two months of continuous meetings,

Simpson immediately accepted the Lexington invitation. He even cancelled some weeknight meetings in his own church in order to go. He thus added another dimension to his ministry, one that would loom large in later days: the role of evangelist.

Upon his return to Louisville, Simpson continued his evangelistic efforts weeknights at Chestnut Street Presbyterian and Sunday nights at the Public Library Hall. Crowds attended and hundreds responded to the invitation to believe in Christ.

Black people came to the gallery of the public hall on Sunday nights. This must have pleased the young pastor. During the Whittle/Bliss campaign he had complained publicly that the poor were too embarrassed by lack of good clothes to attend the meetings. He had pleaded for "free seats" for everyone—whether rich or poor, black or white, educated or uneducated. Now, in his own continuing campaign, he made sure everyone was welcome. No doubt he was already laying plans in his mind so that the unchurched would feel even more welcome in his services.

In June of 1875, after fifteen weeks of Sunday evenings in Library Hall, Simpson confined his preaching schedule to the church. One month later the whole Simpson family left for a six-week vacation. Seven months of strenuous and continuous campaign work must have depleted his physical and mental energies. The family as well must have welcomed the respite, having grown tired of the incessant demands that took him from home day and night.

Even Chestnut Street Presbyterian had a vacation of sorts: In Simpson's absence, the supply pastor preached only on Sunday mornings.

A Creeping Chill

Something more than evangelistic momentum may have been lost during the intervening six weeks.

When the pastor returned, the church agreed to resume the Sunday-evening evangelistic services; they met in the privately owned Macaulay Theatre, since the public hall was unavailable. The church had even agreed before the pastor left on vacation to construct a large tabernacle-type structure.

The new building was to seat 2,500 people, a capacity equal to that of the city's public halls. The Chestnut Street sanctuary could only accommodate 650 people, and the church needed more room for the enlarged congregation and the many more they anticipated as the evangelistic services continued.

A divergence of opinion, however, surfaced between the pastor and some influential members of the church. Years later he touched on this development as he reminisced on his experiences in Louisville. He told how he had "received a profound spiritual blessing in the midst of an ambitious and half-consecrated ministry, how the baptism of the Holy Spirit awakened in his heart an intense longing for the salvation of souls and simpler methods of reaching the masses with the Gospel."

But Simpson continued, "After attempting for several years to accomplish this purpose in a fashionable Presbyterian church, during which something was accomplished but much was hindered by the social exclusiveness and the conventional religious methods about him,"[20] he decided it was time to move on.

That situation became apparent in 1875, when as often happens, tensions emerged during the building program.

After the new project was announced, $18,000 was immediately subscribed and a downtown lot purchased on the corner of Broadway and Fourth Avenue. The pastor wanted a plain but large edifice requiring an outlay of $65,000 to $70,000 and ready for occupancy in nine months. Other voices prevailed, however, and the elaborate structure cost $105,000 and took over two years to complete.

Wider Horizons

When Simpson, in 1877, attended the Believers' Conference at Watkins Glen, New York, for physical and spiritual refreshment, he received more than anticipated. Along with teaching on a closer walk with God, messages by speaker after speaker carried a strong missionary challenge. The Louisville pastor was deeply stirred as his burden for the neglected masses expanded to embrace the unreached peoples of the world.

He left the conference and traveled to the Chicago area, where he visited friends and found time to ponder and pray. The messages he had heard combined with strong memories from childhood days.

A. W. Tozer wrote of this particular pattern in Simpson's life: "He would first get an idea, a concept, then must come a heart experience to set it off, to detonate the charge it contained. Until the explosion came, he could wait, sometimes for years, mulling his idea over, half forgetting it, burying it under a mountain of work; then the great day would come and he would be prostrated, almost slain under the impact of that idea, his and yet God's idea, leaping up now, and powerfully compelling as it came out at him like a blast of creative force."[21]

Simpson spoke of what happened next during his visit to Chicago: "I was awakened one night from sleep, trembling with a strange and solemn sense of God's overshadowing power, and on my soul was burning the remembrance of a strange dream through which I had that moment come.

"It seemed to me that I was sitting in a vast auditorium, and millions of people were there sitting around me. All the Christians in the world seemed to be there, and on the platform was a great multitude of faces and forms. They seemed to be mostly Chinese. They were not speaking, but in mute anguish were wringing their hands, and their faces wore an expression that I can never forget.

"I had not been thinking or speaking of the Chinese or the heathen world, but as I awoke with that vision on my mind, I did tremble with the Holy Spirit, and I threw myself on my knees, and every fibre of my being answered, 'Yes, Lord, I will go.' "[22]

The next day he wrote to his wife and asked her to join with him in this wonderful new venture of faith.

Margaret's reply came swift and blunt: "I wrote to him that it was all right—he might go to China himself—and I would remain at home and support and care for the children. I knew that would settle him for a while."[23]

However her refusal may have been viewed by Simpson, Margaret spoke not only the thoughts of a practical woman concerned for her children's welfare and her husband's promising future. She was a restraining voice from the Lord, and her husband did well to listen. His ministry in North America achieved immeasurably more for missions than he might have accomplished in the remote provinces of China.

If not the mission field, then what could he do now to advance this cause he wholeheartedly embraced? He could not be content with mental assent alone.

Simpson surveyed the considerable missions activity in progress on both sides of the Atlantic. Outstanding pioneers like David Livingstone, J. Hudson Taylor and Mary Slessor of Great Britain, Adoniram Judson of the United States, Jonathan and Rosalind Goforth of Canada helped make the 1800s the "Great Century of Missions." John Geddie, the great pioneer missionary whom fellow Canadians ranked with Taylor and Judson, had personally influenced Simpson.

Yet too often missionaries and their sending agencies knew little of what each other was doing. A plan crystallized in Simpson's thoughts—one that seemed impractical or impossible to those he consulted: He proposed publishing an illustrated missionary journal that gathered into its pages the work of missions in all lands.

The project became a driving force in his life. It would loom large in his future planning, drain his finances, break him physically. Yet of his accomplishment, Dr. Harlan P. Beach, professor of missions in Yale University, would say in retrospect, "Do not forget to mention as one of his great achievements the institution of a pictorial review. Dr. Simpson was the first to make the missionary story beautiful and attractive."[24]

Sense of Release

Three thousand people crowded into the Louisville congregation's new Broadway Tabernacle on June 9, 1878, for the first service. But the debt and its cause hung like a dark cloud over the pastor. He refused to dedicate the elegant edifice and rejected any further salary until the debt was liquidated.

In his remarks during the service, Simpson made it clear that a church building, whatever its design, served the supreme, single purpose of bringing within its walls "the great masses of every social condition who attend no other church and practically know no God."[25]

The issue did not divide the pastor and his people. Relations continued cordial, but they were not the same as during the momentous days of the Whittle/Bliss campaign and the church-sponsored popular meetings that followed. The pastor began to sense in his spirit a release from the Louisville ministry. In another eighteen months he would move on.

Simpson would return two years later to help dedicate the debt-free structure. And in another two months the beautiful edifice would be completely destroyed by fire.

New Directions

Simpson's ministry in Louisville determined the course of the rest of his life. Almost every major aspect of his message, his ministry and the movement he founded can be traced to his experiences while pastor of Chestnut Street Presbyterian.

Seeing Christ in a new light through the Holy Spirit's filling his life, he was impelled to work for revival in the bitterly divided city. The dramatic awakening that followed profoundly altered his attitude toward the ministry and the church's role in the world.

To his calling as minister he added the call to evangelism. To his view of the formal church he added the nondenominational tabernacle. To his parish of prosperous members he added the masses of poor and unchurched. To his vision of witness he added the world.

The deeply respected and beloved pastor bid farewell to his Louisville pastorate in November of 1879, just one month shy of six years after he left Hamilton, Ontario. In both cities he stood out among his clergy peers as a man marked by God for even greater achievements.

He had come a long way from the sparsely settled farmlands of western Ontario, but in a sense, the greater he grew in stature the more he owed to a godly home and heritage.

CHAPTER 2

Foundation Years

The child when grown leaves home, but not its influence.

1843—1873

Context of the Times

In the 1980 presidential election year, people talked about the "Year of the Evangelicals," as if it were some freakish turn of events that dragged Christians into the mainstream of national life.

Some historians, however, speak of the entire nineteenth century as "The Evangelical Age." The 1800s seemed dominated by great religious movements and populated by spiritual giants. (*Evangelical* refers to commonly held beliefs such as the divine inspiration and authority of the Bible, the sovereignty of God, the imperative of the new birth and accountability of individuals for their actions, and the necessity of personal holiness.)

"The Second Great Awakening" in the early 1800s followed an earlier sweeping revival of the mid-1700s. Just when the second wave seemed to ebb in midcentury, "The Laymen's Revival" began in the Fulton Street midday prayer meetings for business people in New York City and spread throughout the United States and Canada.

England and North America still bear the imprint of outstanding evangelical leaders of the 1800s.

William E. Gladstone, an evangelical Christian and several times prime minister of Great Britain, led an entire nation. George Williams founded the strongly evangelistic YMCA. Catherine and William Booth mobilized the Salvation Army. George Mueller seemed to have inexhaustible resources of faith to care for his thousands of orphans. J. Hudson Taylor founded the China Inland Mission.

The Evangelical Alliance emerged in London in 1846 to unite Christians—but not churches or denominations—in promoting religious liberty, missions and other common interests. The alliance quickly spread to North America, Germany and other countries. It would later become the World Evangelical Fellowship.

In the early 1800s Methodist circuit riders and camp meetings spread the evangelical Gospel through the small towns, farming communities and frontier territories that formed America's backbone and soul.

Charles G. Finney took the frontier camp meetings to cities of the Northeast, appealing for personal, public responses from his vast audiences. His use of camp-meeting methods to call Christians to a second crisis of faith leading to holiness established the pattern of revivalism for years to come.

* * *

Much of the ferment and fervor of "The Evangelical Age" must have seemed a remote din and a bit strange to the staunchly conservative homestead of James Simpson in the farmlands of western Ontario. Yet from that home would come a man of God not only deeply influenced by the spiritual dynamics of his day, but one who in turn would become an eloquent spokesman of the movement impacting on his generation.

LOOKING BACK on those early influences," Simpson wrote in an autobiographical note, "I cannot say I wholly regret the somewhat stern mould in which my early life was shaped. It taught me a spirit of reverence and wholesome discipline for which I have often had cause to thank God....

"The religious knowledge, which was crammed into my head without my understanding it, furnished me with forms of doctrine and statements of truth which afterwards became illuminated by the Holy Spirit and realized in my own experience."[1]

That "somewhat stern mould" of Covenanter Presbyterianism was forged in steel and fire. During the 1600s, English dragoons scoured the Scottish Highlands to force dissenters into the official Church of England or make them die for their faith. All the soldiers succeeded in doing was to further deepen the Covenanters' commitment to their faith.

When some of the Simpson clan emigrated from Scotland to Canada in 1775, they brought along their rugged, severe beliefs. The fierce winters and plain settlements on Prince Edward Is-

The Simpson homestead in Chatham, Ontario

Albert Benjamin Simpson at age seventeen
when entering Knox College

Margaret Henry Simpson during Hamilton, Ontario years

Rev. and Mrs. A.B. Simpson at the time of their Hamilton pastorate

Sophie "the Scrubwoman" Lichtenfels

Sarah G. Beck

The New York Gospel Tabernacle of the 1940s remained in appearance much as it was during the days of its founder and first pastor, Dr. Simpson

"THE CONGO CLASS," 1895-1896

Top row to left of banner, left to right: N. E. P. Millar, C. A. McKinney, F. Sodaborg, A. H. Jamieson. *Second row; H. Hess, R. C. Haime, H. P. Schilde, S. S. Grey, A. P. Woodcock. Third row;* A. H. Hess, L. Collins, L. Villars, M. Kohm, L. S. Gardner. *Seated:* R. Dixon.

Top row to right of banner, left to right: W. A. Cramer, James McKee, A. J. Stevenson, J. C. Green. *Second row:* N. W. Macomber, E. B. Nichols, Thomas Luttit, W. J. Roth. *Third row:* Mrs. E. G. Stanley, Mr. E. B. Stanley, D. Houghtly. *Fourth row:* L. A. Samson, W. Wilmat, M. Shuman.

One of the earliest graduating classes of the Missionary Training College in New York

Beulah Beach (Ohio) youth pavilion

Mahaffey Camp (Pennsylvania) dining hall

Canby Camp (Oregon) tabernacle

land insured that their religion did not grow soft and comfortable.

Yet Albert Benjamin Simpson was not born into a dour home and bleak circumstances. The parents, James and Jane Simpson, furnished their home in Bayview, Prince Edward Island, with every necessity, including faith and love in generous measure.

Already the fourth child when he arrived on December 15, 1843, Albert knew from the start the acceptance that makes for wholesome character. The family eventually numbered five children, not counting another four who died at birth or in early childhood.

James Simpson prospered as a shipbuilder, exporter and importer on the island until a financial depression forced him to sell the business and move to the mainland. At Chatham, western Ontario, he planned to enter a partnership in shipbuilding, but an epidemic in town forced another move. The loss of their little Margaret, one of many children who died in Chatham, filled Jane Simpson with fear she would lose all their children if they stayed in town.

Also deeply shaken, James purchased a log cabin and farmland nine miles out in the countryside. The move brought hardship to him because he was a carpenter, not a farmer. But James converted the cabin into a comfortable home furnished with beautiful walnut furniture made by his own hands, and did what he could with the land.

Years later Albert's sister Louise spoke lovingly of their father. She said that in all the time she knew him, until he died at age eighty-five, she had never once seen him lose his temper or say an unkind word, though she often saw him deeply hurt by others.

When James, another brother, stood by her at their father's coffin, she heard him say almost enviously, "There lies a man who never wronged his fellow."[2]

If the move from town to countryside proved hard on James, it doubled in hardship for Jane. Well bred and well-to-do, daughter of Prince Edward Island's legislator for many years, she enjoyed the company of creative people and sociable surroundings. Sensitive, poetic and high spirited, she suffered at times on the lonely farm, like a prisoner in solitary confinement.

Albert's earliest childhood recollection was "of my mother as I often heard her in the dark and lonely nights weeping in her room; and I still remember how I used to rise and kneel beside my little bed, even before I knew God for myself, and pray for Him to comfort her."[3]

Whatever her private griefs and broken dreams, Jane Simpson saw to her family's needs in a loving and selfless manner. Albert's appreciation for books and natural beauty he traced to his vibrantly alive mother.

Stern Religion

Jane quietly dedicated their infant son Albert to the Lord for whatever purpose He should choose, whether minister or missionary. She did not speak of it to her son, lest in later years he be unduly influenced in a decision that was not of God.

Rev. John Geddie, on his way to the South Sea Islands as Canada's first missionary, baptized the baby and in prayer committed him to missionary service. When on furlough twenty-one years later, he would visit Simpson to remind him of that prayer consecrating him to the Christian ministry.

Religion in the Simpson home followed the strictest Puritan code. Each Sunday the family, soberly attired, rode the nine miles to church in a rattling wagon. On the rare occasion they were unable to attend services, the family gathered in the sitting room, where for hours on end one or another read from such ponderous works as Baxter's *Saints' Rest* and Dodderidge's *Rise and Progress of Religion in the Soul.*

On Sunday afternoon the children stood in a row to answer questions from the Shorter Catechism. By covering several questions each week they finished all the approximately 150 questions in a year's time—and promptly started over again.

The remainder of the Sabbath was to be spent in solemn meditation. Failure to do so brought punishment—sure, but not swift. Even that was deferred until Monday, since administering a whipping was considered breaking the Sabbath.

One Sunday afternoon, however, the sun shone too warmly and all nature seemed to join in a conspiracy to lure a restless young Albert outdoors: "I ventured to slip out of the house and was unfortunately seen by my father while scampering 'round the yard in the joy of my ungodly liberty," he later recalled.[4]

He was summoned back to the house and told with great solemnity that he would be justly punished the first thing on Monday morning. He got the whipping, and afterward his older brother Howard took him aside for some advice on how to escape the punishment on another occasion.

Simpson admitted years later, "I am sorry to say that my heart was as yet sufficiently unsanctified to take the hint, and sure enough one morning when a whipping was coming to me, I stole out of my bed and sat down with a very demure and solemn face to practice my pretended devotions.

"I can still see my quiet and silent father sitting at the table and casting side glances at me from under his spectacles as though to make quite sure that I was truly in earnest. After finishing his devotions, he quietly slipped away to his work, and nothing more was said about the chastisement."[5]

The strict Sabbath laws and young Albert's sham devotions suggest that religious influence in the home was building walls, not bridges, in his attitude toward God. His father's sternly devout life as a Presbyterian elder of the old school, his relentless drilling of the children in the Shorter Catechism, his religious habits that seemed to grant no quarter to humor or the happier side of life, adversely affected his timid, impressionable son. There seemed slim hope of drawing close to a heavenly Father cast to the degree of perfection in the image of his earthly father.

A vivid childhood recollection seemed to epitomize the effect on him of his father's faith: "I can still see him rising long before daylight, sitting down with his lighted candle in the family room, tarrying long at his morning devotion."[6] The mental image filled him with awe and magnified the distance felt between a son and his father, a boy and his God.

Young Simpson's problems with an overly austere Gospel did not prevent him from deciding early in life that he wanted to be one of its ministers. At age fourteen he had already settled "for a good while to study for the ministry."

His sister Louise pinpointed this crucial decision to the time he was nine years old and reading a missionary biography of Rev. John Williams, the martyr "apostle of Polynesia." The account inspired him to dedicate his life to the Lord's work. It was the first of several crises that would arise when a book profoundly influenced a major decision in his life.

Was this in answer to Jane Simpson's prayer of committal at his birth and to the prayer at his baptism by Rev. John Geddie, Canada's great pioneer Presbyterian missionary?

Simpson started having second thoughts at a rebellious stage of his teenage life. He thought resentfully of all the restraints the ministry would impose on him. A shotgun came to symbolize all the imagined liberties and freedoms he would have to give up. In a surge of rebellion, he secretly stole away to town and bought a gun.

The purchase was an act of defiance against his parents as well as against the call of God. His mother had lost a brother in a gun accident and banned the possession of a weapon in the house. Albert, with the connivance of his sister, kept the shotgun hidden in the attic between his forays in the forest.

His mother discovered the outlawed weapon and summoned Albert to judgment. He was forced not only to return the shotgun to the seller but, grief compounded, he was forbidden to seek a refund of his money. The loss of both gun and money cured him of ever again allowing anything to come between him and the call to ministry.

The next test happened when he and Howard were called before their parents for a solemn discussion of the future. With his wife sitting silently by, James informed the boys that, in the finest biblical tradition, the eldest son of the family was to be set apart for service to God. This meant Howard would become a minister, while Albert would work on the farm and, together with the rest of the family, support Howard in his training for pastoral work.

It was a cruel moment of truth that forced a timid boy to speak in contradiction to a decision by a man he held in trembling awe second only to God. But Albert did speak up, pleading for his father's permission to prepare for the ministry. He promised to pay his own way and add no financial burden to the family's meager resources already committed to Howard's schooling.

After what must have seemed like an interminable moment, James Simpson, deeply moved by the prospect of not one but two sons in service to God, said simply and fervently to Albert: "God bless you, my boy."[7]

Once committed, the boys' father did what he could to insure their future success. He arranged for private tutors, first a retired minister and later Rev. William Walker, their own pastor in Chatham. He provided each of his sons with a horse for commuting the eighteen-mile round trip to their tutor. And he released them from many farm chores so they could concentrate on studying, though this greatly increased his own work load.

Call to Conversion

Several traumatic experiences ganged up on Albert, forcing him to set his priorities straight—namely, to know the Master he later intended to serve.

Howard, faltering in poor health under the steady pressure of commuting and studying, decided to temporarily discontinue his studies. Albert, more avid a student than ever, decided to attend Chatham High School full time.

Taking a break from the books one day, he and another high school student went to gather wild grapes on the riverbank. His companion decided to have a swim and urged Albert to do the same. Albert foolishly agreed, perhaps embarrassed to admit he could not swim.

He suddenly found himself in deep water, thrashing and choking beneath the surface. His companion froze in panic and screamed for help to some men in a boat nearby.

"They pulled me out just as I was sinking for the last time, and laid me on the river bank," Albert remembered. "As I came back to consciousness a while afterwards, it seemed to me that years had passed since I was last on earth."[8]

Shortly after, according to his sister, Albert attended a service in Chatham where Rev. H. Grattan Guiness, of London, England, preached. He became deeply convicted by the evangelist's messages. Still profoundly disturbed, he walked home that weekend and got lost, though he had gone that way many times. He stumbled upon some desecrated Indian graves, and the gruesome sights further unhinged his sensitive spirit. His father finally found him wandering distraught in the woods and took him home.

The near-drowning, exhausting studies, plundered graves, being lost in the woods—all crowded in upon him and his health collapsed under the strain in 1858.

"Then came a fearful crash in which seemed to me the very heavens were falling," Simpson later recalled. "After retiring one night suddenly a star appeared to blaze before my eyes; and as I gazed, my nerves gave way. I sprang from my bed trembling and almost fainting with a sense of impending death, then fell into a congestive chill of great violence that lasted all night and almost took my life."[9]

The sense of impending death tormented him. He became obsessed with the idea that at a certain hour he would die.

The doctor had warned him not to open a book for a year. Deprived of this mental activity, he could think of nothing but death. Each day as the hands of the clock inched toward the fatal hour, Albert sank deeper into mental and physical agony. Then the terrifying deadline passed, and he marveled at still being alive—only to fear the next sweep of the clock's hands.

One day he could stand it no longer: "Terrified and sinking, I called my father to my bedside and besought him to pray for me, for I felt I was dying. Worst of all I had no personal hope in Christ. The God I knew was a being of great severity...."[10]

God did hear the prayer of a broken-hearted father for his broken-spirited son. The obsession with death peaked like a fever and receded momentarily. Albert began slowly to mend, but for days he could not sleep unless someone was nearby. He kept hoping God would spare him long enough to find that rest of faith that would bring the inner peace he desperately lacked.

Again, God used a book. In late 1858, browsing through a yellowing, brittle book in his minister's library, Simpson came across Marshall's *Gospel Mystery of Sanctification.*

One sentence fairly leaped out to his roving eyes: "The first good work you will ever perform is to believe on the Lord Jesus Christ.

Until you do this, all your works, prayers, tears and good resolutions are vain. To believe on the Lord Jesus is just to believe that He receives and saves you here and now, for He has said, 'Him that cometh to me I will in no wise cast out.' "[11]

In one great surge of relief, like an exhausted swimmer reaching shore, the tormented young man threw himself at Jesus' feet and experienced a conversion so decisive and total he later likened it to that of Saul of Tarsus on the road to Damascus.

The blessed newness of being born again never left him. It would later enable him as an evangelist to bring others out of conscience-wracked uncertainty to the peace and hope of new life in Christ.

Despite his lengthy siege of illness and absence from school, he earned his high school diploma on time and at age sixteen began teaching in a one-room public grade school. Still boyish in appearance as well as years, he marveled at the respect he received from his class of over forty pupils—especially the ten adults considerably his elders.

"I would have given anything for a few whiskers or something that would have made me look older," he recalled.[12]

Young Simpson need not have worried. The students followed his lead with the same instinctive trust shown by large and prosperous congregations just a few years later. The money earned from teaching was saved for college, while he continued studying with his pastor in preparation for the college entrance examination.

As he contemplated college and the ministry, Albert determined to strengthen his dedication to God by a written covenant. He devoted the entire day of January 19, 1861, to fasting and prayer. He then drafted "A Solemn Covenant" of over 900 words.

The heart of the document, remarkable for a young man of seventeen years, lay in the words: "I yield myself unto Thee as one alive from the dead for time and eternity. Take me and use me entirely for Thy glory. Write down in heaven that I have become Thine, Thine only, and Thine forever."[13]

Measuring Up

Those days, ministerial candidates of the Presbyterian Church in Canada needed the approval of their elders even before they could enter college to study for the ministry. It was the first of several checkpoints set up by the church to maintain a high level of pastoral leadership. The faith preserved by their Covenanter forebears at great price in Scotland must not be lost through careless administration and lowered standards.

Therefore at the end of September, 1861, Pastor Walker presented

Albert and Howard, his private students, to the Presbytery of London, Ontario. (The presbytery was a district-level council comprised of one clergyman and one elder from each church in the area.)

After being studiously ignored at length by the august body while it attended to other business, the Simpson brothers and other young men underwent intense examination as to their spiritual experience, soundness of faith, call to ministry and academic qualifications. Mercifully—perhaps for the presbyters as well—the candidates were exempted from preaching the sermon each one had to write.

All the candidates survived the exhaustive ordeal and received permission to enter Knox College, Toronto. Howard remained at home for one year because of illness, but Albert began his college studies immediately. He had done his homework so well that he was admitted to the senior year of the literary department.

Simpson's academic pursuits advanced without faltering, but not his spiritual life. His roommate, something of a campus swinger, had stag parties in their room, complete with beer, whiskey, ribald ditties and lewd jokes. Confronted with a situation unlike anything he had ever known, young Simpson confessed that he "had not firmness nor experience sufficient to suppress these orgies."[14]

Just being forced to stay in the same room with such rowdy classmates took a toll on his spiritual life. At one point he sensed such a spiritual dullness creep over him he felt impelled to renew his solemn covenant. "September 1, 1863. Backslidden. Restored. Yet too cold, Lord. I still wish to continue this. Pardon the past and strengthen me for the future, for Jesus' sake. Amen."[15]

Both the literary and seminary departments of Knox College shared the same campus. When Simpson fulfilled the equivalence of three years in literary studies, he moved immediately into the three-year ministerial program. The seminary was housed in Elmsley Hall, the residence of a former governor-general of Canada. Though small in size, the seminary attracted some of the finest theological professors in the dominion.

Albert was not a slavish student who memorized reams of material with little comprehension. He developed an ability to grasp the key passages of a lecture or reading and express them with disarming simplicity. He seemed gifted with almost total recall of material he studied. His quickness to learn left him time to tutor slower students and thus earn money to help pay for his schooling.

He entered several essay contests in both college and seminary, but not with the intention of earning a scholastic reputation. He needed the money. On one occasion he wrote a prize-winning essay on infant baptism—and later in life would recant the position he had so well championed in his essay.

Romance Awakened

Most of the seminarians boarded in the homes of sympathetic Presbyterian families in Toronto. When Albert's older brother Howard joined him in the seminary, they searched for rented quarters to share. The pastor of the church they attended, Dr. John Jennings of Cooke's Presbyterian, took an interest in them. He reminded Mr. John Henry, a leading elder in the church, of a vacant room in his house and told him of two Knox students who needed it.

Mr. Henry invited the Simpson brothers for an interview and then offered them the hospitality of his home. One result of that invitation would have lifelong implications for Albert.

There was something about Margaret, the eldest of John Henry's two daughters, that immediately attracted both Simpson brothers. Some might even say that for Albert it was love at first sight. Some fifty years later, he would tell University of Toronto students that "he had left his heart at the door of a Toronto residence as it was opened by the fair daughter of the house."[16]

Although Howard also felt drawn to Margaret, whose sparkle seemed all the more animated by her diminutive stature, he did not have a chance. Albert's handsome features, gracious manners and richly resonant voice not only carried the day but won the contest. Marriage was but a matter of time—the far side of three years' study in seminary.

Money was never in great supply during Albert's student days. He told how more than once he found himself penniless and had to cry out to God for money to pay his boarding bill. Yet he found ways to make Margaret feel special. On one occasion he received a generous ten-dollar fee for his Sunday preaching services. The next day he spent the entire amount on a present for his sweetheart.

Pulpit Fame

Though Simpson did well in classwork, he excelled in preaching. At first glance some congregations had difficulty in accepting such a boyish-looking seminarian as worthy to speak from their staunchly guarded pulpits. In one church a zealous elder tried to stop him from mounting the platform because he could not believe such a stripling could be the guest preacher for the day.

But once the young man began to speak, questioning abruptly ceased. His well-ordered exposition in polished diction demanded a hearing for his message and earned him a respect well beyond his years. An upperclassman at Knox, J. W. Mitchell, alternated with Simpson as supply preacher one summer. He said, "I did my work faithfully and acceptably, but was quite thrown into the shade by my junior, for already his pulpit gifts were notable."[17]

Even before graduation in April of 1865, Simpson served Knox Church in Hamilton, Ontario, as supply preacher. That in itself represented a considerable honor, since Knox Church ranked as having one of the most important Presbyterian pulpits in the whole Dominion of Canada. The large and prosperous congregation attracted some of the denomination's finest preachers, though in the interval between pastors in 1865, attendance declined noticeably.

Simpson's temporary responsibility at Knox Church became permanent when in June the church session extended a unanimous call to the twenty-one-year-old preacher fresh out of seminary. The church, however, acted a bit hastily, since Simpson had yet to be licensed in the Presbyterian ministry. Were the elders anxious to get their church first on the list of invitations sure to come?

The Presbytery of Toronto subjected Simpson and other ministerial candidates to an examination that may well have exceeded in difficulty the seminary's comprehensive tests. Each young man underwent a searching review of his aptitude in Hebrew, Greek, theology, church history and government, and an interrogation of his religious experience.

The examiners also assigned special exercises to each candidate. Simpson had to prepare an exposition of Romans 7, a lecture on Matthew 4:1-11, a popular sermon on Romans 1:16, a discourse based on 2 Timothy 1:10 and a thesis in Latin.

Duly licensed by mid-June of 1865, Simpson expressed willingness to accept a call from Knox Church. Reporting on a lecture he gave to a teachers' association, the Hamilton *Spectator* commented, "The reverend gentleman justified the high opinion that has already been formed of him and created a feeling of satisfaction that a man of so much promise has become permanently associated with one of our city congregations."[18]

Set Apart

In August the Hamilton Presbytery issued a unanimous call to Simpson to become pastor of Knox Church. Not one to waste time, he immediately accepted and met with the presbytery to schedule three of the most momentous events of his entire life.

On Sunday, September 10, he was to preach his first sermon at Knox Church as its official pastor. On Tuesday he was to be ordained by the Hamilton Presbytery in a special church service. On Wednesday he was to travel to Toronto and marry Margaret Henry.

Hosting the ordination service for their young pastor was a new experience for the congregation. Previous pastors at Knox Church had come as seasoned pastors with distinguished records. Organizers for the special day set to work with enthusiasm, determined that the event be unforgettable. It was indeed.

The solemn ordination service at two o'clock, Tuesday afternoon, had a profound impact on the hundreds of people who crowded into the sanctuary. Following the sermon by one of the ordaining council, Simpson was directed to stand and publicly answer to questions by a council spokesman. The congregation was then asked whether or not they stood by their choice of this man as their pastor.

Receiving an affirmative answer, members of the council laid hands on the young pastor for an ordination prayer. Brief charges to pastor and congregation brought the service to a close.

That first-ever ordination service in Knox Church forged links between the people and their pastor that endured even after he left the Presbyterian ministry. He would be invited back numerous times on the anniversary of his being set apart for the Gospel ministry, including his fiftieth anniversary in 1915.

The "Grand Soiree" reception attended by 600-700 people included two very important mentors in the young pastor's life: Rev. Walker, his pastor and tutor in Chatham, and Dr. Jennings, his college pastor in Toronto.

At the close of the reception, Dr. Jennings presented Simpson with a silk cassock from the women of the church. He then concluded that "he had just presented his young friend with an empty gown—nothing in it. But tomorrow he expected to perform the pleasant duty of presenting him with another gown, not an empty one, but one with somebody in it."[19]

The wedding of Albert Simpson and Margaret Henry, with Dr. Jennings officiating, took place at the Cooke's Church in Toronto. It began fifty-four years of marriage filled with joyful experiences and fruitful partnership in ministry as well as misunderstandings, struggles and heartbreaks.

The honeymoon boat trip on the St. Lawrence River set the pace for their married life: It was kept short, since the pastor was expected to return to Hamilton and preach Sunday night.

Albert, with his clear-cut conversion, call to ministry and excellent education, stood on the threshold of an outstanding ministry. Margaret, with no preparation for the pastorate but her conversion, Christian home and high school education, stood at the entrance of an uncertain future. He would soar, and she would struggle. His vision of the heavenlies at times would obscure his earthly duties as father and husband, while her practical preoccupations would at times allow no honor for the prophet in his own home.

But for the newlyweds in the autumn of 1865, those honeymoon days on the placid St. Lawrence River were all that mattered, and they were happy ones.

Balanced Ministry

Simpson worked hard to develop his pulpit ministry. He studied carefully, read widely and wrote out in longhand each of his sermons and lectures. The congregation responded by growing rapidly, crowding out the church facilities.

Their spiritual mentor wisely guarded against specializing in preaching at the expense of pastoring. So intensely did he take the people of the parish to his heart in visitation and counseling that several times he approached nervous collapse. The church session finally urged him to take an extended vacation of two months to recuperate, but he settled for one.

In 1871, however, he agreed to a four-month vacation in order to visit Great Britain and Europe. His letters home to Margaret not only spoke of places visited, but of his love for her and their two sons, Albert Henry and James Gordon Hamilton. Another child, Melville Jennings, died of sickness when only three and one-half years old.

During his Hamilton pastorate, Simpson became acquainted with an organization named the Evangelical Alliance. Organized in London, England, in 1846, the movement sought to form a worldwide fellowship of evangelical Christians for closer unity and cooperation, to demonstrate the oneness prayed for by Christ in John 17:21.

Nine hundred delegates representing fifty denominations attended the London conference in 1846. From there the movement spread to other cities and countries, where the local organizations became known as branches. Both the concept and terminology must have been in Simpson's thinking when later he initiated the Christian Alliance with local fellowships also called branches.

The Evangelical Alliance sponsored a New York City convention in October, 1873. Simpson attended and was deeply impressed by the movement. That convention played an important but unforeseen role in his ministry.

He was invited by the Thirteenth Street Presbyterian Church in the city to be guest speaker on a Sunday morning during the convention. Delegates to the convention from Louisville, Kentucky, attended the service at which Simpson preached. Greatly moved by what they heard, the delegates returned home to Louisville and set in motion events that would bring the young preacher to their city and parish.

Likewise impressed, the Thirteenth Street Presbyterian congregation would remember that sermon and eventually issue an invitation that would bring Simpson from Louisville to New York City less than seven years later.

The pastor of Knox Church returned home to Hamilton to sponsor a meeting of the Evangelical Alliance and influence the organizing of a Hamilton branch. A fellow Presbyterian minister, Rev. A. T. Pierson,* spoke at the interdenominational service and at the same time established an enduring friendship with Simpson.

Moving On

At the December 4, 1873, meeting of the Hamilton Presbytery, Simpson expressed a desire to accept the invitation from the Louisville church. The presbyters reluctantly agreed to release him from Knox Church, effective December 20. He gave his final sermon as pastor on Sunday evening of the 14th. *The Hamilton Spectator* printed the sermon in its entirety.

Along with a moving exhortation to the congregation based on "Now is the day of salvation," the pastor recited some statistics covering his eight years of ministry in the church. Membership more than doubled, from 297 to 646, the Sunday school increased from 180 to 459 attendees. He estimated that total contributions from 1865-1873 totaled $50,000.

Concerning the treatment he and his family received from the congregation, he said, "Kinder hearts I can never meet than these I am leaving." Then he concluded, "May God be with you in sorrow and joy, in life and death until we meet again, 'where congregations ne'er break up and Sabbaths have no end.' "[20]

Simpson and Knox Church would retain a special affection for each other throughout his life. Their mutual respect was justly earned, by the pastor no less than the congregation.

A pastor tends to repeat in a new church the pattern of ministry he established in his former pastorate. Knox Church's lasting contribution to their young pastor's future was to provide his high expectations with gratifying results.

*See "The Founder's Team" in the Appendix for further details.

CHAPTER 3

The New York Pastorate

New York City: "If you make it here, you can make it anywhere." And he did.

1879—1881

Context of the Times

The last quarter of the nineteenth century in New York City is described by one historian as " an era of velvet and vice, of magnificance and misery."

It was a period when a concert performance could attract an audience of wealthy men together worth $500,000,000—while a shirtmaker earned 35 cents for a dozen handmade shirts. It was the generation of Astors and Vanderbilts, when the rich got richer and the poor got poorer at a dizzying rate.

Yet 1875-1900 were also years of exciting growth in the city.

In 1879, for instance, St. Patrick's Cathedral, eleventh largest in the world, was dedicated. Construction of the Metropolitan Museum of Art neared completion, and a public fund drive sought to finance the base on which the Statue of Liberty would stand.

The city received its first commercial telephone exchange. Inventor Charles Bush installed the first string of arc lights and another inventor, Thomas Edison, gave a demonstration of his incandescent bulbs that would light up the city.

Immigrants from southern and eastern Europe poured through the Port of New York, many never getting beyond the city limits: Italians, Poles, Greeks, Croatians, Magyars, Portuguese, Lithuanians and Ukrainians. To the many Roman Catholics among them, the church provided their one familiar landmark in a strange and alien nation, and they in turn provided the church with a numerical strength it had not before known. The Roman Catholic Church thus became a power the Protestants were forced to reckon with.

An even larger number of the working class struggled for survival in New York City: the city-born citizens untouched by the ministry and message of the organized churches. How could they be reached?

This question attracted little attention among the larger, prosperous churches. In fact, they competed with one another for the distinction of having the most popular and sensational preacher. It was the era of Henry Ward Beecher and T. DeWitt Talmage in New York, Phillips Brooks in Boston, Russell H. Conwell in Philadelphia.

Adoniram J. Gordon, noted Baptist preacher in Boston, proved that churchmen could be both eloquent and practical. While he preached a powerful gospel of salvation, his church sponsored a halfway house where alcoholics could find help and rehabilitation into society.

Dwight L. Moody continued to dominate the evangelistic scene, with his emphases on the new birth and on life consistent with biblical standards. While maintaining cordial relations with denominational leaders, he chided them for their infighting and church-league competition. In one sermon he said, "I hope the motto of the ministers of this country will be, 'Quit your fighting and go to work and preach the simple gospel.'"

John Inskip and other Methodist ministers formed the National Camp Meeting Association for the Promotion of Holiness. In 1867 the move spearheaded a renewed interest in camp meetings and helped spread the holiness movement beyond both denominational and national bounds.

The holiness movement also sparked renewed interest in the doctrine of divine healing—the direct intervention of God to restore health and wholeness to the physically sick. Leading pulpit preachers like Andrew Murray and A. J. Gordon, and a layman, Dr. Charles Cullis, made divine healing an important part of their ministries.

In England the famous Keswick movement held its first annual conference "for the promotion of practical holiness" in 1875.

* * *

A young Presbyterian clergyman, well aware of the world he lived in, realized that his future lay not in Louisville, Kentucky, despite his impact on that gracious city of southern refinement. Only one place answered to the dimensions of the vision growing clearer to him: abrasive, explosive and progressive New York City.

SIMPSON'S MINISTRY for almost six years in Louisville brought the same gratifying results he had known in Hamilton, Ontario. From 1874-1879 the congregation grew, income increased, his ministry extended to churches all across the city.

But the pastor of Chestnut Street Presbyterian was changing, and his expectations changed as well. No longer was he content with a prestigious church growing more prestigious, and its large congregation larger.

His experience of the Holy Spirit's infilling and his participation in the Whittle/Bliss evangelistic campaign had revolutionized his life. For him now the "regular work of the ministry" was not enough. He must also evangelize the unchurched of his city and work with all his might to make the Gospel available to the overlooked people overseas.

Chestnut Street Presbyterians were not prepared to follow their made-over pastor. The new church structure, elegantly finished and deeply in debt despite his protests, evidenced the church's unwillingness to march to a new beat of the drum.

The pastor did not try to push the congregation on a forced march. He would rather move than fight. In September of 1879, the year following completion of the Louisville tabernacle, he made a trip to New York City and preached three Sundays in the Thirteenth Street Presbyterian Church—the same church in which he had been guest speaker when visitors from Louisville heard him preach and decided they needed him for their pastor.

Now it was Thirteenth Street Presbyterian's turn. The congregation extended to Simpson a unanimous call. He responded with characteristic decisiveness: Within six weeks he resigned from his charge in Louisville, moved to New York and was preaching in the church.

Though Simpson's departure from Louisville was sudden, he was not farewelled in strife. Not wanting to lose him, the Chestnut Street Church refused at first to accept his resignation, but then agreed with great reluctance. Before leaving, their pastor visited every family in the congregation—some on the very day of his departure for New York.

Domestic Discord

Opposition to the New York move came from within the home as well as from the church family. Maggie, as her husband affectionately called her, vigorously opposed their leaving Louisville. At one point Simpson considered asking members of the church session to intervene and try lessening her hostility toward him on this matter, but reconsidered when he perceived the effort would be futile.

In a diary that he kept sporadically, he wrote of continually praying for her and for himself as well, that he might be "kept in compassion, love and holy forgiveness."[1]

Why did Margaret Simpson so vehemently oppose the move to New York? One stated reason was her fear of the city's evil influence on her four children. Albert Henry by now was thirteen; James Gordon, nine; Mabel Jane, seven; and Margaret May, not quite two.

Her fears would prove justified. Both Albert and James later succumbed to the temptations rampant in New York City. A third son, Howard Home, would be born in New York and prove just as susceptible to its temptations as his older brothers. They would not return to the Lord until their last days.[2]

Simpson's granddaughter Katherine remembered, years later: "Grandfather has been heard to say many times that if he had his life to live over he would not have chosen New York as a playground for his family."[3]

Did Mrs. Simpson's hostility toward the New York invitation stem from another reason as well? At this time she thoroughly disagreed with her husband's desire to be free of pastoral duties in order to concentrate on evangelism among the unchurched and to promote missions. Any move by him from their established place in Louisville would therefore be viewed with suspicion and hostility.

But Simpson gave no more heed to her opposition than he did to that of the congregation. In his diary entry of November 10, 1879, he wrote: "Tonight my pastorate was dissolved by the presbytery and I am Christ's free servant. I have moved very slowly and waited for Him to lead."[4]

He was still undecided about what he was to do in New York, even after boarding a night train to head north with his family. Leaving his wife to look after the four children, he went off alone to spend more time in prayer and reflection. His diary on Saturday of that week read, "On the way the message was clearly given while praying about the matter. 'Write the vision and make it plain. Though it tarry, at the end it shall speak, and not lie' " (Habakkuk 2:2,3).[5]

Events moved quickly toward resolving the question of Simpson's immediate future. Two days after stepping off the train in New York, he preached in the Sunday morning service at Thirteenth Street Presbyterian. On Monday the church session requested the presbytery to set an early date for his installation.

In his diary Simpson wrote, "Does the Master clearly bid this or does He hold me back at present to keep me free for wider work as I have often desired—as an evangelist? Or does He bid me receive this special charge at present and let Him open the way in the future for whatever else He may have?"[6]

The missionary magazine filled his thoughts as well: "Much more light about the foreign missionary magazine tonight. Left it wholly with Him. But I know the word is Forward!"[7]

By Wednesday of the same week, the inner struggle seemed resolved: "A great and blessed day," the diary began. "This morning in prayer so clearly shown me that I was wrong in my attitude about this matter [of the evangelist] which has been so much on my heart for years; and that God would have me open to all His words and intimations, that He was not misleading and would not let me be misled about it, and that there was much in the vision that He would make plain in His own way and time; and enable me to write [the magazine] without question. All doubt and fear was taken from my heart at this time."[8]

So the great debate in his heart was resolved for the present. He would pastor the church and edit the magazine. His wife would be less hostile if he were a pastor with an assured income for their growing family. Their savings and the initial subscriptions would finance the magazine. Later, when they were all better adjusted to New York City, the time would come when he could begin an independent ministry and a life of faith.

Simpson was ready, but not his family. God would give them time to catch up with his vision.

On Monday, December 1, 1879, the New York Presbytery received Simpson into membership, and at the same time he accepted the call to pastor the Thirteenth Street Presbyterian Church.

City Parish

If the church secured the pastor from Louisville just to have eloquence in the pulpit that stood up to the competition, they were in for a surprise. Simpson was not only a pulpiteer, he was a visitation pastor as well. Prior to his installation on December 9, he visited all but forty families on the membership roll. Even on that day, he visited sixteen families. His diary ended that night with "very tired."

Two days later he made calls to twenty more families and thanked God for "strength to visit two congregations in one month and for all the blessed fruit."[9]

That "blessed fruit" included a steady infusion of new members for the church. The diary recorded a running record of church growth: "Large prayer meeting tonight, the house full, much blessing and several decisions for Christ...."[10] "We had many conversions today in all the services...."[11] "Much blessing on Sabbath and many hopeful conversions...."[12] "Many accessions to our church—thirty-five up to tonight...."[13] "Praise for thirty-seven new members, twenty by profession."[14]

Minutes of the church session tell a similar story. The governing body usually met the first Monday of each month. But on December 31, 1879, they met to approve new members and again on Monday, January 4, 1880, through Friday of that week for the same reason. Twenty-one persons joined the church by profession of faith and fourteen more by letter of transfer from other churches.

Every meeting of the church session throughout Simpson's ministry recorded the accepting of new members. Even on his final Sunday as pastor of the church, ten more people were received into membership.

Not everyone was happy with the sudden surge of requests for membership. Some looked askance at the variety of newcomers—poor, shabbily dressed individuals as well as the affluent and educated. To these uneasy guardians of Thirteenth Street Presbyterian's prestigious image, the church's growth was a mixed blessing. How were they to attract their social peers if the church gained the reputation of a city mission?

The showdown came when the pastor asked permission of the church session to bring into the church about 100 converts from the Italian quarter. They had been won through his street preaching in the poor neighborhoods. The committee kindly but firmly refused.

This attitude completely contradicted a clear understanding Simpson had reached with the church leaders before he agreed to become the pastor. He later said he "had accepted a call to New York with the explicit understanding on the part of his new church officers that they should unite with him in a popular religious movement to reach the unchurched masses."[15]

The disappointed pastor made arrangements for the discipling of the new believers by another church, but the experience must have removed all lingering doubts about the futility of trying within a long-established church setting to answer the call God had given him for neglected and unreached people.

The presbyters won their point that day, but the church lost its pastor.

Magazine First

Simpson had no lingering doubts about editing and producing an illustrated missionary periodical. He had been convinced for quite some time that this was one goal he must attain.

The magazine certainly played an important part in his decision to come to New York. Not only did the city rank first as the nation's publishing capital, it formed the hub of religious and general communications extending into every part of the globe.

Even before his installation as pastor, he wrote in his diary concerning the foreign missionary magazine: "I feel since tonight that this was His message—Write!"[16]

Should Simpson have taken on such a huge task? True, he had won prizes for written essays in college and had long disciplined himself to write out each sermon, but he was totally inexperienced in the technicalities of publishing. He had no financial backing, no advertisers, no staff and few subscribers. At the same time, his large church needed a full-time pastor.

But one supreme factor overrode every negative or cautionary argument: his intense and still growing concern for the unevangelized masses in foreign parts of the globe.

The first issue of his magazine, *The Gospel in All Lands,* was dated February, 1880. An editorial addressed the question of the publication's role. It read in part, "Another voice of cheer to the scattered workers in the great Harvest Field; another standard raised in the great conflict; another channel opened for the diffusion of the living facts of Aggressive Christianity; another echo of the Great Commission; another plea for the one thousand million of our immortal fellowmen, 'those great billows of humanity surging every generation upon the dark shores of eternal death.'

"This is the meaning of our proposed work. Surely there is no need of excuse for even the feeblest effort in such a cause."[17]

The fledgling editor tackled his first issue with much prayer and enthusiasm. He felt led by God to feature Africa as the theme. The church's Christmas gift of $555.00—"far more than I prayed for the magazine," he said—went entirely into the financing of the first issue.

He then noted in his diary, "I must record God's amazing goodness to me today in enabling me to write so much and I trust so well. Ask God to get pictures selected tomorrow and all important articles written by tomorrow night."[18]

The writing of major articles took two days, but in that week he finished almost all the material. His appreciation for the value of good illustrations as he prayerfully searched for the right ones put *The Gospel in All Lands* in a class by itself. No similar publication of the era had such attractive graphics. To his amazement, the first issue spilled over into eighty pages instead of the sixty-four he had probably intended.

The marathon effort needed to field the first issue took a heavy toll on his strength. Apparently he felt reproved in conscience for keeping late hours at work, because he resolved "to sleep earlier, not later than eleven retiring."[19] But the pressure of deadlines proved greater than his resolve. He began to have some doubts about his ability to carry on.

His diary entry for Sunday, February first, noted, "Broken down much....I do desire the Lord to hold me back from this whole work if it be not of Him. He seems to say that I cannot sustain the tremendous load, but would sink under it....It may be I am before His time, but He will guide and sustain."[20]

By the end of the week he rebounded in confidence and began work on the second issue. Positive remarks concerning the first issue strengthened his resolve to continue.

In four months, February through May of 1880, he published four issues, each averaging sixty-four pages. Most of the writing, all the selection of material and artwork, negotiations with the printer—all this he did himself, in addition to pastoring a large city church.

The price he paid for this incredible output was broken health. Extreme weariness brought on illness that kept him from the June issue.

In the July number he apologized for the missing month: "It was made imperatively plain that the undivided business responsibility and editorial management of such a work, in addition to the duties and cares of a pastoral charge, constituted a burden which no single heart or brain could or should longer bear....The providence of God has clearly shown that the burden must be shared or the work be abandoned or imperfectly done."[21]

Simpson found the help he needed in Eugene R. Smith, an experienced Methodist publisher. Smith offered to take over publication of *The Gospel in All Lands* and continue its stated purpose. The exhausted editor was more than willing to transfer both ownership and management to Smith, while retaining an editorial voice in the publication.

His continuing link to the magazine grew out of a hope "to be able to continue this labor of love and cooperate in the sweetest and sublimest service given to the church of God—the work of the world's evangelization."[22] His relationship with *The Gospel in All Lands* would continue through the October issue of 1881.

While Simpson was the editor and publisher, he refused to print comments about his magazine, fearing that pride would enter his work and obstruct God's blessing. But when Smith took over the monthly, he began to publish some of the high commendations from readers, including twenty-one publishers and editors.

"The first issue is far beyond anything in the missionary line published in this country.—Dr. S. H. Kellogg, Professor, Allegheny Seminary.

"I receive a large number of the missionary periodicals of the world and regard yours as the best."—Rev. R. W. Allen, Missionary Editor, *Zion's Herald.* [23]

"We are amazed at the amount of work which must have been expended on it, the variety and fullness of its contents—making it a continuous cyclopedia of missions—and the exceedingly interesting way in which it is gotten up."—*Christian Intelligencer.* [24]

"We have been reading missionary papers for the past forty years, but never before have we met with a periodical that so completely fills the bill of missionary information as this."—*Western Recorder.* [25]

"*The Gospel in All Lands* for May, 1881, contains the fullest and most complete account of mission work in China that has ever been published."—*Methodist Protestant.* [26]

Brokenness and Wholeness

The Gospel in All Lands, with its demanding editorial activities and incessant deadlines, may have been the last excessive claim on Simpson's frail body, so unequally yoked to his passionate nature. Added to his pastoral concern for hundreds of parishoners, his pursuit of excellence in the pulpit, his evangelistic zeal for the unchurched, the magazine pushed his physical strength to the limit—and beyond.

Medical competence of the era proved inadequate for his needs. He later preached a message on "My Medicine Chest," in which he said, "I began with allopathy, then went to homeopathy. Then I went into the herb doctors' business and the patent medicine line.

"I went around with a bottle of ammonia in one pocket in case I should drop from my weak heart. In the other pocket I carried a horse chestnut. An old Highlander told me it was a sure remedy for inflammatory rheumatism which had brought the heart weakness upon me.

"I was very nervous, impulsive, and did not know how to be quiet; and one form of my heart trouble came from excitement and wasted strength. I used to take tonics, bottles of quinine, iron, hypophosphates and every sort of thing. When I had inflammation inside the doctors would get up an inflammation outside—a counter irritant."[27]

Little more than a year after coming to New York, Simpson's health totally collapsed. The crisis surpassed in severity his illness during high school days and later in the Hamilton church, when he was forced to suspend all pastoral activities for several months. Now a prominent New York physician warned that his weakened heart was even worse, perhaps beyond medical help.

Along with physical and nervous prostration came mental gloom.

He took a leave of absence from the church and went to Saratoga Springs, but nothing seemed to help. "I was deeply depressed," he confessed, "and all things in life looked dark and withered."[28]

The despondent pastor happened to pass an evangelistic service where some black singers were leading the song service. The phrase of one chorus cut through his despair like a shaft of sunlight: "My Jesus is the Lord of Lords / No man can work like Him."

The words powerfully affected him, bringing a spiritual lift that not only brought release from benumbing depression but also a promise of help on the way.

In late July or early August of 1881, the Simpson family vacationed at Old Orchard, Maine, one of the favorite seashore resorts and convention grounds of the era.[29] The weary pastor had no intention of working on this vacation, but he did occasionally visit the campgrounds and take part in a few services.

Providentially, Dr. Charles Cullis was conducting meetings at the time. Boston physician and former director of a tuberculosis sanatorium as well as devout Christian, Dr. Cullis had prayed for his patients as well as treating them medically. Some terminally ill patients had remarkable recoveries, causing Dr. Cullis to study the scriptural teaching on divine healing. Once convinced God wanted to heal both body and soul, he began a healing ministry while continuing his medical practice.

Simpson attended one of Dr. Cullis's healing services at Old Orchard and listened to at least 200 people give accounts of their healing. "I had believed that there were cases of healing—but the facts did not convince me," he said later.

"They sent me to the Bible to settle the matter. If it was true, it was the most stupendous thing in life. And so I went to my room and took my Bible thinking, 'If that is here, I will stand on it; if not, I will let it go. If it is true, I will accept it, cost what it will.' "[30]

Deep in thought, he later sat on some rocks by the ocean. While trying to sort out some decisions regarding his future—which seemed painfully short—he noticed some seaweed being carried back and forth by the incoming tide. A wave would deposit it on the beach, seemingly saved and safe from the ocean. Then another wave would drag it back out to the turbulent breakers.

"To Simpson's poetic mind," a friend wrote, "this piece of seaweed became human. A great concern took possession of his mind and he felt the little waif must come ashore. Instantly he sprang into the shallow surf, seized the little waif and brought it to land where no tide could ever reach it again."[31]

As Simpson laid it gently down, the Spirit of God seemed to say: "That little piece of seaweed is yourself. You have tried and tried to get to land, and just when you felt you had attained your end, another cruel wave has come and washed you out to sea again. All the while I have been watching you, anxious to pick you up and carry you to safety, but you would not let me do it."[32]

Simpson determined it was time to make his own personal commitment to the truth he now believed was taught in the Bible. "I felt I dare not hold any truth in God's Word as a mere theory or teach to others what I had not personally proved."[33]

He went into the pines of Old Orchard, raised his right hand to heaven and made "three great and eternal pledges"[34]: He accepted without questioning that divine healing was part of the Gospel of Christ; he took without doubting the Lord Jesus for his healing and health; he promised without fail to use this blessing to the glory of God and for the good of others.[35]

He arose from that prayer of commitment sensing himself to be a new man—"It had only been a few moments, but I knew that something was done. Every fibre of my soul was tingling with a sense of God's presence."[36]

Tests of Healing

He had not long to wait the testing of his faith. That weekend he was to preach in a Congregational church several miles north of Intervale, New Hampshire. He felt impressed to speak of his healing, but chose instead to preach "a good sermon." It was a total failure, he ruefully concluded after the service. That same evening he made amends by testifying of his healing during a service conducted in the hotel.

The next and harder test of his healing came the following day, when he was invited to hike up Mt. Kearsarge, a 3,000-foot mountain. Of late, even a slight elevation or steps to climb had been hard on his heart. But he knew refusing the invitation would be pure unbelief on his part.

The first steps of the hike threatened to be his last. Then Simpson sensed another Presence, a source of strength if he claimed it, and he did. "When I reached the mountain top," he testified, "I seemed to be at the gate of heaven, and the world of weakness and fear was lying at my feet."[37]

Yet another test of his faith followed, perhaps the most difficult because it involved not himself but one of his precious children.

Shortly after their return from vacation, his three-year-old daughter Margaret fell ill with diphtheria. Simpson's wife insisted they call a doctor. She had already lost her son Melville Jennings at the same age from the same sickness. She was determined not to lose a second.

Little Margaret's father told how "that night, with a throat white as snow and a raging fever, the little sufferer lay beside me alone. I knew that if the sickness lasted to the following day there would be a crisis in my family. With trembling hand I anointed her brow and claimed the power of Jesus' name. About midnight my heart was deeply burdened. I cried to God for speedy deliverance.

"In the morning her throat was well and she was ready to get up and go about her play. The mother gave me one look as she came to see the child which I shall never forget. From that hour I was never asked again to get a physician."[38]

Blessing and Buffeting

Simpson's healing ranked as the third greatest crisis of his life, surpassed only by his experiences of salvation and infilling of God's Spirit. It drastically changed his life and ministry for the next thirty years. A. W. Tozer wrote that for half a lifetime he was enabled to do a work so enormous as to stagger belief. To his knowledge, only the Apostle Paul and John Wesley compared with Simpson for quantity of work turned out.[39]

Four years after his healing—and four years after an eminently qualified physician had given him up for dead—Simpson would testify of his divine source of strength. At that time he would be editor and principal writer of a large magazine; pastor of a church with services every night and three times on Sunday; manager of a healing home where hundreds found help; and director of the Missionary Training College.[40]

Word spread fast in 1881 of his healing and that of his daughter Margaret. He was besieged by many with pleas for help. By many others, he was vilified and ridiculed as another quack miracle worker.

Ironically, his critics were willing to let him alone as long as he struggled along sickly and weak. But when he became healthy, strong and energetic, they bitterly criticized his ministry and motives.

Simpson suffered these public attacks in silence. He needed neither to defend his life-renewing experience nor seek approval from people. Neither did he need to exploit this gift of healing God had given him. Although miracles of healing later helped launch his independent movement, he never allowed this teaching to supersede the miracle of the new birth or the necessity of yielding to the Holy Spirit.

The penalty most costly to him for his healing was a sense of loneliness. He first experienced this isolation from his friends and associates when the Holy Spirit took control of his life. They were not hostile, they just did not understand, and this caused a widening gulf between them and a man of God who would go deeper in spiritual matters than they dared to follow.

The same sense of isolation overtook Simpson in the matter of healing. He remembered, "When I found this blessed Jesus Christ was a living Christ, with not only His Spirit for my spirit, but His body for my body, a risen body, touching mine into life, and holding and quickening it with His resurrection life—then I felt again so lonesome.

"My old friends seemed to leave me and for months I seemed to be alone—separated from hundreds and thousands of ministers and people I had loved and worked with all my life. I felt I did not know them now and they did not know me as before."[41]

But neither criticism and loneliness on the one hand, nor pressures to exploit his healing on the other, could turn Simpson away from a relationship basic to his very existence. Jesus had proven Himself to be the unfailing source of physical life and health. Healing became more than a release from a particular weakness or disease. It became also daily health and strength with which to work and to do the will of God.

Immersion and Resignation

The pastor of Thirteenth Street Presbyterian would soon feel a sense of isolation greater than ever. For some time he had been troubled by his denomination's practice of baptizing babies. Even though during college days he had written an award-winning essay defending infant baptism, he was now convinced that only individuals mature enough to publicly declare their faith in Christ should be baptized, and by immersion.

Simpson quietly approached the pastor of an Italian Baptist congregation that worshiped in a frame schoolhouse because they were too poor to own a church. Speaking of himself in the third person, he described his experience: "It was a bitter autumn day when even the water was cold as ice. No audience present but the wife of the humble evangelist who baptized him, no sympathy from a single human friend, but a consciousness of being utterly alone, misunderstood and condemned even by his dearest friends for an act of eccentric fanaticism that must surely separate him from all the associations of his Christian life and work....

"After it was over, he hastily robed himself and threw himself upon his knees and thanked the Lord for the unspeakable privilege of following Him in full obedience into death. No language can ever express the unutterable joy that came sweeping into his soul and spirit as the Master seemed to say, 'You have gone with Me into the death, now you shall come with Me into the resurrection.' "[42]

Stepping into the cold water was indeed an act of dying to all his religious heritage, life and work. He had publicly vowed in his installation service two years previous to uphold and practice the beliefs of his church. Now he found himself in open conflict with one of its cherished ordinances. He was left with no alternative but to resign.

When Simpson later pastored his own independent church, he would make a point of accepting Christians into membership regardless of the mode of baptism. He wrote that he did not consider this "as such a necessary ordinance that it would separate him from the communion of any evangelical church."[43]

While his colleagues may have considered this change of thinking grounds for dismissal from the presbytery, Simpson decided to separate from Thirteenth Street Presbyterian for what he considered a more serious cause.

"For two years I spent a happy ministry with this noble people," he reminisced later, "but found after a thorough and honest trial that it would be difficult for them to adjust themselves to the radical and aggressive measures to which God was leading me. What they wanted was a conventional parish for respectable Christians. What their young pastor wanted was a multitude of publicans and sinners."[44]

After a week of reflection and prayer, he startled the church session on Monday evening of October 31, 1881, by stating his intention to resign from the church and presbytery. Confused and dismayed, the session requested a delay in the decision and adjourned until the following evening. Tuesday night they accepted his resignation, and on Wednesday evening at the prayer service, the pastor informed the people of his action.

Sunday, November 6, proved to be the last time he would be permitted to preach from the pulpit of Thirteenth Street Presbyterian. The sanctuary was crowded with members, curious visitors and representatives of the press. He preached from Luke 4:18: "The Spirit of the Lord is upon me because he has anointed me to preach the gospel to the poor."

In his sermon Simpson expressed his great concern that the church was not doing enough to reach nonchurchgoers of the city. He then referred to his recent baptism by immersion and his disagreement with the official Presbyterian practice of infant baptism. The sermon concluded with an appeal that members of the church not follow him or bring upon him the stigma of having split the church.

On Monday he met with the New York Presbytery. His colleagues expressed deep appreciation for him and the hope he would soon return to their fellowship. As he left, one fellow pastor expressed his best wishes, but added: "You will never succeed without keeping your work under the auspices of the Presbyterian Church."[45]

The morning of that same day the elders called on Mrs. Simpson at home to express their profound sympathy. Her husband said, "They remarked as they condoled with her that they felt they were attending his funeral." He added humorously, "It is possible she may also have felt that he might as well be dead."[46]

Dr. Kenneth Mackenzie,* an Episcopalian clergyman and friend of Simpson, said: "It seemed as though he had wrecked high possibility for a venture that could only end in disaster."[47]

The warm feelings of fellow pastors in the presbytery must have been tinged somewhat with exasperation, for Simpson was not allowed to preach on the following Sunday, nor was he allowed to serve communion to his people, even though they had requested it.

The resigning pastor's situation was suddenly and drastically changed. From a salaried position paying $5,000 annually, he was reduced to not knowing where the next dime would come from to support himself, his wife and four children. From one of the most prestigious and influential pulpits of the nation's leading city, he stepped into seeming oblivion. He found himself alone in a great city known even then for its expensive ways; he had no following, no backing, no prospects of employment and no visible means of carrying out the vision that had propelled him to such a drastic step.

No wonder Dr. John Hall, one of his close friends and associates in the presbytery, said to him, "We will not say goodbye to you, Simpson; you will soon be back with us."[48]

Dr. Hall's intention was fine, his prediction wrong.

*See "The Founder's Team" in the Appendix for more details.

PART TWO

THE MOVEMENT LAUNCHED

1881—1912

CHAPTER 4

The Gospel Tabernacle

He used the New Testament as a pattern for the church, and it worked.

1881—1886

Context of the Times

What began as a rescue mission in London's East Side developed into a militant, highly organized Salvation Army by 1878. Two years later the Army landed in New York, led by two of founder William Booth's children: Ballington and Evangeline.

The Salvation Army in New York grew fast because of its "Soup and Salvation" program and its "Blood and Fire" emphasis on regeneration and sanctification as taught by John Wesley—namely, the ability to live free of all known sin.

It was a new hymnody, however, not formal theology that perhaps best expressed the spiritual flavor of the era. Soloist and song leader Ira Sankey's compositions in the Moody campaigns gave gospel songs great popularity. So did the music of the deceased P. P. Bliss and England's Frances Ridley Havergal.

The songs of blind Fanny J. Crosby, eventually over 2,000 in number, seemed to be on every lip. In simple lyrics and singable tunes, themes of consecration and surrender to God's love became gospel favorites for generations—songs such as: "Safe in the Arms of Jesus," "Near the Cross," "Draw Me Nearer," "He Hideth My Soul" and many others.

In contrast to the harmony of their hymnody, relations among the saints were turning to sour discord. Historical denominations like the Methodists and Presbyterians drifted toward a more sedate, middle-class Protestantism, while individuals and groups within their ranks pleaded ineffectively for a return to spiritual fervor.

Meanwhile, holiness groups crossing all denominational lines laid claim to a radical experience of faith, with emphasis on a strict code of personal morality, plain attire and abstinence from "worldly" pleasures. Though these groups stressed their disinterest in forming new religious groupings, they were viewed with increasing suspicion by the long-established churches. Neglected and rejected, they began to gravitate toward organization.

One historian saw trends linking doctrinal emphases to social levels. Separatist holiness groups seemed to draw support primarily from those of low social and economic standing. Keswick-type teaching called for a spiritual transformation through crisis and subsequent growth that appealed more to the conservative middle-class. Liberal Protestantism, with a strong emphasis on personal and social ethics and a nonradical view of sanctification, secured the most affluent base.

The Niagara Conference offered one alternative to the trend toward religious splintering. It enabled evangelicals with differing distinctives in Canada and the United States to meet on neutral ground and enjoy their common heritage of faith.

Begun in the late 1860s as a series of summer meetings to study the Bible and prophecy, the conference chose Niagara-on-the-Lake, Ontario, as a permanent location in 1883.

The one-week sessions were controlled by leading evangelical churchmen like A. J. Gordon, A. T. Pierson and James H. Brookes. Bible study, prayer and a missionary emphasis characterized the meetings.

The Niagara Conference eventually disbanded, but not before it scored two major achievements. First, it encouraged the formation of similar conferences. Second, it made possible interaction and alliances among conservative evangelicals. These family ties would later play a significant role in the fundamentalist movement after World War I.

* * *

The brilliant but (to many people) unpredictable ex-Presbyterian pastor, who had recently disaffiliated himself from his church in New York, did not view the flux and flow of religious life from a neutral corner. He was in the middle of it.

Now "Christ's free servant," he would oversee the biblically oriented formation of believers into a fellowship also very much in tune with the times.

SIMPSON was a churchman.

Just as the family constitutes the basic unit of society for its preservation, he believed that the local church forms the basic unit of God's Kingdom for the evangelization of the world. If Christians lived and worked together as God intended, Simpson estimated that the job could be done in one decade.

He taught that the New Testament contains specific guidelines for Christians to follow in their community of faith: "Just as the tabernacle of old was to be constructed strictly according to the pattern that was shown to Moses on the Mount, so the Church of Jesus Christ has a divine pattern and should be in every particular constructed accordingly."

He warned, "The failure to do this has been the cause of all apostasies, declensions and mistakes of the past eighteen centuries; and is the reason that the heathen world is still lying in darkness and crying to God against the unfaithfulness of His people."[1]

New York Style

How did that "divine pattern" translate into terms understandable to the nineteenth century metropolis of New York?

The word "free" stood high on Simpson's list: "God put it on my heart to prove that it was practicable and I left my church to form a church for the people of all classes based on absolute freedom."[2]

He would never forget his irritation in Louisville with the accepted custom of rented church pews and other social distinctions that kept many low-income people, including blacks, from attending his church. When conducting his own evangelistic meetings after the Whittle/Bliss campaign, he made sure the publicity emphasized "free"—free seats, free admittance, freedom from disdainful looks by ushers directed toward those poorly dressed, freedom from denied entrance for lack of membership.

"My plan and idea of a church," he said, "are those which are exemplified in the great London churches of Newman Hall and of Spurgeon, comprising thousands of members of no particular class, but of the rich and poor side by side."[3]

However, with the true instincts of a church planter, Simpson had a specific target group in mind. He did not aim, as some have supposed, at rescue mission work or at some indeterminate, catchall mass of people. "From the first it was not designed as a mission to the lowest and vicious classes," he wrote, "but as a self-supporting work among the middle classes, who have no church home."[4]

Every program, every activity, every organization in the church had a primary purpose. Whatever additional value, it had first to serve the function of evangelism. "All of his institutions at home and abroad have been a light brigade in the great movement for world evangelization," wrote his official historian, A. E. Thompson.[5]

Now "Christ's free servant," Simpson was free to implement all he believed a New Testament church should be. Like a builder who owned his own company, he could lead the formation of a new church that followed the divine pattern as he understood it. And he was confident it would succeed, though he had no investors, no working capital, no bank credit and no network of supporters to back him.

Reporters asked him how he expected his new work to be supported. His reply: "Just as in business anything that was worth succeeding always found people enough to sustain it; so in the work of God, if anything was worth doing, God would see that it was supported."[6]

Small Beginnings

Simpson lost no time in committing his ideas to action. On November 20, 1881, two weeks after his resignation from Thirteenth Street Presbyterian, he conducted a meeting in the Caledonian Club Hall on West Thirteenth Street and Eighth Avenue. After speaking on the spiritual needs of the city he urged those "in sympathy with an aggressive spiritual movement" to meet on November 23 to confer and pray.

Only seven other people showed up. Huddled around a little stove in a "cold and cheerless dance hall," they opened their Bibles. "This is the word of the Lord," they read. "Not by might, nor by power, but by my spirit, saith the Lord of hosts. For who hath despised the day of small things?" (Zechariah 4:6,10).

Simpson, once again happily a pastor, recalled that the small group then knelt in prayer to thank God that they were poor, few and weak. "We threw ourselves upon the might of the Holy Ghost, and He has never failed us."[7]

The undaunted group developed a schedule that might intimidate even a large congregation: a service each evening and three on Sunday. The Sunday afternoon session concentrated on training workers for anticipated branches in the city. A street meeting usually preceded the evening service and tent meetings joined the schedule every evening during summer months.

Demanding as the schedule was on the workers, Simpson made sure the services were anything but tiring to the public. Music played a key role, both group singing and special renditions. The pastor kept his sermons short and refused appeals for money. Also lacking: any put-downs of other churches or groups.

"There is need in every town and city of the land for a simple, popular and undenominational evangelistic movement," Simpson wrote, " not for a few passing weeks, leaving them to relapse into their old habits when the meetings close, but continuing throughout the year; gathering its fruits around its own center and providing a home for the non-church going classes."[8]

The neglected and unchurched people of New York, comfortable in neither rescue mission nor fashionable church, began to notice they were remembered. Simpson's marathon of meetings quickly attracted a following. Audiences overflowed the Caledonian Club Hall, forcing the first of numerous moves in January, 1882. The larger Academy of Music Hall lasted only two weeks for the burgeoning congregation. In mid-January they moved across the square to Steinway Hall. Needing still larger facilities, the evening services next moved in March to the Abbey Park Theater on Broadway near Thirty-second Street.

As the audiences grew in size, so did the corps of workers. Mr. Ide came from Brooklyn to lead the song service and organize the choir. Dr. George F. Pentecost, a prominent churchman and friend of the pastor since Louisville days, opened the year of 1882 by preaching for Simpson in the Academy of Music's large auditorium. Mr. George C. Stebbins, famed gospel songwriter, and his wife assisted in the services from time to time.

It became evident Simpson needed to establish a church home for his growing number of new converts. On February 10, 1882, some thirty-five people met in his home to organize a simple, New Testament church. The constitution consisted of only eight brief articles, totaling less than five hundred words in all.

Giving testimony to faith in Christ and demonstrating a life consistent with that profession formed the only conditions of membership. Immersion was the preferred method of baptism, but not compulsory. The yet unnamed church's specific mission was to evangelize unreached peoples both locally and afar.

Finances ranked low among the priorities. The pastor drew no salary, and would not for many years of ministry. He chose rather to trust God for his meals and help support himself, such as through the sale of his books at a later date. Initial expenses of the work also came out of his pocket and would continue to do so for several more months.

As the summer of 1882 neared, the pastor and his people looked for a more adequate meeting place. The Grand Opera Hall on Eighth Avenue at Twenty-third Street met both requirements and became the hall-hopping congregation's home for the next two years.

Summertime tent meetings offered another means of evangelistic outreach. A New Jersey businessman offered a two-pole tent with a 500-seat capacity for the meetings. Someone else offered a vacant lot. The pastor promptly accepted both gifts and moved all his services from the hall to the tent, where he conducted services under the big top from July 14 through October 29. Josephus Pulus, one of the original seven in Simpson's organization meeting, added some variety with his temperance meetings each Friday evening and Sunday afternoon.

The congregation's incessant outreach efforts had marked success. By 1883 church membership rose to 217 and the Sunday evening services were attracting some 700 people. By midyear the congregation voted to incorporate legally under the innocuous name of Gospel Tabernacle, which the State of New York approved on July 9, 1883.

In July also the church moved back to the evangelistic tent and followed the previous summer's heavy schedule of services. At the close of the season the tent audience moved to the Hippodrome (predecessor of Madison Square Garden) for Sunday services.

The last such meetings held in the large arena had been the Moody/Sankey campaign in 1876, and the inevitable comparisons favored the latest effort. One reporter concluded his article with, "From the attendance yesterday, it looks as if Mr. Simpson will rival those celebrated apostles."[9]

The comparison was not one the great D. L. Moody would have minded. On one of his trips to New York, Moody said to his friend Dr. A. T. Pierson, "I have just been down to hear A. B. Simpson preach. No one gets to my heart like that man."[10]

The Gospel Tabernacle preacher had a way to getting to the heart of a wide variety of people. A clergy editor wrote his impressions of Simpson: "He was a minstrel—a spiritual minstrel; preaching was melodious and musical when it fell from his lips. The very sway of his body was poetic and passionate. He was like a reed shaken by the wind of the Holy Ghost...a poet preacher."[11]

Blue-collar workers, more impressed with straight talk than poetic style, were equally captivated. A railroad flagman put it pointedly, "I could sit on the point of a picket fence twenty-four hours and listen to that man."[12]

A little known but historically interesting event took place in 1883. Seeking a site for a permanent building, the congregation raised $13,000 and engaged a lawyer to purchase land on Thirty-fourth Street near Eighth Avenue. The lawyer made off with the money, and the available site was lost to another purchaser: builders of the landmark Pennsylvania Railway Station.

Friday Meetings

Fruitful though the tent meetings were, another feature of the Gospel Tabernacle also proved effective: the Friday meetings. Originating in the pastor's home, these afternoon sessions grew until they became New York's largest attended religious meeting on a weekday.[13]

The afternoon hour may have been chosen because of the meeting's unusual character. Begun as a consecration service with emphasis on giving preeminence to the Holy Spirit in one's life, the services gradually added divine healing as a second major theme.

Simpson believed that teaching on divine healing in particular should not "be crowded upon the popular audiences who were not prepared for such strong meat."[14] The Friday afternoon hour suited this purpose, but still the crowds came, ranging from 500 to 1,000 people in attendance.

Dr. Kenneth MacKenzie, who worked closely with Simpson from the beginning of his independent ministry, said: "Had he renounced divine healing he could have obtained a wider and more tolerant recognition. But that would have required a diplomacy of which he could not be guilty....It was the healing element in his initial work that proved most influential. The Friday afternoon meeting became a shrine for thousands of people connected with the churches of the city and its suburbs."[15]

Simpson was obviously not playing to the grandstands. On the one hand, by refusing to treat his obvious ministry of healing with benign neglect, he lost points with the ultraconservative and liberal church groups. Conversely, he would not manipulate his gift as a promotional device to pack halls and fill offering plates.

Early in 1883 he wrote concerning the healing ministry: "It is very solemn ground and can never be made a professional business or a public parade. Its mightiest victories will always be silent and out of sight, and its power will keep pace with our humility and holiness."[16]

Yet neither did Simpson believe in building walls around the truth of divine healing. While he taught that ministers and elders of the church should anoint and pray for the sick, he emphasized the right of every child of God to claim this blessing for personal needs. He himself had exercised that right when, alone in the pines of Old Orchard, he had sought the Great Physician and found Him.

"The Lord Jesus has purchased and provided for His believing children physical strength, life and healing as freely as the spiritual blessings of the Gospel," he maintained. "We do not need the intervention of any man or woman as our priest, for He is our Great

High Priest, able to be touched with the feeling of our infirmities, and it is still as true as ever, 'As many as touched him were made perfectly whole.' "

Berachah Home

Some people seeking healing needed more time for instruction and spiritual preparation than the public services provided. A "healing home" answered this need and developed naturally as an adjunct to the healing ministry of the Gospel Tabernacle. In this quiet retreat center, guests had time to read and pray, and to receive counseling from staff members.

Healing homes seemed especially popular in the middle and latter years of the 1800s. Lutheran Pastor John Christoph Blumhardt operated homes in Mottlingen and Bad Boll, Germany, where hundreds of people experienced unusual healings and recoveries. Among the first to open such a home, he began this ministry in 1844. A contemporary of Blumhardt, Dorothea Trudel, operated a similar home in Mannedorf, Switzerland, despite opposition from civil authorities.

Not until 1882 did England have a healing home, the one opened by Mrs. Elizabeth Baxter in Bethshan, London. Among others, Andrew Murray, the widely known pastor and writer from South Africa, came to Bethshan with a throat disorder that threatened to end his public ministry. He emerged completely healed after three weeks, to continue preaching almost to his dying day at age eighty-eight.

In the United States, Dr. Charles Cullis, an Episcopalian layman, became active as a proponent of divine healing as early as 1864. In 1870 the Boston physician opened a home in Dorchester Heights for people suffering with tuberculosis.

His writings circulated widely, helping convince Andrew Murray in South Africa to seek the Lord's healing touch. He influenced Captain R. Kelso Carter,* who wrote one of the most influential studies of divine healing in the nineteenth century. And it was in Dr. Cullis's Old Orchard meetings where the ailing and frail pastor from Thirteenth Street Presbyterian Church in New York heard many testify of God's healing power.

Miss Carrie Judd,* a young lady in Buffalo, New York, had been bedridden for months in 1880. She covenanted with Mrs. Edward Mix in Connecticut to pray for healing on a specific date. Her miraculous recovery came a day early, and shortly after she founded a healing home, the Faith Rest Cottage, in Buffalo.

*See "The Founder's Team" in the Appendix for more details.

The Gospel Tabernacle pastor, well aware of these various healing centers, considered making a spiritual refuge of his own residence (probably at 123 West Thirteenth Street, next door to the church he had pastored). Mrs. Simpson opposed him in this, and rightly so. Their children should be raised in a home, she argued, not an institution. "The difficulties Simpson later experienced in bringing his children to Christ," Tozer commented, "may be attributed in part to the fact that they had been sacrificed too far in the interest of their father's public ministry."[17]

Mrs. Simpson finally agreed to the idea of a healing center, if larger quarters could be found. Early in 1883 the answer to Simpson's prayers came in the form of $2,000 contributed by a Mr. Guild to rent and furnish the residence at 331 West Thirty-fourth Street. On May 16 Simpson dedicated the Home for Faith and Physical Healing.

To this home came Mr. E. G. Selchow,* a prominent New York businessman whose physician had counseled him to get out of the business world or die within two years. God healed him in Simpson's retreat center, and he became a faithful member of the Gospel Tabernacle until his death thirty-two years later.

Grateful for his new lease on life, Selchow proposed separate, larger quarters to accommodate the increasing number of people wanting admission to the healing home. He found such a place at 328 West Twenty-third Street, paid $8,000 toward its purchase and pledged to make the mortgage payments.

The Berachah Home was dedicated on May 4, 1884. During the next sixteen months, until it moved, Berachah, meaning "blessing," would shelter approximately 700 guests, while a much larger number of visitors would seek counseling.

World Concerns

While still meeting in the Grand Opera Hall, the congregation started moving in another direction the pastor believed essential to a church following the "divine pattern": foreign missions.

Simpson expressed in the strongest of terms his understanding of Christ's words, "Go ye." "Unless I am sure I am doing more at home to send the Gospel abroad than I can do abroad, I am bound to go; and if He wants me, I am ready to go wherever He calls and makes it plain. This and this alone is the attitude of fidelity on the part of each of us to this sacred word of our departing Lord."[18]

*See "The Founder's Team" in the Appendix for more details.

In March of 1883 the congregation formed its own missionary society. The Missionary Union for the Evangelization of the World had the dual purpose of "praying and preparing for the promulgation of the Gospel in all nations."[19]

The missionary union found a ready-made promoter in *The Word, The Work and The World.* Begun in 1882 by Simpson, the periodical was similar to his earlier *The Gospel in All Lands.* The new illustrated monthly contained the same interdenominational world view of missions so popular in its predecessor, and added some of his best literary writing of study and devotional material.

The monthly reported on newsmakers and newsmaking events important to the evangelical community. And throughout its pages the editor continued the same prayerful and imaginative use of woodcut illustrations that had made his earlier publication an innovation in religious publishing.

Tozer, himself a successful editor, said of *The Word, The Work and The World:* "It was undoubtedly one of the finest missionary journals ever published by any religious society anywhere. The sweep and range of it are amazing. Its editor had taken the world for his parish. In its pages his mighty earth-covering wing-stretch became apparent, probably for the first time."[20]

In addition to the healing home and missionary society, the Gospel Tabernacle launched still a third enterprise in the pivotal year of 1883. Early in the year Simpson wrote in his magazine: "Another object contemplated is the opening of a Missionary Training School for Christian Evangelists, where godly and consecrated young men and women can be prepared to go forth as laborers into the neglected fields."[21] The school was to become a formal extension and development of the training classes he had begun in 1882 for workers in the Gospel Tabernacle.

Within a month he could report to his readers, "The Missionary Union is steadily growing in numbers and means. A noble friend in the West has just sent $100 for the proposed Training College for Missionaries. A goodly band of consecrated men and women are already looking forward to commence the full course of study as soon as the Institute is opened."[22]

In Simpson's total view of the church, that "divine pattern" he spoke of, the missionary journal and society, the various tabernacle ministries, and then the training college, were interdependent among themselves and all dependent on the church that gave them purpose for existence.

By July Simpson and his associates drew up the curriculum—twenty-two separate courses—and arranged accommodations for students from outside the city. He wanted all the students to live nearby, where they would have ample opportunity for "actual Mission work in the wide field afforded by a great city and by special evangelistic work connected with the Institute."[23]

On Monday, October 1, 1883, the Missionary Training College formally opened at 446 Eighth Avenue. The tabernacle pastor and Rev. George N. Mead served as professors. The list of lecturers included some of the foremost evangelical speakers and pastors on the East Coast: Dr. A. T. Pierson, Dr. George F. Pentecost, Dr. A. J. Gordon* and Dr. James Brooks.[24]

The curriculum presented a complete outline of Bible study in one year, plus related subjects such as English, Church History and Christian Evidences. The courses were designed "to give the students a thorough instruction in the Word of God, and a practical and experimental training in the various forms of evangelistic and Christian work; besides such other theological and literary studies as are included in a liberal course of education."[25]

The student body, which numbered between forty and fifty students, had only to demonstrate one common qualification: "that they had given up all for Christ, and His work meant all to them."[26]

The first graduating class of twenty-seven students was honored in commencement exercises on July 20, 1884, at the Gospel Tabernacle on Twenty-third Street. Five of the graduates formed the church's first missionary team, destination Congo. Two other graduates, Harriet A. Waterbury* and Ellen A. Griffin,* remained in New York to become valued assistants of Simpson.

In his commencement address, Dr. A. T. Pierson stated that "this and the institution connected with his own church, Bethany Church, Philadelphia, were the only two training colleges connected with churches in the country."[27]

Like its parent church, the training school would have years of building-hopping in the labyrinth of New York. In all, five buildings would house the school until 1890, when it would finally reach its permanent New York facility adjacent to the Gospel Tabernacle at 690 Eighth Avenue.

First Fiasco

Despite their enthusiasm and eagerness to head for the mission field, the school's first graduates were inadequately prepared for the harsh, life-threatening realities of overseas ministry.

The initial group of five young men graduates set out for Congo via England at the end of November, 1884. John Condit led team

*See "The Founder's Team" in the Appendix for more details.

members Francis Gerrish, William Quayle, J. W. Jensen and Mr. Pearson—all members of the tabernacle.

The stormy voyage from Liverpool down the west coast of Africa augered more perilous days to come. Disembarking at Cabinda near the mouth of the Congo River, the missionaries immediately met a stone wall of hostility from Portuguese traders fearful of what the Gospel would do to their hold on the Africans. The newcomers were forced to start without delay for the interior.

The fifty-mile trek on foot to a friendly Baptist mission station on the river sealed the expedition's fate. John Condit, leader of the group, fell victim to fever. Quayle and Pearson continued upriver to Vivi, where they secured tentative approval for a mission site, but it was not to be. Condit died and three of his dispirited colleagues decided to sell their outfits to finance the passage home.

Only Gerrish determined to carry on. Supported by the Missionary Union of Simpson's church, he worked with the Baptists until 1888. Arriving home in New York, he received a royal welcome from his many friends at the Gospel Tabernacle. Within a year he received an even more glorious welcome in heaven. The other three men simply disappeared from view.

In his public statements Simpson had few words of criticism for the unsuccessful team, perhaps feeling partly responsible for their failure. He did try to insure that later missionary recruits received a more adequate preparation for their work.

Missionary articles continued to dominate his journal, and the Missionary Union continued to support overseas workers. The theology of missions in the Gospel Tabernacle could not be thwarted by initial defeat.

Associate Ministries

Although the church organized three major enterprises of its own—the healing home, missionary union and training school—numerous other activities flourished through the independent efforts of groups and individuals in the congregation.

Evangelism characterized these auxiliary projects, just as it did the direct ministries of the church. The members involved took seriously their pastor's insistence that work for Jesus indicated genuine spiritual experience.

Young men preached on street corners and riverside docks, even carrying their message of reconciliation with God on board anchored ships. Tabernacle members pooled their resources to start a mission on Thirteenth Street.

Ladies teamed up for house-to-house visitation and special meetings for "fallen women." The South Street Mission was one of at least four havens begun through their efforts. Mrs. Sidney Whittemore began a similar work, The Door of Hope Mission, for the ruined women drifting on the city's unfeeling streets.

Wealthy tabernacle members gave both time and money to start their own ministries. Mr. and Mrs. Henry Naylor founded Berachah Mission.

O. S. Schultz and his wife funded the Berachah Orphanage for homeless children, and then managed it. The institution gradually grew to a twenty-five room house and several acres of wooded land on 161st Street.

Rev. Albert E. Funk,* formerly a member and minister in the Mennonite Church in Pennsylvania, conducted German-language services in the tabernacle for immigrants who sought the Lord, but not in English. He would later play a key role in the developing movement.

The list of activities at the Gospel Tabernacle grew and changed, making difficult an inventory of ministries. But together they fulfilled the pastor's initial vision for a self-supporting, mainly middle-class church that busied itself with neglected people wherever they were found, down the street or across the ocean.

October Conventions

By 1884 the Gospel Tabernacle had outgrown the Grand Opera Hall and, like its biblical namesake, packed up to move on, one step closer to a more permanent home.

The Twenty-third Street armory, with its large meeting hall and stables, was secured in a remarkable manner that presaged unusual blessing for the congregation within its walls.

Pastor Simpson had tried two years earlier to lease the building, but he was outbid by sponsors of the Oberammergau Passion Play. One lady in particular continued to pray that the theatrical group would remodel the armory for the church's use. "O Lord Jesus," she prayed repeatedly, "make the carpenters fit up that place for us!"

Had the theater company known of those prayers and taken them seriously, they could have saved a small fortune. After investing $70,000 for remodeling work to turn the armory into a theater, they found themselves blocked by city authorities, who vetoed performance of the "blasphemous theatrical."

Forced to give up the lease, the company offered the improve-

*See "The Founder's Team" in the Appendix for more details.

ments to the tabernacle congregation for $5,000. Even that was too much.

"We prayed over it, and God stopped us from going too fast," Simpson recounted. "The building was finally put in the market and sold at auction, and the gentleman bought whom we prayed would buy it. The result is that we have been enabled to come in here without paying a penny for improvements."[28]

The congregation moved into the freshly remodeled building on April 6, 1884, and, with their penchant for plainness, named it the Twenty-third Street Tabernacle. It would serve as their base for the next two years.

Perhaps the most significant development while at that address was inauguration of the October conventions. In tandem with *The Word, The Work and The World,* the conventions would extend the ministry of the Gospel Tabernacle and its pastor nationwide, and become the seed ground for a worldwide movement.

Religious conventions, including summer camps, attracted large audiences in the middle and late 1800s. Simpson had visited several, including the Niagara Conference and D. L. Moody's Northfield (Massachusetts) Convention. The Mildmay Convention in London, England, each spring especially impressed him.

He concluded one magazine editorial in 1883 with this hope: "We earnestly trust that before next year shall close, such a gathering of God's dear children shall be brought together in this city from all parts of the land to consider the great truths which God is speaking to this generation; and also consider the solemn question of evangelistic and missionary work to which His promised coming calls His people with ever increasing urgency."[29]

"Consider great truths" and "consider the solemn questions of evangelistic and missionary work"—these became the platform for the conventions that would have far-reaching impact.

The first convention in the Gospel Tabernacle took place in September of 1884, not October. Few other details have survived. Dr. H. Gratton Guinness* of London, Dr. John Cookman* and Dr. Henry Wilson,* both of New York, were the principal speakers, but certainly the tabernacle pastor and others shared the pulpit. Prior to the October convention of 1885, the pastor, his wife and their oldest son, Albert, attended the International Conference for Holiness and Healing at Bethshan, London. After its conclusion he joined with some other delegates in a preaching tour of several cities in England.

Simpson's London experience may have given him the idea of taking his own October convention on the road. Bethshan certainly

*See "The Founder's Team" in the Appendix for more details.

strengthened his conviction that similar gatherings and tours could inspire and unite American evangelicals better than most other methods.

The October convention of 1885 demonstrated the kind of Christian unity Simpson had in mind. The lead speakers included three Episcopalians from New York: Dr. W. S. Rainsford, Dr. Henry Wilson and Dr. Kenneth MacKenzie; two Methodists: Dr. John Cookman and Rev. Stephen Merritt.* Henry J. Pierson came from Boston, Captain R. Kelso Carter from Philadelphia, Miss Carrie Judd from Buffalo and Rev. H. W. Brown from Chicago.

In terms of the future, perhaps the two most important people attending the 1885 October convention were Isaac Luce, president of the Old Orchard (Maine) Camp Meeting Association, and Hezekiah Chase, a board member. Blessed and impressed, they returned to the next meeting of their board of trustees and secured an invitation asking Simpson to bring a similar convention to Old Orchard the following summer.

This open door provided Simpson the opportunity to enlarge his ministry. It also provided an arena where several dynamics would converge and bring to life a new movement.

Simpson had already arranged for a tour of key cities after the October convention of 1885. Several of the speakers accompanied him to Brooklyn, Philadelphia, Boston, Pittsburgh, Buffalo and as far away as Detroit and Chicago.

The Canadian Connection

During their multicity tour, Simpson and his convention associates visited Buffalo, where Carrie Judd had made arrangements for a series of meetings. No one expected that Buffalo would become the bridge for the new movement to cross over into Canada and attract a following that would eventually grow into a strong and enduring partner with a distinctly Canadian character.

The torchbearer was Rev. John Salmon, an ex-sailor who had run away to sea when he was a boy of fourteen in England. God caught up with him at sea in a "Damascus Road experience" that transformed the foul-mouthed, heavy-drinking, antireligious sailor into a Pauline evangelist who redirected his energies for good.

Salmon passed years in wilderness wanderings from one denomination to another in search of a spiritual home compatible with his tremendous zeal for evangelism and discipling among the unchurched masses. His personal experience of healing and his healing

*See "The Founder's Team" in the Appendix for more details.

ministry to others further alienated him from the doctrinally rigid churches he served.

In 1885, suffering from a severely diseased kidney that God had not chosen to heal immediately, Salmon read a booklet on divine healing authored by Carrie Judd. With characteristic directness, Salmon determined to see Miss Judd in Buffalo. He trusted God for the needed travel funds, which arrived providentially and in short order.

The Canadian cleric arrived from Toronto just in time for Simpson's first convention in Buffalo, October 26 to 30, 1885. He was anointed, prayed for and instantly healed. Salmon immediately stood and joined in praying for the others.

Salmon's credentials seemed especially appropriate for the future alliance of Christians Simpson would initiate. Historian Lindsay Reynolds listed his varied background in a summary that almost read like a statement of faith: "With firm respect for the authority of Scripture derived from his early Presbyterian heritage, he espoused an irrepressible evangelism as a result of his conversion and Methodist training. Because of the circumstance of his spiritual restoration after an early lapse of faith, his beliefs were characterized by both Armenian and Calvinistic traits.

"An Adventist belief in the pre-millennial Second Advent and a believer's baptism by immersion (enhanced by Baptist experience), a Methodist concern for holiness (sanctification) now redefined, a Congregational conviction of the independence of the local church, a firm belief in divine healing taught by W. E. Boardman and A. B. Simpson, and lastly a spectacular personal healing experience through the ministry of A. B. Simpson...."[30]

Not surprisingly, the instant appreciation of Simpson and Salmon for each other during their first contact in Buffalo grew into a deep, lifelong friendship and association in ministry. Salmon had found a spiritual home at last.

Expanding Aspirations

Simpson had more in mind for his convention tours than just conducting deeper life meetings in America's large cities. In an editorial he did some thinking out loud: "A Christian Alliance of all those in all the world who hold in unison the faith of God and the Gospel of full salvation would be a great blessing and a mighty power for good. It might be made a bond of blessed fellowship in prayer and work; and, while not separating any from their present denominational associations, would blend all as the Evangelical Alliance does into a large unity."[31]

These same thoughts would find expression in the first constitution of the Christian Alliance in 1887.

As these convention tours increased in size and scope in later years, they would attract bad press from unsympathetic critics both secular and religious. Simpson's teaching on divine healing and sanctification would be like lightning rods, attracting the most bolts.

Occasionally, however, when critics got close enough to observe what happened in the conventions, they went away with a different attitude. *The Michigan Christian Advocate* had such a change of heart. Admitting that they went to a convention in Detroit with a chip on their shoulder, representatives of the paper were disarmed by what they saw.

They conceded in an editorial, "Cranks they may be in the popular definition, but it is for the lack of just such crankiness that the Christian Church languishes today."

Calling for toleration, the editorial concluded, "They have their health, their spiritual elevation, and their keen enjoyment of unceasing labor for God. On the other hand, we have our invincible theories, our conventional piety, our unimpeachable orthodoxy, and our doctor's bills. Ought we not to be satisfied?"[32]

Tozer added another reason for the opposition to Simpson from various religious quarters once the conventions began to generate large offerings: "Some of the leaders could not forgive him for his ability to raise more missionary money in ten days than they could in ten years."[33]

Others in the religious public noted what Simpson was doing and readily came forward with encouragement and praise. One southern college offered him a Doctor of Divinity degree in recognition for his scholarship and outstanding achievements. Simpson declined, explaining he wanted no honor "that would elevate him in any measure above the lowest of his brethren."[34]

The Christian community brushed aside his objections and from that point on, with a sense of rightness, addressed him as Dr. Simpson.

The Gospel of Songs

Dr. Simpson added one more activity to the life of a New Testament church as he envisioned it: the blessing of music.

Raised in a Covenanter heritage of traditional hymnody, he would never turn his back on the great hymns of the church. But deeply impressed by the part music played in the Louisville campaign—many people were drawn to Christ by Bliss's songs, not only Whittle's sermons—he also saw the value of gospel music.

Intensely personal and immediate in nature, the messages were sung to lively rhythms and tunes easy to remember. "What ministry today has been more honored than gospel song?" Dr. Simpson asked. "How God has shown in a Bliss, Sankey or a Phillips the honor He will put on this simple taste to draw millions by the power of the consecrated melody of the gospel!"[35]

Dr. Simpson used gospel music extensively in his meetings, even though some objected to its popular style. "Popular?" challenged Tozer. "Sure it was popular and it was frowned on by many of the sterile scribes of the synagogues, but to Mr. Simpson the word 'popular' carried no terrors. It meant 'of the people' and it was people he was interested in...so the singing went on and the crowds loved it and kept coming back week after week to enjoy it."[36]

Throughout his ministry Dr. Simpson would be credited with 181 songs for which he wrote the words, music or both.[37] Most of his music would appear in the various editions of the Alliance hymnal, *Hymns of the Christian Life.* The 1908 edition, largest of the hymnbook series, would carry 117 of his songs.

Though lacking formal training in composition and harmony, he wrote the music to many of his first songs—a fact obvious to people as they tried to sing them. Later he would enlist the help of musicians like R. Kelso Carter, Louise Shephard, May Agnew Stephens* and his daughter Margaret.

Dr. Simpson often composed songs linked to his sermons, either the outline or condensed devotional thoughts. A soloist or the congregation would sing the original composition before or after his sermon, helping people to remember his main points. This accounted for the intense feeling and deep personal commitment present in all his songs.

Dr. Simpson's daughter Margaret described how her father might at times arrive at a song in keeping with his sermon. "He used to call me often and say, 'I have a message for you for my sermon tomorrow. Meet me at the piano soon.' There we labored together till he was satisfied it carried his inspiration.

"Sometimes he would say, 'Here, take this. I can't do a thing with it, but this is what I want.'

"And where it was crescendo he would demonstrate it by singing out loudly enough to be heard down the hill, with obvious punctuations and emphasis. When you grasped his idea, he would glow with ecstasy and say, 'You've got it, there, that's fine.' "[38]

Lacking many features of a tightly knit organization, the Alliance found in Dr. Simpson's songs some of the cement needed to hold

*See "The Founder's Team" in the Appendix for more details.

the loosely formed structure together. Alliance people, more than most, quite literally sang their theology, and in doing so discovered ample reason to stay together.

One of his songwriters, May Agnew Stephens, emphasized the seriousness of the text in his songs: "He was a prolific writer of hymns but none were mechanical. They all came from a hidden fire and bore a definite message. And none ever satisfied him unless they expressed the full scope of the Fourfold Gospel.

"Especially the hope of the return of our Lord he felt must be added to every hymn of salvation or service, if at all possible, and he often commented on the failure of many a gospel song to carry its message to the highest point—the coming of Christ."[39]

The quality of music often did not match the strength and beauty of the text in Dr. Simpson's songs. Many of his compositions with unsingable tunes or poor tempo left the congregation stumbling in confusion, and they would eventually be dropped from even the founder's later hymnal editions. Some, like "To the Regions Beyond" and "Yesterday, Today, Forever" would enjoy popularity year after year.

Even Tozer, critical of Dr. Simpson's music, would admit, "After saying all this I would yet confess that hardly a day goes by that I do not kneel and sing in a shaky baritone comfortably off key, the songs of Simpson. They feed my heart and express my longing, and I can find no other's songs that do this in as full a measure."[40]

Healthy Balance

The Missionary Union and Training College, the Berachah Home and Friday meetings, tent campaigns and October conventions—these differing and complementary activities all contributed to Dr. Simpson's understanding of the divine plan found in Scripture concerning the church.

In the congregation could be found no tension between home and foreign priorities, or evangelism and community projects. All the parts functioned in balance because of the Holy Spirit at work building the local church to complete the church universal and bring back the King.

The October convention of 1885, that first tentative step toward wider ministry and fellowship, spread to other key cities, attracted a following, generated momentum. The invitation by the men from Maine to bring the convention to Old Orchard would open a whole new chapter for the fledgling movement.

Old Orchard was ready for Dr. Simpson, and he for Old Orchard.

CHAPTER 5

The Two Alliances

"Regroup for the sake of common cause,"
said the spirit of the age.
One man heard that same message
from the Spirit of the Church.

1886—1890

Context of the Times

New York City and the nation draped the year 1886 in flags, festivities and fireworks as the Lady of the Harbor took up permanent residence off lower Manhattan. The Statue of Liberty, an expression of esteem and friendship by France for its American ally, witnessed massive immigration in an age of old problems and new alliances.

Another event quietly joined history in the green hills of Massachusetts, but for the world it held more enduring promise than any statuary could represent. Evangelist D. L. Moody hosted the first international conference of Christian college students at Mt. Hermon. That gathering formed the embryo of a youthful alliance. The Student Volunteer Movement for Missions emerged two years later under the banner motto, "The evangelization of the world in this generation."

Only 21 of the 250 student participants were settled on overseas ministries when the 1886 conference opened. Before the concluding prayer, 100 of the young people recorded their "purpose, if God permit, to become foreign missionaries."

Eighty-three years later, the movement would disband—after having helped some 20,000 student volunteers join scores of established missions.

Among the more popular young missions of the era was the China Inland Mission. Brought to North America by founder James Hudson Taylor in 1888, the mission had already been sending workers to China from England for twenty-three years. It became the pattern for a new breed of missions, based on faith and interdenominational support.

While evangelical, conservative and liberal groups within Protestantism gradually coalesced into separate doctrinal alliances during the 1880s, considerable goodwill and cooperation still existed among them.

One historian wrote, "They exchanged pulpits, labored together in union revivals, and wrote tolerant reviews of each others' books and articles. Indeed, in the context of the times, it is not particularly surprising that Walter Rauschenbush, the prophet of the Social Gospel, translated the higher life hymns of Fanny J. Crosby and Ira Sankey into German."

One dramatic example of this religious coexistence took place in 1887. The Evangelical Alliance of the United States met in Washington, D.C., to assess the "perils and opportunities" of the age. Leading exponents of all three tendencies (mainstream conservatives, new-theology liberals and higher-life evangelicals) generally agreed that dry rot rendered the church powerless and unattractive. Each in their own way turned from ordinary religion in search of extraordinary religion.

For a surprising cross section of the church this meant a search focused on the Holy Spirit. C. I. Scofield, editor of the reference Bible, said at that time, "Within the last twenty years more has been written and said upon the doctrine of the Holy Spirit than in the preceding eighteen hundred years."

Alignment and realignment seemed to be the spirit of the age as well as of the church. The Austro-German Alliance, the Three Emperors' League, the Triple Alliance, the Franco-Russian Alliance reshaped the European political landscape.

* * *

The energetic pastor of the Gospel Tabernacle in New York noted events nationwide among Christians to emphasize the Holy Spirit and missions, and it all made eminently good sense to him. He sensed in the neglected ranks of the church a desire to transcend creedal differences for the sake of true Christian concerns—holiness of life and a Gospel for the world.

It was time to act.

THE natural amphitheater of Old Orchard camp appeared as if God had jabbed the earth with His finger and said, "Here I will be heard."

On the surrounding slopes, pine trees stood tall, like steeples pointing back to God while spreading cool shade over those who entered the arena's embrace. Single-board benches without backs offered scant comfort to the 4,000 early comers, but at least they could sit. Those who arrived later had to content themselves with standing on the perimeter or sitting on the pine-needle carpeted ground. But the natural bowl was so acoustically ideal that even 15,000 people could hear a speaker using his normal voice.

Tucked in the evergreens bordering Maine's boulder-strewn coast, the amphitheater provided a sounding board for differing causes. Abolitionists like Sumner and Garrison delivered fiery denunciations of slavery in prewar days. Evangelist D. L. Moody exalted the God of love and mercy. President William McKinley would later extol the benefits of his protectionist policies.

To this famous Old Orchard camp in August, 1886, came Dr. Albert B. Simpson for the first of many such conventions. He brought a program unlike anything the camp old-timers had seen. His speakers showed a catholicity of background and a commonality of views, including Major Cole from Chicago, Dr. Arthur T. Pierson from Philadelphia, Miss Carrie Judd from Buffalo. Isaac Luce and Hezekiah Chase, who had attended the October convention in New York the previous year, also spoke. Another local speaker, David Lelacheur,* would have a prominent role in later years.

The main attraction, however, was Dr. Simpson himself. One longtime resident of Old Orchard remembered, years later: "We had no megaphones or speaking apparatus in those days, but when he spoke one could hear a pin drop. He was lowspoken, and all you could think of was Jesus speaking to you."[1]

Even the weather seemed to favor the meetings, she said. "On 'Simpson Sunday,' as I recall, it never rained. It was always in the grove and there were vast crowds."[2] (The last Sunday of the convention was called "Simpson Sunday.")

The Igniting Spark

The crowning achievement of the 1886 Old Orchard camp narrowly missed being a nonevent. W. E. Blackstone* may or may not have been invited to the meetings, but he definitely lacked a place on the speakers' roster. With a certain audacity he pressed Dr. Simpson for an opportunity to speak on Sunday, the convention's biggest day.

Dr. Simpson declined but did give him permission to speak on

*See "The Founder's Team" in the Appendix for more details.

Monday morning, one day before the convention was to close. Whether an act of generosity or wisdom, that decision brought a turning point in the Alliance founder's life and produced consequences still multiplying a century later.

Combining the precision of his business background with the fervor of a hard-sell salesman, Blackstone preached a missionary message such as the Monday audience had never heard. He recited details—appalling statistics in the multimillions—about unevangelized peoples and compared this to the meager attempts by Christians to give them the Gospel.

Blackstone concluded with a sweeping proposition: "If the church were fully commited to the work, it is fair to say that in twenty years the world would be evangelized!"

After a week of rejoicing in the goodness and blessing of the Lord, of realizing all that God had done for them, of listening to deep truths from the Bible, the large audience received Blackstone's challenge like a spark falling on dry tinder. The convention blazed into action that Dr. Simpson had only dared pray and talk about until now.

Before the 1886 convention ended, he had in hand a request by the participants to frame a proposal for an organization to be formed the following year at Old Orchard. The proposed structure must enable them to unite around the deep truths they shared and to place missionaries where they were most needed.

Ground-breaking Months

Months before the 1887 convention at Old Orchard, Dr. Simpson began advertising in *The Word, the Work and the World.* He promised "a much more thorough and systematic plan of Bible study and missionary instruction." Furthermore, he announced that the last two days "will be given to the theme of Foreign Missions. The foreign missionary movement inaugurated last summer will be more fully organized."[3]

In his preliminary coverage of the convention, the editor spoke of only one group, but he envisioned two, each with a specific purpose and both interlocking.

By implication he stated his case for two groups with rhetorical questions in an editorial: "Is it not fitting that the great multitude whom the Holy Spirit has called in these days into a closer union with Jesus, into a deeper revelation of His fulness, should unite in some work for the evangelization of others? That this would be a

*See "The Founder's Team" in the Appendix for more details.

worthy expression of their gratitude and love, and in turn be a bond of delightful union? Has not God given us a secret which the world needs and which the world is not receiving?"[4]

Expanding the missionary theme in the June issue, he wrote: "An informal movement was begun last summer with a view to encouragement of some new missionary effort to reach some of the yet unoccupied fields...and to see if the time has come...for a simple, spiritual and undenominational movement to send the full gospel—which has proven such a blessing to us—to the neglected millions of heathen lands."[5]

In further preparation for the August meeting in Maine, *The Word, the Work and the World* published the ten sections of the proposed constitution for the missionary endeavor tentatively called the Evangelical Missionary Alliance. It characterized the missionaries to be supported as "consecrated persons of both sexes, lay as well as clergy, without regard to their denominational preference."

The principle of self-support and a "spirit of absolute reliance upon God alone for support" would be required of all missionaries. There would be "no fixed remuneration for any missionary after reaching the field." The organization would "simply act as a channel through which such aid may be sent from time to time."

Gospel preaching was to be the primary task of the missionaries. "The formation of native churches [and] the form of church government" would be decided by the "native [local] community and each missionary."

As for the sending agency, they too "will depend entirely upon the promises and faithfulness of God through the voluntary gifts of His people." In addition they would "publish reports of the work of the Alliance, presenting the claims of the work to the Christian public throughout the land."

The sending agency also planned to extend the work "through the formation of local auxiliaries and bands of seven or more throughout the land."[6]

Following the suggested constitution for the Evangelical Missionary Alliance, Dr. Simpson stated reasons for proposing such an organization. In resume, these reasons have a certain enduring relevance:

1. Obedience to Christ's Great Commission to the church.
2. Present accessibility to unevangelized peoples.
3. "The awful need of the human race and the utter inadequacy of all that has yet been done to meet that need."
4. Blessing and prosperity that God has bestowed upon a half-century of foreign missions work in spite of a woefully inadequate effort on the part of the church.

5. Special features of the proposed missionary movement: lay people, both men and women, will be used; economy of administration, self-support and dependence upon God will govern the work; the undenominational principle of organizing churches will be followed, avoiding the "old bigotries" of transplanted western church structures; competition with older missions will be avoided.[7]

Dr. Simpson added yet another reason for the Alliance, this one uniquely theological: Missions is "the Lord's own appointed way of hastening His speedy coming."[8]

Dr. Walter Turnbull would later say at Dr. Simpson's funeral: "He is the only great teacher we know who linked the evangelization of the world as a necessary preparation for Christ's return and with the study of Bible prophecy."[9]

On one occasion a *New York Journal* reporter approached Dr. Simpson with the question, "Do you know when the Lord is coming?"

"Yes," he replied, "and I will tell you if you will promise to print just what I say, references and all."

The reporter's poised notebook gave the ready promise.

"Then put this down: 'This gospel of the kingdom shall be preached in all the world for a witness unto the nations, and then shall the end come.' Matthew 24:14. Have you written the reference?"

"Yes, what more?"

"Nothing more."

The reporter lowered his pencil and said, "Do you mean to say that you believe that when the Gospel is preached to all nations Jesus will return?"

"Just that."

"I think I begin to see daylight," answered the reporter. "I see the motivation and the motive power in this movement."

"Then," said the Alliance leader, "you see more than some of the doctors of divinity."[10]

The Founders' Convention

The preconvention groundwork in *The Word, the Work and the World* served to intensify the excitement of people already enthused about the Old Orchard meetings of July 30 to August 9, 1887. Attendance in the amphitheater on the first Sunday exceeded 2,000. It more than doubled to 4,500 for the concluding Sunday. Participants came from all over the East—New England states, New York, Pennsylvania and Ohio—from the South, the Midwest and Canada.

Speakers from the previous year returned and were joined by

new ones. The presence and power of God filled the teaching and preaching sessions. One healing event in particular seemed to epitomize the high level of excitement and anticipation in the convention.

Ina H. Moses, a twenty-year-old resident of the area, had been severely injured in a sledding accident in 1884 and had been unable to walk without crutches. In the convention of the previous year she had been converted and was trusting the Lord to heal her.

Although in much pain, she attended the 1887 meetings and testified in the Friday afternoon healing service that the Lord had already given her faith she would be healed.

Dr. Simpson described what happened next: "Suddenly the power of God fell upon her and she sprang to her feet, crying out, 'I am healed! Jesus has healed me!'

"Throwing away her crutches, she began to walk to the platform; and, ascending the steps, she stood before the vast assembly with a face shining like the sun. The audience rose spontaneously to their feet, some shouting, many of them weeping and others singing the Doxology. It was a moment that will live like a sunburst in a tempest as long as memory lasts."[11]

The Christian Alliance

Dr. Simpson had implied, but not spoken directly, about two Alliances in his magazine. In the business sessions of the 1887 convention, the first organization considered was the Christian Alliance. He envisioned it as the parent organization that would sponsor and support the missionary effort. It would operate in North America as a nondenominational fellowship for the dual purpose of giving testimony to certain truths and of encouraging like-minded believers to put those truths into action.

Dr. Simpson presented a rationale for the Christian Alliance in a promotional pamphlet. He identified as potential members those "who are more fully one in spiritual fellowship than they are in any single denominational communion."

He singled out some "present truths" that formed a doctrinal basis for fellowship: "One of these truths is the Gospel of full salvation and present and complete sanctification in Jesus Christ.

"Another is the provision Christ has made in the Gospel for our physical redemption through Divine Healing and the physical life, support and strength of our risen and living Lord.

"A third is the doctrine of our Lord's personal, pre-millennial, speedy return, and the necessity for the preparation of the Church and the world for His advent."

These "present truths" unfortunately were not universally accepted, and even occasioned grief for those who held them. This, the founder maintained, constituted another basic reason for the Christian Alliance: "Such an alliance may not only cherish the larger fellowship of sympathy and common testimony, but also promote the union and growth of the scattered flock in all parts of the land and the world."[12]

The constitution of the Christian Alliance clearly stated it had no intention of causing antagonism in the churches, but "to embrace Evangelical Christians of every name."

Dr. Simpson conceded that in some circumstances it might be necessary "to organize independent churches for closer fellowship or more aggressive work," but in most cases "its members will be found to be the most earnest, faithful and spiritually minded people in the various evangelical churches, the most valued helpers of every faithful pastor and of every good work.

"At the same time there are special truths which need to be doubly emphasized and there are chords of spiritual unity more deep and dear than any denominational affinities. And to these truths the Alliance is called to witness."[13]

On the other hand, Dr. Simpson, president of the newly formed fraternal union, made it abundantly clear the Christian Alliance had no intentions either of starting new churches or planning a new denomination.

"Whether this proves superior insight or the total lack of it, history will decide," commented Tozer. "He sought to provide a fellowship only, and looked with suspicion upon anything like rigid organization. He wanted the Alliance to be a spiritual association of believers who hungered to know the fullness of the blessing of the Gospel of Christ, working concertedly for the speedy evangelization of the world."[14]

Dr. Simpson never swerved from that original purpose. Even in later years, he would grant the possibility of exceptions but not abandonment of the principle.

"There are cases continually arising where it is necessary to provide special and permanent religious privileges for little bands of Christian disciples who have either been converted in some evangelistic movement or pushed out of their churches by false teaching and harsh pressure and prejudice.

"Yet these local and independent congregations should never be considered as Alliance churches in any technical sense, but simply independent movements which God Himself has specially raised up 'through the present distress' and over which we exercise for the time a certain spiritual oversight."[15]

The founder's unequivocal attitude of "There is no such thing as an Alliance church" was well-meaning but costly in terms of growth. "The law of growth is always from simple to complex," observed Tozer, and Dr. Simpson's efforts to keep the movement simple would create problems for the movement in later years.

The Evangelical Missionary Alliance

In point of time, the Evangelical Missionary Alliance (EMA) was formed after the Christian Alliance. In comparison of relationships, it was an "association within the Christian Alliance designed to be purely missionary."[16] In sequence of action, it had to flow from lives vitalized by truth that found its ultimate expression and source in Jesus Christ.

"All for Jesus" did more than summarize the life of Dr. Simpson. The total commitment it expressed gave birth, life and direction to all he envisioned for the two Alliances.

In later years the founder would save his major missionary address for "Simpson Sunday," but in the charter convention of 1887 he delayed until Monday morning. He gave an eloquent, fervent appeal that must have brought "the sky low."

Then he concluded, "I stand here today to plead for ample methods and economical ones that shall send forth simple-hearted, earnest men and women trusting in the Word of God and in His power to save."[17]

The proposed constitution of the Evangelical Missionary Alliance had already been published in the magazine. Convention delegates now adopted it with only one slight editorial change and the inclusion of two additional clauses.

Before dispersing, participants of the Old Orchard organizing convention elected officers representing all parts of the country and instructed that a general meeting of the two Alliances meet in New York prior to the October convention in the Gospel Tabernacle.

Historian Lindsay Reynolds noted that although the movement would not be organized in Canada for another eighteen months, Canadians were represented on both boards.

William John Fenton, of Toronto, an associate of Rev. John Salmon, was selected as a vice-president of the Evangelical Missionary Alliance. He was the only Canadian to hold office in the organization, but the Canadians had a much higher representation in the Christian Alliance. Two Canadians were made vice-presidents and two others elected to the general committee. Salmon continued as a vice-president for twenty-five consecutive years, a record among the founding vice-presidents.[18]

Convention Theology and Doxology

Dr. Simpson always cherished Old Orchard more than any other camp meeting location, and no wonder. God had done so much for him there personally and had made its grounds the birthplace of a movement that epitomized his beliefs and goals.

Old Orchard and summer conventions elsewhere in the United States and Canada proved second only to the editor's pen in promoting the rapid expansion and influence of the movement. The conventions "were a puzzle to the professor of religious psychology and an enigma to the reporter," wrote A. E. Thompson, "but to the hungry-hearted they were a feast, to the weary a refreshing, to the sick a fountain of healing, to the Christian worker an inspiration, and to the worn missionary a haven of rest."[19]

At first the thousands of people who attended the conventions belonged only to denominational churches. They drank in biblical teaching too often lacking in their churches, enjoyed the company of like-hearted believers, and went home to share with others what they had learned.

As inevitably happens whenever people become enthused about their religion, the secular press ridiculed the conventions and skeptical church leaders warned against strange teachings and goings-on.

While attending an Old Orchard convention, one Presbyterian minister received a letter warning him against the dangerous theology of the Alliance. "Bless you," he wrote in reply, "their theology is all gone up in doxology."[20]

Follow-up Convention

Some delegates at the 1887 Old Orchard convention went home to Oberlin, Ohio, too excited to wait for the October meeting. They quickly organized a similar convention in Linwood Grove, Vermillion, during September. Other enthusiasts from Ohio, western New York and Michigan joined them in organizing the first district "branch" of the Christian Alliance and appointing delegates to the October gathering in New York City.

The Christian Alliance officers and directors took action in October to further develop the movement and plan for its extension to every part of the country. Then, with a prayer and a figurative changing of hats, some of the same individuals became the Evangelical Missionary Alliance directors, eager "to begin practical work immediately."

They had not far to look for workers. Helen Dawley, a staff worker of Carrie Judd's mission in Buffalo, had come to the October convention with her trunk packed to go overseas. After accepting assignment to India, she became the first appointee of the newly formed Alliance to set foot on foreign soil.

William Cassidy was already studying at the Missionary Training Institute when the October convention took place. He, his wife, Elizabeth, and two small daughters, had come to New York from Toronto, where he had been a school principal by day and a medical student at night. Sensing a call to medical missionary work in Japan, he had offered his services to the Canadian Methodist mission board. Rejected for lack of such an opening, he came to New York to further his medical studies and found lodging for his family in Simpson's school dormitory.

The Cassidys, along with five other volunteers, became the first appointees of the Alliance. He had the additional distinction of being ordained as a missionary to China, the first missionary ordained in the new movement.

The board acceded to his request that he go first to China and open up the work, and then send for his family. While he and others waited at Grand Central Station for a train to the West Coast, someone suggested they sing, "Take the name of Jesus with you, child of sorrow and of woe."

Cassidy objected, saying he was no "child of sorrow and of woe." Instead they sang, "God be with you 'til we meet again." This side of heaven, that was never to be.

Going by ship to China, Cassidy chose to travel steerage, the lowest and cheapest class, so he could mingle with the Chinese. When smallpox broke out in steerage he refused to seek safer quarters and instead tried to use his medical training to help the sick. He contracted smallpox and was put ashore at Kobe, Japan.

There in the land he had originally felt called to, Cassidy died and was buried in January of 1888. He thus earned one final distinction in the newly formed Alliance: its first missionary casualty.

In the following year, 1889, the Gospel Tabernacle in New York found a different kind of resting place: a more permanent location of its own.

After moving ten times in eight years, after watching attendance swell or shrink depending on the location, after developing a highly diversified and successful program of ministries, after growing into a large congregation needing facilities suited to its particular needs—after all this, the Gospel Tabernacle purchased property on the corner of Eighth Avenue and Forty-fourth Street and hired a builder.

The plan included a bookstore on Eighth Avenue with dormitory and classroom facilities for the Missionary Training Institute above it. Berachah Home, a six-story building, would face Forty-fourth Street. The Gospel Tabernacle would occupy the rear of the property with entrances on both streets.

The cornerstone ceremony took place on January 12, 1889, and the complex stood ready for use ten months later. It was not only built fast, but it was built well. The builder served as the first treasurer of the Alliance and as an elder in the church: David Crear.*

The complex would serve the needs of both the church and the movement until the mid-1970s.

A Different Approach

Commenting on formation of the Evangelical Missionary Alliance, its founder said, "It is not in any kind of opposition to the great societies already in the field. It is simply one more added. Would to God there were one hundred more."[21]

In balance, however, the new missionary movement was not "simply one more added." It did bring a new dimension to the spectrum of foreign missions: the diversity of a nondenominational alliance of missionaries backed by the stability of an alliance of supporters in organized branches holding in common the fullness of Jesus.

The religious community in North America had not seen anything quite like the two Alliances. It was soon to see even more.

*See "The Founder's Team" in the Appendix for more details.

CHAPTER 6

The Missionary Explosion

The final decade of the century introduced the first decade of a new missionary movement with startling vigor.

1891—1897

Context of the Times

The "Gilded Age" of the 1890s spread euphoric confidence across the nation that all things were possible through science and industry.

Not one but three railroads straddled the nation, opening new markets and vast natural resources. Businessmen and investors jostled one another in their hurry to form cartels, combines, corporations, pools and trusts of every description. "Big Business leaped from the cradle with steel sinews and a giant's appetite," wrote one historian concerning the era.

A corresponding enthusiasm in Europe expressed itself in unbridled imperialism. Colonial powers dismembered Africa, four times the size of Europe, in just thirty-five years. Asia was also carved into spheres of influence.

The United States refused to join the colonial empire club, but did occupy the Philippines at the triumphant close of the Spanish-American War. That conflict temporarily ended America's isolation from the world. During that same era of the 1890s, the nation emerged as a major force in foreign missions of the church.

The modern missionary movement in the United States had begun with formation of the American Board of Commissioners in 1812. Adoniram Judson was to missions in America what William Carey was in England. The earliest mission enterprises started as interdenominational efforts, but as the work grew, each denomination felt the need of having its own board.

Denominational missions faltered around mid-century, before

and after the divisive Civil War that split communions into family feuds, North versus South. Preoccupation with the spiritual needs of expanding frontier areas further diverted personnel and funds from overseas work. By the 1870s denominational mission boards had only several hundred active foreign missionaries.

The holiness movement seemed to inspire a new wave of missionary enterprise: independent faith missions. The Evangelical Missionary Alliance (1887) mobilized along with other vigorous young groups like the China Inland Mission (1888 in America), The Evangelical Alliance Mission (1890), Sudan Interior Mission (1893) and Africa Inland Mission (1895).

These newcomer missions saw themselves as relating to denominational missions in a complementary and cooperative manner. But, like the holiness movement that inspired their formation, faith missions were viewed by the denominations as competitive and divisive. This lack of acceptance did not stop the movement: Every major nineteenth century faith mission continues to the present.

Accepting evangelical volunteers from any denomination, trusting God for support and majoring in evangelism and church planting, these missions quickly advanced American Protestantism to a leading role in world evangelism.

The churches of other nations did their part as well. Church historian Kenneth Scott Latourette noted that at the end of "The Great Century" every Christian nation in the world was represented on the mission field.

In his panoramic view of missions, J. Herbert Kane wrote, "Never before in a period of equal length had Christianity or any other religion penetrated for the first time as large an area as it had in the nineteenth century."

* * *

The newly formed Evangelical Missionary Alliance and its parent body, the Christian Alliance, played a major role in the new surge of overseas activity. Little would be heard among Alliance branches in the 1890s about forming independent churches similar to Dr. Simpson's New York Gospel Tabernacle. Alliance people in the branches were too busy finding, training, equipping and sending missionaries to neglected areas and unreached peoples.

THE DECADE following formation of the two Alliances would be mostly dominated by missionary activity, but it began differently.

From 1887 to 1890, both movements got off to a slow start, although the Christian Alliance achieved more noticeable growth than the Evangelical Missionary Alliance, and rightly so.

The missions organization had to start from zero—no candidates, no support network, no organized work overseas. The North American fellowship had an obvious starting point in Dr. Simpson's monthly magazine, *The Word, the Work and the World,* which attracted thousands of enthusiastic supporters across the nation. When the monthly appeared more frequently as *The Christian Alliance and Missionary Weekly* in 1889, its readers enjoyed an increased sense of unity.

Dr. Simpson's city and summer conventions did more than the magazine to get the movement going. These special gatherings of two to ten days generated a certain spirit and common bond that gave substance to their common cause. Simpson achieved, for the first time, according to Tozer, "a synthesis of the best features of several other kinds of public meeting, and succeeded in producing in one place and at once a Bible conference, a camp meeting, an evangelistic campaign and a missionary promotional meeting."[1]

The Fourfold Gospel exalting Christ as Savior, Sanctifier, Healer and Coming Lord ran like a rich vein of gold through all the teaching and preaching. Evangelism at home and missions abroad channeled the awakened concern of participants into concerted efforts. And a spirit of unity gave the name "Alliance" special meaning.

"They say the number of speakers on my convention platforms makes my announcements look like a small-town telephone directory," Simpson conceded. "But I have a good reason for all that. I want to enjoy the broadest fellowship possible myself, and I want my people to receive the benefit of the ministry of all God's gifted servants, regardless of whether they agree with me in everything or not."[2]

The conventions gradually spread from Old Orchard and the New York Gospel Tabernacle to other areas: Vermillion, Ohio (1887); Western Springs, near Chicago (1889); Round Lake, near Albany, New York (1890); and Atlanta, Georgia (1899). Eventually the conventions would move upward into Canada (1889) and westward to California (1908), until they spanned the nation.

Cautious Reception

Dr. Simpson faced a dilemma. He recognized in the "Fourfold Gospel people" a potential power base for a sweeping new movement in world evangelism. He also realized that almost all these consecrated, like-minded Christians already belonged to various churches—a relationship he desired to strengthen, not dissolve. He could not imagine the two Alliances as anything other than spiritual catalysts among existing denominations for holy living and world missions.

But how to unite their efforts for a costly, concerted missionary enterprise? On whom could he count? How many and where?

The solution seemed to lie in encouraging the formation of "branches." These fraternal, informal groups of Christians subscribed to a simple sixty-four word creed. They held public meetings weekly or monthly, at times that did not conflict with regular church activities. Under the leadership of a local superintendent chosen by the group, they met to encourage one another in the deeper truths of the Bible and "to promote the interest of Christ's kingdom" in the local church and overseas.

Dr. Simpson urged these believers to send in membership cards and join the gathering movement. When publishing in his magazine the 1887 constitution of the Christian Alliance, the editor added a note: "It is very desirable to push the membership so as to have at least a nucleus in every important center of the population."[3]

Dr. Simpson's magazine readers and convention attendees had little hesitancy in identifying with the Fourfold Gospel or the cause of world missions. But dual membership? How would being an Alliance adherent affect their church membership?

Lack of understanding kept initial growth in the Christian Alliance to a slow pace. By mid-1890 the magazine reported meetings in only forty-one branches in fourteen states and Canada.[4]

Only a few independent, incorporated churches identified officially with the Christian Alliance. Among them, the Gospel Tabernacle in New York, Bethany Church in Toronto and Bethany Church in Peterborough.

The latter two churches were in fact more "Alliance" than the Gospel Tabernacle. The constitution of Dr. Simpson's church in New York committed the congregation only to the basic tenets of evangelical faith, but the two Canadian churches were bound by constitutions that specified in detail the Alliance themes of Christ as Savior, Sanctifier, Healer and Coming King.

First Steps

The Evangelical Missionary Alliance progressed even more slowly during the first three years, and it was perhaps just as well. The first missionary party sent out by the Gospel Tabernacle in 1884 had met with disaster, partly due to lack of proper training and planning.

Basic questions needed study before a new wave of recruits plunged into dangerous areas overseas. What would be the criteria for approving candidates and training them? for determining the level of support and the method of securing it? for selecting the target areas overseas and getting personnel into those areas?

The Alliance founder later spelled out some of these guiding principles that have timeless significance.

1) "The Alliance emphasizes the special agency and superintendency of the Holy Ghost in the work of missions, seeking only for wholly consecrated missionaries and holding the work under the constant direction of the Spirit of God.

2) "Along with this naturally follows that the work should be a work of faith and that it should be maintained by a spirit of prayer and continual dependence on God.

3) "The Alliance missionary work is evangelistic and aggressive rather than educational and institutional.

4) "Our chosen fields are 'the regions beyond,' the unoccupied portions of the heathen world.

5) "The principle of economy is rigidly aimed at. The expenses of home administration are reduced to the lowest possible figure. Missionaries on the field are not promised regular salaries, but simply [allowances to cover] their expenses.

6) "The principle of sacrifice is the deepest element in our work."[5]

The Alliance sent out nineteen missionaries from 1887 to 1890, while three others already overseas joined the mission and continued their work.

Helen Dawley and Carrie Bates sailed for India in 1887 and 1888 respectively. They began working with the American Faith Mission, which eventually merged with the Alliance.

Seven sailed for China between 1888 and 1890, completing the unfinished journey of William Cassidy, who died in Japan. Mrs. Elizabeth Cassidy and her two daughters formed part of that group.

Four missionaries led by M. H. Reid arrived in Congo in 1888 to attempt what the previous group failed to do. They succeeded, but at a cost: Mathilda Reid, the superintendent's wife, died in childbirth and the baby with her. The single woman in the group had to leave the field seriously ill. John Kuno, a graduate of the Missionary Training College, arrived in 1890 to reinforce the work.

A $2,000 gift to open a mission in Japan enabled Helen Kinney to board ship in 1889 for Yokohama. She was teaching English from the Bible when Clara Howard joined her in 1891. Another designated gift made possible a witness in Palestine. Lucy Dunn in 1889 and Elizabeth Robertson in 1890, both members of the

Gospel Tabernacle, went to the Holy Land as independents but later joined the Alliance.

Canadian Cooperation

When the two Alliances organized at Old Orchard in 1887, John Salmon and his Canadian colleagues accepted leadership roles even though the movement had not yet penetrated the Dominion. Two years later Canada was ready and, appropriately, the first invitation to conduct an Alliance convention came from Hamilton, city of the founder's first pastorate.

Some discussion between Hamilton and Toronto representatives preceded the event. Each group wanted to host the meeting. An ad hoc committee from the two cities—a Methodist, two Presbyterians, a Congregationalist and a Plymouth Brethren—reached agreement on Hamilton as the conference host. They secured the First Methodist Church from February 3-5, 1889.

The pastor in whose church they met made ungraciously clear in his welcome that he might not be able to endorse all that would follow. But when the guest speaker stood, such comments were quickly forgotten.

A reporter described Dr. Simpson as "a tall gentleman with a lofty forehead thrown into relief by bushy black hair and beard. He is an eloquent speaker of the high pressure, emotional type, and by his earnestness and power created a marked impression on his hearers."[6]

After several days of devotional services and a healing meeting, the convention concluded with a business session. The participants organized The Dominion Auxiliary Branch of the Christian Alliance. This national governing body would oversee all local branches in Canada and itself be subject to the Board of Managers in New York.

The charter convention elected W. H. Howland, president; W. J. Fenton, secretary; and A. I. MacKenzie, treasurer. Ten vice-presidents, including John Salmon, were chosen from the four charter branches: Toronto, Hamilton, Montreal and Ottawa. Other vice-presidents, including two women, were later added.

Members of the Canadian Auxiliary showed little enthusiasm at first for the Evangelical Missionary Alliance. Historian Reynolds explained that "this was not the result of disinterest in foreign missions, but indeed because of an already well developed missionary interest."[7]

Christians in Toronto especially felt little need for another mission organization. In addition to missionary programs by five major denominations and numerous smaller groups, the China Inland Mission made its headquarters in "Toronto the Good."

Even John Salmon showed little interest in Alliance missions, saying, "To me it appears a small matter who does the work in a foreign land so long as it is done unto the Lord."[8] Maggie Scott, one of the vice-presidents, obviously had similar thoughts: She went overseas with the China Inland Mission.

William John Fenton, whose Plymouth Brethren assemblies had no vigorous missionary program at the time, became the chief advocate for Alliance missions in Canada. He served as a founding vice-president of the missionary organization since Old Orchard days.

Due in part to his influence, five young ladies left Toronto in October, 1889, to study at the Missionary Training College in New York. Their enrollment marked a turning point in Canadian attitudes toward Alliance missions.

Quick to understand the significance of their arrival as only a Canadian could, Dr. Simpson secured permission from the Board of Managers in November, 1889, to change the name of the missionary organization to International Missionary Alliance. The close harmony in missionary work begun that year would continue even after the Canadian Alliance, some ninety years later, would become autonomous and administer its own church affairs.

Prayer Alliance

The new partnership between Canadians and Americans in the Alliance brightened an otherwise dull picture. From November, 1889, to August, 1890, no new Alliance missionaries went overseas. Two-thirds of the workers in the field were women, a ratio that would continue through the 1890s. Two of the most difficult countries, Japan and Palestine, were first entered by single women.

Something had to be done, or the newly born movement would die in the cradle.

Dr. Simpson followed a predictable and admirable course. In May of 1890 he began a series of sermons on prayer that continued into July at the Gospel Tabernacle. Readers of the magazine saw the same material in print. When the series ended, he published the sermon in a book, *The Life of Prayer,* and further extended the impact of his message.

He editorialized in a May issue of the magazine, "God has laid it on our hearts to suggest a Prayer League for the world's evangelization in the next ten years."[9]

More teaching on prayer appeared in an August issue, together with a prayer pledge card the editor asked readers to sign and return "so that an exact list can be kept."

He then followed with these words, "We believe that this Prayer Alliance will prove to be the mightiest force in the spread of missions. It is not understood that this large-hearted, worldwide petition is for a moment intended to be limited to the Alliance. It is not a prayer that the Christian Alliance shall evangelize the world within the next ten years, but that God Himself shall work through all the agencies which He employs."[10]

The prayer theme surfaced and resurfaced in the 1890 convention at Old Orchard. Unusually large attendance forced even the weekday meetings from the tabernacle to the outdoor amphitheater in the grove.

In his missionary address on the final Sunday, Dr. Simpson spoke of sitting by an open window far into the night and hearing from one of the cottages "the voice of prayer go forth all night long...that the mighty God would work with all His power and glory."[11]

Dr. Simpson told the assembled thousands that he hoped the man's prayer would prove prophetic and that his prayer burden would "go forth from this mighty convocation and be caught up by all the world until it shall be answered by the voices of heaven above proclaiming, 'the kingdoms of this world have become the kingdom of our Lord and of His Christ.' "[12]

Not one to trust eloquence alone, the speaker concluded by proposing the formation of a Prayer Alliance to "pray for the evangelization of the world during the present century and for the speedy coming of our Lord Jesus."[13] Then, for the first time in Alliance history, Dr. Simpson had pledge cards distributed among the Old Orchard attendees—and the pledge was for prayer, not money.

Sudan Volunteers

A drama already unfolding in 1890 gave praying Alliance people an immediate and tangible cause. One day early in the year, with no advance warning, seven student volunteer missionaries appeared at the Gospel Tabernacle. Enroute from Kansas to the African vastness of the Sudan, the young people had no money to get there and no training in what to do when they did arrive. But if they were short on funds and expertise, they were rich in missionary zeal and sacrificial spirit.

This attitude delighted the Gospel Tabernacle pastor and his congregation. They provided the five young men and two women with lodging in Berachah for several weeks until passage could be secured for Africa—and no doubt contributed generously to their project.

By the sailing date of May 15, 1890, the Alliance had practically adopted the seven young people and two others that had preceded them to Africa as an advance team: Eliphalet Kingman, group leader, and James A. Trice, his black companion. Alliance support for the group turned even more determined and concerned when word filtered back that four of the seven died of fever before the year ended.

Dr. Simpson came under some severe criticism at the time of the deaths. People assumed that because the young people had stayed at Berachah, a healing center, they had been influenced by Simpson to embrace the teaching of divine healing and, at his insistence, refuse medical aid.

The controversy obligated him to make a clear statement concerning divine healing and missionaries overseas: "We do believe that God heals His sick and suffering children when they can fully trust Him.

"At the same time we believe that no one should act precipitately or presumptuously in this matter, or abandon natural remedies unless they have an intelligent, Scriptural and unquestioning trust in Him alone and really know Him well enough to touch Him in living contact as their Healer.

"We give no instructions to our missionaries in this matter, but leave them wholly free to use or not to use medical aid as they are led of the Lord and can individually trust Him....

"Therefore we say to our own dear workers who go to the foreign field, 'Let every man be fully persuaded in his own mind.' "[14]

The investment of love and prayer in the student volunteers by the Gospel Tabernacle reaped ample rewards. The five surviving Sudan missionaries eventually joined the Alliance and served with great distinction.

Kingman became superintendent of the Sudan field. Roy Coddling and James Trice, the first black missionary of the Alliance, transferred their work to the Alliance with him. Jennie Dick, the second woman in the original group, died in 1892.

John Jaderquist* returned to the United States in 1892, graduated from the Missionary Training Institute and became an Alliance pastor. Years later he would be elected publications secretary of the Alliance and serve on the Board of Managers.

In retrospect, the concerted emphasis on prayer for missions and the timely arrival of the Sudan volunteers made the promise of Isaiah 65:24 seem most appropriate: "And it shall come to pass,

*See "The Founder's Team" in the Appendix for more details.

that before they call, I will answer; and while they are yet speaking, I will hear."

Round Lake Breakthrough

If the Sudan volunteers appeared as an unexpected answer to prayer, the summer conventions held an even greater surprise. The sudden surge of missionary interest in response to prayer came not at the expected locations of Old Orchard or the Gospel Tabernacle. The breakthrough began at the Methodist campgrounds in Round Lake, New York, in July of 1891.

Even the eleven-day program gave no hint of events soon to happen. The New York State Alliance Branch leaders decided, with some misgivings, to devote the last two days to missions: city mission work on Monday and foreign missions on Tuesday.

At the early morning Bible study session on Tuesday, the speaker read the Lord's last words concerning world evangelism. He concluded by saying, "How simple and practicable it would be to send the Gospel to every creature in the next ten years."[15]

Not particularly profound words, yet they produced an electrifying effect. Almost everyone present stood and pledged to unite in prayer and effort to win the world for Christ. Several offered themselves as missionaries, and one minister laid his little girl on the altar as an offering to the Lord for future missionary work.

At the 10:30 meeting, several speakers briefly presented the needs of various mission fields. Louise Shepard rose and admitted that since her conversion, "never until this morning had she really been aroused to foreign missionary work." She had put her jewels aside after her conversion, and she now offered them to the Lord. Estimating their worth at $250, she asked who would add an equal amount so that together they might support one missionary for a year.

"An extraordinary scene then began. One after another began to take off pins, rings, watches, chains and other precious heirlooms, many of them gifts and dear by every tie of holy affection, and laid them on the missionary altar."[16] Others placed money on the altar, until the total value rose to $1,000, sufficient to sustain two missionaries for one year.

In the afternoon a woman added enough to support a third missionary, and a little later money was given for a fourth worker. Two young men consecrated themselves to overseas service.

The service had an especially profound impact on Louise Shepard. She had become a Christian only the previous December and had begun almost immediately to travel with Dr. Simpson's convention team. A gifted musician and singer, college trained and gifted in writing, she had already proven a valuable worker, but from this day on, she would be an even greater asset to the new movement with its commitment to missions.

The enthusiastic giving evident at Round Lake would become one of the standard but always exciting features of Simpson's conventions. But the gold and jewelry offerings left Dr. Simpson uneasy. It gave the newspapers a field day in their constant search to sensationalize events in his conventions.

The idea of offering valuable jewelry, sometimes precious family heirlooms, for missions fitted nicely their most familiar charge of mass hypnosis. The media accused Simpson of casting a spell on his audiences so that people would give impulsively, against their better judgment, and even without being aware of what they were doing.

Since Simpson wanted no taint of discredit attached to the Alliance if it could be avoided—especially in the sensitive area of finances—he quietly discouraged this practice. In some cases he had jewelry returned to owners whose spouses or friends had become angry over the donation. The practice gradually died out, and with it, the adverse publicity.

All this was accomplished on the closing day of camp by a small congregation of about one hundred people. Dr. Simpson, perhaps sensing "the sound of a going in the tops of the mulberry trees," believed God had begun to move on His people.

In an editorial he reasoned that what happened at Round Lake could be expected in the twenty-four other conventions and local branches. He concluded it would be reasonable to expect one hundred new missionaries during the following twelve months.

Readers of *The Christian Alliance and Missionary Weekly* began to pray specifically about the 100-missionary goal for the year. In anticipation of this prayer being answered, Dr. Simpson made changes in the Missionary Training College to handle more students and prepare them better. He brought in Dr. Frederic W. Farr* as vice-president to teach and to manage daily administration of the school while he would be away answering the many speaking invitations that must certainly come.

Dr. Farr was pastoring the Pine Street Baptist Church in Milford, Massachusetts, at the time. He had attended several Old Orchard conventions and also meetings held by Dr. Simpson in Boston. The two men were drawn to each other by their similar convictions.

*See "The Founder's Team" in the Appendix for more details.

A graduate of both Colby College and Newton Theological Seminary, Dr. Farr brought to the Missionary Training College that higher level of academic discipline that Dr. Simpson desired. Even after becoming pastor of the Bethlehem Baptist Church in Philadelphia, he would continue to lecture regularly at the college.

Old Orchard Response

The 1891 Old Orchard convention followed the Round Lake meetings by one month. The high level of blessing on which the July camp ended seemed to characterize the August meetings at the start. The opening prayer service was "crowded from floor to ceiling and full of the Holy Ghost," Dr. Simpson jubilantly reported in the magazine.[17]

An audience of nearly 5,000 attended the first Sunday's services, and many of them stayed for the entire period of August 8-16. After a week of rich blessing, in which some sixty people were converted and then baptized, the final Sunday seemed to bring heaven near.

It was, in Dr. Simpson's words, "the most wonderful outpouring of the Holy Spirit and missionary consecration that we have ever seen. One after another rose and asked the privilege of supporting a missionary until about forty workers had been provided for by individuals.

"Then smaller sums were given by scores and hundreds. After an hour or more of ceaseless, overflowing liberality, it was found that about fifty-four missionaries had been provided for and over $25,000 pledged for one year."[18] (This was the first missionary pledge offering in the Alliance.)

The "Simpson Sunday" offering of the 1891 Old Orchard convention featured a precedent-setting event that would become a distinguishing feature of Alliance giving and a critical factor in the entire financial foundation of the movement: the pledge offering. Dr. Simpson introduced the concept of a faith promise as a free but solemn vow before God concerning financial support of world evangelization.

"This is simply an estimate on the principle of faith and love of what we will endeavor and may reasonably expect to give," he explained. "This we make in dependence on God, and then we go home and work it out in our business and in the self-denials of every day."[19]

The excitement and significance of the final Sunday missionary rally was captured in reportorial style by a visiting journalist of the *Baltimore Sun.* Although written about a later convention, it conveyed something of the high drama that characterized the Old Orchard conventions throughout the Simpson era.

"These mission meetings have been increasing in interest until now annually they attract attention on account of the immense sums of money annually raised. The meeting was different in several ways from any ever held before.

"Through the windows of the Old Orchard House shortly after daybreak this morning there came to the ears of the *Sun* reporter the strains of the gospel carol, 'Let the blessed sunshine in.' They came from the throats of all the alliancers at the grove, half a mile away, who thus early had begun the services of the day. From this time on the people at the camp grounds steadily increased in numbers, so that when Dr. Simpson arose to make his appeal for missionary money he looked out upon a mass of humanity of over 15,000 persons.

"The sight as the vast assembly rose, was inspiring when under magnetic leadership they would join in singing some old hymns. In all, fully 20,000 people were in the grove. At least 10,000 of these remained for hours and hung breathlessly on every word Dr. Simpson uttered.

"His hold on the vast audience was remarkable. He could sway them at will. If he said 'sing very softly and tenderly,' the mass would just breathe the melody of some hymn. Then at a word they would fairly shake the ground. So during his sermon they would drink in every word. His discourse was more like a talk than a sermon, not nearly as much of a rhetorical or oratorical effort as in former years.

"His text was Luke 10:2: 'Pray ye, therefore, the Lord of the harvest that He would send forth laborers into His harvest,' but the theme constantly repeated was, 'Simon, son of Jonas, lovest thou Me more than these?'

"The *Sun* reporter is able to say from absolute proof that the Alliance received today what could be taken to any bank and sold for $70,000."[20]

The momentum of missionary fervor did not fold with the tents at Old Orchard. In the September 18 issue of the magazine, the editor reported that five more people wanted to sustain missionaries overseas. He also wrote that an additional $30,000 to $40,000 would be needed to cover travel expenses of all the new missionaries.

Before that issue of the magazine went to press, Simpson added an updated report: An anonymous person had already given the entire amount needed.[21]

Tabernacle Surge

The first hundred missionary candidates and their travel funds were now available—and the year not yet ended. So Dr. Simpson raised his sights and called for another hundred recruits. He especially appealed to young men, promising them room and board while they studied in the Missionary Training College and met with the Board of Managers.

Anticipation ran high as the October 4 -12 dates of the Gospel Tabernacle convention approached. Pastor Simpson had been away in city conventions during most of September, and he feared that preparations for the meetings would be inadequate.

His fears were ungrounded, however, as speakers like Dr. Henry Wilson, R. Kelso Carter, Rev. John Salmon, Mrs. Sarah Grier Beck, Dr. F. W. Farr and Dr. A. J. Gordon lined up to address the crowded meetings. Louise Shepard's numerous solos added to the impact of the messages.

The first part of the convention especially emphasized deeper truths such as divine healing, sanctification and the Lord's return. The last Saturday through Monday evening services focused on missions. Following Dr. Simpson's Sunday appeal for more missionaries, $18,000 was quickly pledged, an amount adequate to send thirty-six missionaries. This offering not only came from a congregation one-fourth the size of Old Orchard crowds, but also from many who had already attended the summer camp.

When offering time came in the rally, no doubt Sophie Lichtenfels* led the parade as the congregation marched forward to place their gifts on the altar. She would deposit her sack of savings with a solid thud and a hearty "Praise the Lord!" A scrubwoman whose German accent was as rough as her manners, Sophie had a way of making people forget her castaway clothes and rawboned features. She usually left them thinking about the Lord and about how much more they could do for Him.

When the pastor asked for missionary volunteers, 187 people immediately stood, including many "whose age would probably render their going unwise," he observed. On Monday night seventy young men and one hundred young women "sprang to their feet, all ready and glad to go forth if the Lord would accept them," and he added that another 500 people arose, vowing "henceforth they would consecrate their lives to make the evangelization of the world their chief business."[22]

*See "The Founder's Team" in the Appendix for more details.

Prayer, which rendered all this possible, continued in a dominant role. The October convention closed with a nightlong prayer meeting led by Dr. Wilson. The convention and its conclusion may have provided the final nudge in persuading this remarkable man to become more closely related to the Alliance. If so, the whole convention was worth that one decision.

Wilson obtained leave from the senior rector at St. George's Episcopal Church to become associate pastor of the Gospel Tabernacle. He even received permission from his bishop to erect an altar in one of the Tabernacle chapels and there conduct an Episcopal service of Holy Communion each Sunday morning.[23]

Later, during the last seven years of his life, Dr. Wilson would become the senior field superintendent for the Alliance and spend at least half his time in long, difficult travels into every part of the United States and Canada, and even to Sweden.

Emerging Force

By 1893 the Alliance began to emerge as a missionary force. In six years of operation, 180 missionaries worked on forty stations in twelve fields. Twenty-three colleagues had paid for these advances with their lives. The fields occupied were Congo (now Zaire), Sudan, India, China (Central, South and North), Japan, Bulgaria, Palestine, Alaska, Haiti and the Dominican Republic.

Growth of the Alliance and the attendant problems of a missionary society of global dimensions convinced Dr. Simpson he ought to tour the fields for a firsthand inspection. He left New York in January, 1893, on a world-circling tour of seven months, the longest he ever undertook. The journey took him to Alliance fields in the Middle and Far East, but not to those in Africa and South America.

He spent as much time being pastor to the missionaries as administrator of the fields. The initial period of work was pioneer in nature, producing few visible results other than graves. Dr. Robert H. Glover described those years: "The opening of some fields and stations was in the teeth of the most strenuous resistance, involving riots and uprisings, humiliating insults, physical injuries, threatenings and dangers of many kinds.

"And having obtained a first foothold under conditions of this sort, the pioneer missionaries had to negotiate for property, renovate and make habitable old buildings or have new ones erected, and plod through all kinds of tedious and trying preliminaries before a beginning could be made in actual Gospel work."[24]

These grim conditions seemed to fuel the momentum of missionary expansion that broke free from inertia at the Round Lake summer convention after a year of concerted prayer. By 1895 almost 300 missionaries spread out to some of the hardest unevangelized areas of the world.

As the Alliance grew in size and complexity, the need for changes became apparent even to the founder, despite his natural inclination toward simplicity of organization and economy of details. Dr. Simpson reluctantly agreed that some far-reaching decisions must be made if the Alliance were to continue its remarkable advance.

CHAPTER 7

Changes, Crises and Convictions

Of all conflicts,
the most hurtful is found within,
and it cannot be escaped.

1897—1912

Context of the Times

In 1899, the final year of his life, Dwight L. Moody watched the gap widen between diverse factions in the church. Still totally opposed to controversy, he pleaded in one of his last sermons: "Couldn't they agree to a truce and for ten years bring out no fresh views, just to let us get on with the practical work of the kingdom?"

It seemed for a while at the turn of the century that Moody's wish would come true. "A kind of Truce of God," one writer called the first ten years of the twentieth century.

The glow and optimism of "The Evangelical Age" in the 1800s spilled over into the 1900s. Many supposed the new century would be greater still, for both foreign missions and domestic church growth.

The Student Volunteer Movement channeled literally thousands of dedicated young people into long-established denominational missions, such as Northern Baptists, Methodists and Presbyterians. By 1900 nearly 5000 Americans made up more than a quarter of the world's Protestant missionary force.

Meanwhile, denominations continued to flourish at home. Good causes continued to abound in what one historian called the "Age of Crusades." Outstanding preachers with rare abilities continued to generate enthusiasm among churchgoers. Religion still seemed close to the mainstream of national life.

Most Americans, not ideologically inclined, paid small heed to the low-throated theological thunder on the horizon. Only a few perceptive individuals realized a storm would soon break, causing irreparable divisions in the religious community.

The problem began in the schools. For years thousands of American students had been returning from German universities trained in a detached rationalistic scholarship that undercut confidence in the Scriptures and sound theology.

Upstart science did its part by sneering at religion as an outdated, hidebound superstition. And an unbridled spirit of freedom encouraged the individual to determine for himself what was binding truth and authority.

By 1900 critical thinking permeated most older seminaries and church-sponsored universities. In another dozen years, evangelical scholarship was virtually driven from the campus. It was only a small step for liberalism from school to church with attendant consequences that would ever after trouble the religious community.

The holiness movement paid little heed to this new development. It was already having problems of its own. As various groups moved closer to formal identity, they found it necessary to stress their differences from others with whom they had celebrated similarities in a previous era of congeniality.

The Boxer Rebellion (1899-1900) in China served to remind Christians in North America of the deeper bonds that suffering often renews. Rampaging Chinese, infuriated at the piecemeal partition of their motherland by haughty European powers, struck with blind fury against all foreigners and their work, including Christian missionaries.

The more numerous Roman Catholic clergy suffered the heaviest losses, but an estimated 186 Protestant workers and their children were hacked, beaten, tortured or shot to death. Thousands of Chinese Christians, "secondary foreign devils" accused of betraying their culture and country, fell victim as well to the rage of the Boxers.

An event the following year accentuated tensions within the American religious community. Perhaps no other event in recent history has stirred as much continuing controversy and renewal within Protestant circles as the modern pentecostal movement, with its emphasis on the baptism of the Holy Spirit as necessarily evidenced by speaking in unknown tongues.

In 1901 Charles Fox Parham, a former Methodist minister, and students at his small Bible school in Topeka, Kansas, concluded from their study that tongues always accompanied the Holy Spirit's baptism. After much prayer, they received the gift of tongues.

The phenomenon had only sporadic outbreaks until a sustained revival in 1906 in the Azusa Street Mission of downtown Los Angeles. William J. Seymour, a black holiness preacher from Texas and a student of Parham, led the series that launched pentecostalism as a worldwide movement.

The momentous first decade of the twentieth century climaxed with two events that would fuel even more controversy in the splintering Protestant community.

Lyman Stuart, an oil millionaire, saw the rising tide of liberalism in the churches and determined to take countermeasures. He financed publication of *The Fundamentals,* a scholarly "Testimony to the Truth." The series of twelve volumes written by "the best and most loyal Bible teachers in the world," defined and defended a whole range of historic Christian beliefs.

Stuart funded the free distribution of a total 3 million volumes to pastors, missionaries, educators, students, religious editors and Sunday school superintendents for whom he could get addresses. *The Fundamentals* became a reference point for the "fundamentalist" movement that formed to combat modernism in the churches.

In 1910 mission leaders converged from all directions on Edinburgh, Scotland, for the first global missionary conference. Ironically, the gathering of evangelistic and mostly evangelical-minded church leaders became the organizational launching pad for the ecumenical movement that culminated in the World Council of Churches.

* * *

Dr. Simpson, like his colleague and friend D. L. Moody, sought to avoid confrontation and controversy. He and the enthusiastic supporters of the two Alliances seemed to adopt an attitude like Nehemiah on the walls of Jerusalem: "I am doing a great work so that I cannot come down."

Circumstances forced a change in this attitude as more and more Alliance people felt excluded from churches where liberalism seemed to embrace everyone—except those who held to historical biblical faith.

Then a pentecostal wave swept over some areas of the Alliance, carrying away leaders and causing those who remained to look more closely at their convictions: who they were and why; what they were doing and where headed.

A movement began reluctantly to take a more tangible form.

A CHRISTIAN ALLIANCE BRANCH IN SPOKANE, WASHINGTON, 1896

Bottom row, left to right: Nora Cusick, unknown, Lura Morse, Effie Morse, Meda Nickerson. *Second row:* C. D. Ide, Mrs. Buzzell and baby Helen, Mrs. J. N. Tewinkel and baby Ruth, Mrs. Jones (organizer), unknown, Vi Morse, "Father" Morse (preacher emeritus), unknown, J. J. Stage. *Third row:* Thomas Olson, Mr. Buzzell, J. N. Tewinkel, Rosa Cusick, B. F. Morse, Mrs. B. F. Morse, unknown, unknown, Mrs. Hotchkiss, "Billy" Dunn, Mrs. Dunn. *Fourth row:* Hugh Cusick, Alice Morse, unknown, unknown, Mrs. Cusick, unknown, unknown, Mrs. Nickerson, Mrs. J. J. Stage. *Top row:* unknown except for Mr. Cusick, standing sixth from left.

The completed center of the Missionary Training Institute

THE CHRISTIAN AND MISSIONARY ALLIANCE

Program of
THE EASTER CONVENTION
OF THE
Christian and Missionary Alliance

IN THE GOSPEL TABERNACLE
NEW YORK
Cor. of 8th Avenue and 44th Street

APRIL 14th to 18th, 1897

For the Ratification of the Union of the Christian and Missionary Alliance.

Work for the Uplifting of Christian Life.
Work for the Sick and Suffering.
Work of the Printed Page.
Work for the Neglected Classes at Home.
The Open Doors at Home.

7.30-9.30 P.M. Our Work for Israel and the Heathen World.
The Jew First.
The Pre-eminent Obligation to Evangelize the World.
The World's Need.
The Possibility of the World's Immediate Evangelization.
"Let us go up and possess the land."

SATURDAY, APRIL 17.

10—12 A.M. The Ratification Meeting.
The Reading of the Report of Eight Years of Work, and the Formal Adoption of the Constitution and Officers.

3 P.M. Laying of the Corner Stone of the Missionary Institute at Nyack, N. Y. Special Excursion on the Northern R.R. of New Jersey, leaving New York at 1 P.M. Applications for Tickets should be made at the Book Store, 692 Eighth Ave., N. Y.

SABBATH, APRIL 18.

10 A.M. Special Sermon on the Work of Training and Sending Forth Laborers into the Harvest. Special Offering for the new Missionary Institute.

2 P.M. Children's Meeting.

3 P.M. Rally and Re-union of the Students and Graduates of the N. Y. Missionary Training Institute.

7.30 P.M. Farewell Meeting and Addresses.

Laying the cornerstone of the Institute Building, the multipurpose center of the Missionary Training Institute on Nyack Heights, April 17, 1897

An artist's rendition of the training institute and other buildings on the Nyack hillside: (1) Institute Building (Simpson Hall); (2) Tabernacle; (3) Bethany; (4) Harmony Hall; (5) Berachah; (6) Sara Lindenberger home; (7) Simpson's home; (8) Wilson Academy

Berachah, a healing home in early years,
later Berachah Hall, the institute's music building

Wilson Academy, later used as dormitories for the institute's married students

BLACK STUDENTS AT THE MISSIONARY TRAINING INSTITUTE, CIRCA 1920

Top row, left to right: Montrose Waite, Eugene Thornley, Joe Garcialo, Headley Wilson, Gerald Steele. *Middle row:* Peter Robinson, Ben Duarte. *Bottom row:* Ms. Morris, Ms. Banks, Rev. E. M. Collette, Anita Bolden, Daniel Mullings.

Robert Page, graduate of the 1890 class of the New York Missionary Training College and the first black Alliance missionary. He taught in the first mission school of the Alliance in Belgian Congo (Zaire).

The Cleveland Coloured Gospel Quintette. *Front row, left to right:* Alexander Talbert, H. D. Hodges. *Second row:* Floyd H. Lacy, J. W. Parker, Spurgeon R. Jones.

Carrie Merriweather,
first black missionary to
Sierra Leone in 1913

Evangelist and educator
Edward Mark Burgess

An honor guard of 300 students at the Missionary Training Institute lining the road as Dr. Simpson's funeral cortege passed to the burial plot on the Nyack hillside in early November, 1919

SOME FACTS become apparent only in the perspective of time. It took ten years for The Christian Alliance and International Missionary Alliance to realize they could both work together better as one—at least in the United States. Their objectives were interdependent, their leaders the same, their constituencies and convictions identical.

Amalgamation of the two Alliances took place in April, 1897, under an unwieldy name that represented a triumph of zeal over reason: The Christian and Missionary Alliance.

Dr. Simpson, however, approved: "It expresses the genius of our movement. We are an alliance of Christians for worldwide missionary work."[1]

The officers chosen to serve at that time: Dr. A. B. Simpson, president and general superintendent; Rev. A. E. Funk, secretary; Mr. David Crear, treasurer; Mrs. A. B. Simpson, financial secretary.

Canadian Discontent

Not everyone agreed with the streamlined version of the Alliance. Canadians especially objected, because the merger meant the dissolution of their Dominion Auxiliary Branch with its Canadian-elected president and executive committee. The designation of auxiliary had special value to them, because it denoted a certain status of ally or associate acting under its own mandate for a common cause.

Now Canadians no longer had a separate identity. They became a district of the C&MA, and as such were to be administered by a district superintendent answerable to Alliance leaders in New York.

This discontent should not have surprised Dr. Simpson. Being Canadian, he must have known their deep traditional dislike of being administered from abroad. He was pastoring Knox Church in Hamilton when Queen Victoria saw the wisdom of declaring Canada the first self-governing dominion in the British Empire.

In addition, Reynolds pointed out that Dr. Simpson certainly was aware that the Canadian public's suspicions of being manipulated were still causing widespread criticism of the "New York divine" for his "huge collections of money and jewels."[2]

Swallowing hard, the Canadian Alliance leaders and branches decided to go along with the unilateral action taken by New York. Even so, Reynolds commented that the resulting scars would reappear later and contribute to a temporary decline in Canadian enthusiasm for the Alliance. From 1900 to 1919, Canadian branches decreased from twenty-five to eight.

Growth Factors

The number of Alliance members and branches continued to grow steadily as Christians responded to the double attraction of deeper-life teaching and missions. Dr. Simpson's summer camps and city conventions accounted for much of this growth—in fact, without conventions there would probably have been no Alliance. In 1897 he and a select team of speakers conducted five camp-meeting conventions.

Pardington noted that between the summer camp at Old Orchard and the city convention in New York stretched a chain of conventions that eventually reached across the United States and into Canada. Citing conventions on the national, district, state and local levels, conventions in the mountains and on the seashore, conventions in summer and winter, he concluded "that it is quite safe to say that a day does not pass that an Alliance convention, and perhaps more than one, is not in session either in the homeland or in the foreign field."[3]

Dr. Simpson's publications also contributed to an expanding fellowship of Christians in whom spiritual truths went deeper than denominational ties. His 24-page magazine, now called *The Christian and Missionary Alliance Weekly* [4] in step with the 1897 merger, represented only one ministry to the Christian reading public. He also published books of various kinds, including commentaries, biographies, doctrinal studies, sermons, hymnbooks and some poetry collections. His published titles would eventually total 101.

Most of these books were not finished products, carefully crafted and finely edited. Dr. Simpson simply did not have time to author books, although in his early ministry he had carefully handwritten his sermons. Sixty-seven of his titles represented sermons that were preached, recorded stenographically and then printed. *The Christ in the Bible* series, for example, consisted of sermons preached in the Gospel Tabernacle, not material specifically written for publication.

Living Truths had a different role in Dr. Simpson's stable of publications. A monthly 64-page magazine printed on quality paper, the periodical carried articles and editorials designed primarily for Christian readers who would not bother to read literature concerning the higher Christian life. He published *Living Truths* anonymously, though he advertised it in the *Weekly* as a tool for Fourfold Gospel Christians to use with their church friends.

Some of Dr. Simpson's best articles appeared in this monthly. He also enlisted the cooperation of other articulate leaders of Christian thought, like Dr. John R. Mott, Dr. James M. Gray, Dr. Kenneth MacKenzie, Dr. Henry Wilson and W. E. Blackstone.

The editor did much of his writing while commuting to work or traveling to conventions by train. He sometimes indulged in writing himself to sleep. On one occasion a friend asked Mrs. Simpson why the bedspreads were spotted with ink.

"It's the doctor," she explained patiently. "You see, he writes in bed and sometimes he nods, and his pen falls onto the bedspread and leaves a spot."[5]

Dr. Simpson could never have carried on his extensive publishing work without capable editorial assistants. Over a period of years, beginning with Miss Harriet Waterbury, one of the first graduates of the Missionary Training College, he depended on editorial assistants to help him publish the magazines and books. Miss Louise Shepard and Miss Emma L. Beere* also provided invaluable editorial help.

Neither could he have carried out his plan for establishing branches across the nation without men like Edward "Daddy" Whiteside.* Canadian by birth, Whiteside was converted and licensed to preach in the New Brunswick Conference of the Methodist Church. Ill health led him to New York, where he met Dr. Simpson and through him the Great Physician.

Completely healed and ready for service, Whiteside was given responsibility for the Pittsburgh Alliance branch. Whiteside sensed deeply his lack of qualifications.

He turned to God and said, "O Lord, I appoint You as superintendent of the Pittsburgh branch of the Alliance, and I will run errands for You."[6]

Western Pennsylvania eventually contained more Alliance branches per square mile than any other region in the country. Whiteside accomplished this through two major means: prayer and his "boys."

Desiring Whiteside's prayer ministry during an annual missionary convention, Dr. Simpson invited him to New York. Whiteside shared a room with a prominent preacher also on the Gospel Tabernacle program. When the preacher retired, Whiteside was kneeling in prayer. When the preacher awoke in the morning, his roommate was still on his knees.

When Daddy Whiteside decided one of his "boys" was ready for the ministry, he displayed a holy persistence that would not be denied. A young man working in a downtown business office never forgot his pastor's dealing with him.

*See "The Founder's Team" in the Appendix for more details.

"Mr. Whiteside came into the office one day near closing time. He asked me to take charge of his street meetings for the following summer. I declined, but he simply stayed with me and said it was the Lord's will and that he was counting on me.

"We left the office and as I kept giving excuses he walked with me for almost a mile to the Pennsylvania Railroad station. As I went through the train gates his last words were, 'We are depending on you.' He took no denial when he believed he was in the will of God."[7]

That young man was H. M. Shuman, who eventually became president of the Alliance.

Still another growth factor for the Alliance resulted from the tragic polarization taking place not only between denominations, but within local churches. Pastors trained in methods of Higher Criticism reduced the Bible to a mere book. Social Gospel was in, biblical Christianity was out, and so were spiritually minded parishoners.

To those rejected, often lonely Christians, the writings of Simpson and the Alliance summer and city conventions brought refreshing streams of living water.

Leadership Gap

Widening interest in branches created a leadership shortage at all levels of the movement. State or district superintendents had the responsibility of organizing these local fellowships of believers. Dr. Simpson wanted a superintendent for each state, but the lack of qualified men forced him to assign large territories to these district leaders. Dr. R. A. Forrest,* for one, had an immense district stretching from Florida to Texas.

District superintendents did all their travel by train, and their expenses were sometimes reimbursed, sometimes not. Allowances often failed to meet family needs for food and clothing, but the workers counted such sacrifices an acceptable price for the work they were privileged to do.

Shortages at the local branch level further hampered growth. The New York Missionary Training College should have provided workers, but most of the graduates had their hearts set on ministry overseas. Branch superintendents frequently emerged from the local fellowships themselves, and in some cases women filled the role.

Since the training college produced too few workers for the branches, the Board of Managers decided to start a school specifically for branch superintendents and other home workers. The Home School opened in New York City on October 19, 1896, at the

*See "The Founder's Team" in the Appendix for more details.

Alliance complex on Eighth Avenue. The six- to twelve-week training course included special training in rescue mission work, visitation and tract distribution.

An early circular for the Home School stated that time would be given over to "meeting and hearing from the leaders of the many special forms of Christian work, for which New York and vicinity are unequalled, and in visiting the places themselves where these activities are carried on."

Dr. Henry Wilson assumed leadership of the school, and faculty members from the Missionary Training College taught courses, but the school failed to attract many students. Enrollment never exceeded fifty students, and courses were held on and off until 1912, when the Home School would become part of the Missionary Training Institute.

Destination Nyack

By 1896 the New York Missionary Training College had outgrown its "substantial and commodious building" adjacent to the Gospel Tabernacle on Eighth Avenue. Only fifty students could live in the school dormitory. The other 150 or more students had to find rooms of their own in the city. Many applications had to be turned down, as lack of space stifled further growth.

The need for a larger campus became critical, but where to build? Construction costs in the city were almost prohibitive. What would cost $250,000 in New York could be built in the suburbs for $75,000.

Rev. Stephen Merritt, an active Alliance supporter who lived in Nyack, New York, across the street from the future location of Simpson Memorial Church, suggested the school move up the Hudson River some twenty miles to his town.

A report in the Weekly enumerated some advantages of the move: "The country affords much greater quiet and opportunity for study and saves students from a certain class of distractions which have been found to seriously interfere with solid work.

"Again, in a city as large as Nyack, with a population of 10,000, there is ample opportunity for evangelistic and missionary work."[8]

Cornerstone-laying day on April 17, 1897, promised to be a gala occasion. Over 800 people planned to attend, including two chartered trainloads from New York City. But the day began with a torrential downpour that turned the roads into a quagmire and the hillside into a saturated sponge.

Dr. Simpson believed people could change the weather—through prayer—so he called for an impromptu prayer service. "Before the prayer meeting was over," he recorded, "the sky cleared and the clouds rolled away, the sun shone in all its glory, and a stiff, drying wind blew briskly over the land. By three o'clock, when the services began at Nyack, one would scarcely have suspected that there had been a shower."[9]

Circumstances did not shine as brightly on another Nyack project conceived by Dr. Simpson. When the Missionary Training Institute and Berachah Home moved to the hillside, he and several Alliance leaders formed a development company and bought a large tract of land. They offered individual lots for sale to Christians who wanted to live in a community uncontaminated by the world and permeated with Alliance ideals and spirit. Fortunately, this ill-conceived evangelical ghetto attracted few buyers.

As in a number of such unsuccessful ventures, Dr. Simpson readily admitted failure and assumed full responsibility. With characteristic integrity he bought out the other partners in the company and personally assumed the substantial loss.

A Role Model

One buyer of land on the Nyack hillside was Dr. Simpson himself. He moved the family to Nyack shortly after the school transferred from New York. This enabled him to maintain close contact with the school, now called the Missionary Training Institute.

One student recalled an incident that illustrated his impact for years on the institute students. "The teacher's chair is empty, for all have come early at Dr. Simpson's hour. A happy chorus is started with exuberance of spirit, and the zest of it makes young blood tingle. Another chorus, perhaps a trifle boisterous, but suddenly a hush falls, for down the aisle comes the dignified form of Dr. Simpson.

"The massive head upon the broad shoulders is bowed as one who enters a holy place. The chorus dies away; he quietly takes his chair, opens his Bible, and smiles in delightful comradeship upon his class.

" 'Will you not sing another chorus?' he asks. 'Song is a little of heaven loaned to earth.'

"He is one of us, young as the youngest. One feels that he knows every thought and desire of the most wayward heart, yet his face and voice betray the fact that he has been caught up into the third Heaven and has seen things unlawful to utter. He comes to our level, but brings the glory of the Presence with him.

"We can only sing, 'My Jesus, I love Thee, I know Thou art mine.' "[10]

The Simpson family's move to Nyack brought a basic change to his work schedule: He became a commuter. On a routine day he would board the 6:18 A.M. train at Nyack, using the one-hour trip to midtown Manhattan for studying and writing. After immersing himself in work all day at the West Forty-fourth Street headquarters, he would return to Nyack for a late supper.

Then it was off to an evening class up the hill and later to his room for more study and work (and ink spots?) until one or two o'clock in the morning—and all this by a man given up for dead by a competent physician just a few years before.

Dr. George P. Pardington could have included his friend Simpson when he wrote of people "who daily experience a supernatural quickening of their bodies, which gives them freshness and strength and in some instances extraordinary physical endurance. Indeed, they seem to have something more than divine healing; they have divine life."[11]

Dr. Simpson's nonstop, seven-day work week should not be mistaken for other than it was. He was not a workaholic, one who overloads himself with work to escape painful questions and disappointments. That would have been an abuse of his God-given stamina.

What impelled the Alliance founder was a sense of urgency that could well be summed up, "All for Jesus." He once exclaimed: "Everything around us is intensely alive; life is earnest; death is earnest; sin is earnest; men are earnest; business is earnest; knowledge is earnest; the age is earnest; God forgive us if we alone are trifling in the white heat of this crisis time."

He then wrote:

"No time for trifling in this life of mine;
Not this the path the blessed Master trod,

But strenuous toil; each hour and power employed
Always and all for God.

Time swiftly flies; eternity is near,
And soon my dust may lie beneath the sod.

How dare I waste my life or cease to be
Always and all for God!

I catch the meaning of this solemn age;
With life's vast issues all my soul is awed.

Life was not given for trifling; it must be
Always and all for God."[12]

Costly China

Events in China at the turn of the century dramatized the seriousness of life that the Alliance founder wrote about. The Boxer Rebellion swept like a raging hurricane over China in 1899.

Within one year rampaging Chinese inflicted on Catholic and Protestant missions one of the severest losses of workers in church history. When the Alliance mission in Shansi Province was wiped out, it marked the end as well of a budding cooperation with missions-minded Christians in Sweden.

Hearing of the C&MA only by name, a large number of Swedish believers had earlier offered themselves for missionary service with the Alliance under the leadership of Rev. William Fransen.

Dr. Henry Wilson went to Sweden as the Board of Managers' representative. He conferred with the candidates and leaders, examined and approved those who would go to Shansi Province in North China. He also spoke to many large groups of Swedish Christians, and sensed an immediate affinity with them.

Dr. Wilson later recounted how the men and women were set well apart in two distinct groups for their trip to North China "for the sake of appearances as well as for the sake of the missionaries themselves."[13]

But before long the ladies grew tired and slowed their progress so much that the men's contingent soon overtook them. For the rest of the long journey they traveled together in spite of all the rules and well-laid plans.

When asked for an explanation, one of the young ladies simply said, "Why of course, we likes the gentlemen and the gentlemen likes we."[14]

The engaging simplicity and harmony of the Swedish workers drowned in a horrible bloodbath that wiped out twenty-one of the thirty-two missionaries in the summer of 1900. Fifteen children died alongside their parents.

One small group of seven adults and five children escaped the initial carnage and wandered about on foot in the rugged terrain for a month. Two infants were born during their flight. Finally discovered, they were all murdered.

One letter miraculously survived and reached its destination. Mr. Lundberg had written, "Should we not come out with our lives...we live and die for the Lord and China. Let not your hand fail and do not lose your courage. When the storm is over, then send out other witnesses to China."[15]

Some of the survivors did just that. After the rebellion was quelled, they returned to China with the Swedish Alliance Mission.

Widespread Advance

Crises and casualties formed part of the picture elsewhere on Alliance fields, but none as costly, and they were overshadowed by a steady and remarkable advance.

Dr. Robert H. Glover summed up the missionary movement in 1912: "The Alliance was among the pioneers of Kuangsi and Hunan, the last two provinces of China to be entered. It has penetrated Tibet and occupies three points within its borders.

"It was the pioneer of French Indo-China and is still the only evangelical mission at work among eighteen million benighted Annamese. It has stations among the aboriginal tribesmen of South China and the pagan Subanos of the Southern Philippines.

"It has built the first Protestant chapels in Venezuela and Ecuador, and is laboring among the Mapuche Indians of Chile and the Quichua tribe in the Ecuadorian Andes.

"It has the only American church in old Jerusalem and is located at Beersheba on the southern border of Palestine among the wild Bedouin Arabs.

"It has recently planted a station on the banks of a large tributary of the Niger River in the vast and unevangelized land of French Guinea. And now it is planning advances at an early date into French Congo, and across Jordan into the new Syro-Arabian state."[16]

Dr. Glover's resume of an era substituted for an honor roll of names that could in themselves fill a book of profiles in faith and courage.

His brief reference to the penetration of Tibet involved remarkable people like William Christie, David P. Ekvall, W. W. Simpson and Miss Effie Gregg. David W. Lelacheur penetrated the "Forbidden Kingdom" to the Lamasery of Darge. There he prayed that God would give the temple to the Alliance for the preaching of the Gospel. God granted the audacious request.

William Christie's* penetration to Labrang, the fourth largest monastery in Tibet, obligated him to traverse territory where two Tibetan clans hacked and shot each other in all-out war. He arrived safely at Labrang, only to encounter his own crucible of hatred and violence.

"As he gave forth his message, he was beaten and pounded with sticks and stones and clods of earth," recounted Dr. Thomas Moseley, another illustrious Tibetan veteran. "The fear of a foreigner's being killed so near the monastery wall caused the commander of the Tibetan troops to rescue him and drag him into the monastery.

"He was sent away under escort and warned never to return.

*See "The Founder's Team" in the Appendix for more details.

But again and again he and his colleagues returned, only to have to flee for their lives.

"Today," Dr. Moseley wrote in 1955, "we are told that even under the Communist regime regular services are being held at the little church which was eventually established right across the stream from the Labrang monastery."[17]

While Tibet's borders were being penetrated by Alliance missionaries, the entire continent of South America attracted similar attention. Venezuela came first with the arrival of Miss White and Miss Lanman in 1895. Ecuador and Argentina followed in 1897. Brazil was entered in 1902, but the work was later closed. Chile's turn came in 1907.

The work in South America progressed enough that Dr. Simpson toured the fields in 1910, by then including Peru and excluding Venezuela. The trip nearly cost the Alliance its founder. In Panama on the return trip he was seized by a tropical fever that prostrated him for days.

Even in this, Dr. Simpson found cause for thanks: He felt the sickness had been permitted so that he could more fully comprehend what missionaries must face in the tropics.

Elsewhere in the world, Alliance missionaries celebrated the arrival of the twentieth century by entering Shanghai, Puerto Rico and the Philippines in 1900. The populous region of French Indo-China was opened in 1911.

Although the active missionary staff remained slightly lower than 300 during the period, the Missionary Training Institute supplied the C&MA and other missions with a steady stream of recruits. Twenty years after the first class hastily assembled in New York, fully 1,000 graduates had entered missionary service in forty countries. Of this number, 800 belonged to the Alliance.[18]

Canadian Contributions

Meanwhile, Canadian involvement in the Alliance began to increase noticeably around 1900. This resulted from a gradual shift in emphasis to missions in the city convention tours.

The 1896 conventions in Hamilton, Toronto, and other cities called for "The Deepening of Christian Life and the Evangelization of the World." The first five days of a convention schedule majored on the now familiar topics of holiness, the return of Christ and divine healing. The remaining two days carried missionary themes, climaxing with a missionary challenge.

No offerings, however, were taken. The Canadian press poised to pounce on the "New York evangelist" who "hypnotized his audiences" and took away their jewelry and money. Dr. Simpson wisely refrained from taking an offering in Canada for several years.

The ordination in 1896 of two new Alliance missionaries, Robert A. Jaffray for South China and George G. Shields for Tibet, further legitimatized Alliance missions in Canadian eyes.

By 1900 Alliance leaders decided to test the idea of offerings in local conventions. When this passed without an outcry, they added an offering appeal to the program of the first all-Canada camp meeting convention near Hamilton.

The missionary emphasis and offering of $5,500 during the convention received favorable comment in the churches and press, setting the stage for even greater Canadian involvement in Alliance missions. Dr. Simpson's press image underwent a startling change. He was no longer "the faith-healer," nor even "the champion money-raiser." He became featured as "the most remarkable and successful advocate of missions now living,"[19] reported the ultraconservative *Toronto Globe* in 1896.

The young Robert A. Jaffray ordained by the Alliance founder sailed for China that same year. For the next thirty-three years he made Kwangsi Province of South China his base of operations.

Despite continual problems of a weak heart and diabetes, Jaffray maintained a punishing schedule and expected as much from those who worked with him. Some of his colleagues could not measure up, prompting him to comment in a report to the home board, "To be born again is essential, but it is a big help to be born well the first time."[20]

Jaffray himself was "born well" into a home of affluence and culture. His father owned and published the *Toronto Globe,* one of Canada's most influential newspapers. This background perhaps influenced him to establish the South China Press and publish *The Bible Magazine.* The Chinese-language monthly gained wide circulation and won him international recognition throughout the Far East.

Jaffray was a restless man, not content with evangelizing the mainland of China. He shared with Dr. Simpson a burden for the 22 million people of Annam (now Vietnam), who had no Protestant witness. In 1911 he and two other missionaries entered Annam, at that time part of French Indo-China, purchased property in Danang and established the first Protestant mission in the area.

During World War I, M. Joffre, French governor-general of the Catholic-dominated colony, became so suspicious of the missionaries—particularly those with German names—that Jaffray had to make a second trip from China to clear the air.

During the interview Jaffray mentioned casually that his name seemed similar to that of the governor-general, M. Joffre, and perhaps they were related—distantly, of course. Amused by his affable visitor, Joffre consented to lift a ban against Protestant preaching.

But to protect himself from political repercussions, the French official refused to give his assurances in writing.

Joffre, blind in his left eye, said humorously, "Go ahead, Jaffray, and I won't see you. When a missionary appears I will put my hand over one eye—the right one."[21]

Recurrence of Revival

Reports of revival in Wales spurred hopes among American Christians for a similar moving of the Holy Spirit in their churches. The North Dutch Reformed Church on Fulton Street, location of the prayer meetings that sparked the 1857 "no-name revival," called for fasting and prayer.

Dr. Simpson reported in a March, 1905, issue of the magazine that the Holy Spirit was doing marvelous things among the Gospel Tabernacle people and causing many conversions. He urged readers to pray for revival in the regular channels of church and branch ministries. In a later issue he encouraged the readers "to make things pleasant to the Lord by being occupied with the things that interest Him."[22]

In late October of 1906, revival came to the Missionary Training Institute and spread to the Gospel Tabernacle in New York. Institute classes were suspended for a fortnight. Meetings featured little preaching but much confession of sins and rejoicing in forgiveness.

The public revelations of personal problems may have gotten out of hand, because Dr. Simpson found it necessary to warn about "raking up one's sinful past already forgiven,"[23] and he expressed concern that revival be channeled into useful ministry.[24] In a December sermon, "Fervor and Fanaticism," he cautioned that emotionalism should be kept within certain bounds of decency.

Spreading Movement

The Alliance, following the lead of its founder, preferred to avoid unnecessary controversy. Perceiving itself as a fraternal union intent only on encouraging Christians to be more like their Lord and promoting His salvation among all nations, the movement sought to avoid distraction by other issues.

Unity in essentials and charity in all other matters of faith and doctrine summarized the Alliance ideal—and the essentials needed few words of explanation. Never was the ideal more needed than in the trial by tongues that was soon to sweep over Alliance groups.

About the same time the tongues movement began to gain prominence and momentum in the Azusa Street Mission in Los Angeles, Alliance leaders were meeting in a previously scheduled precouncil conference at Nyack. Local superintendents and official workers gathered in May of 1906 to achieve through prayer and discussion "unity upon a common basis of testimony and teaching."[25]

The conference recognized the possibility of open questions where "the brethren would agree to differ" and yet "hold in mutual charity their individual convictions." Participants defined sanctification as a definite second blessing, the essence of which was "the baptism of the Holy Spirit as a distinct experience" and the reality of "the indwelling of Christ in the the heart of the consecrated believer."[26]

The meeting had been called to consider differing interpretations of sanctification, but the same principles could well be applied to the tongues issue.

By 1907 the tongues movement spread rapidly across the United States, Canada and other nations. Individuals and teams from Azusa Street traversed the county advocating the experience of speaking in tongues as the necessary evidence of being filled with the Holy Spirit.

In all periods of highly emotional religious issues, excesses are inevitable. Some exponents of the tongues movement, or pentecostalism, discredited the teaching more than they adorned it. And some churches reacted negatively to implications that their spirituality left something to be desired. Yet in many Alliance branches, pentecostal teaching was accepted, and certain Alliance people received the gift of tongues.

William T. MacArthur,* superintendent of the Chicago Alliance branch when the tongues movement reached the city in 1907, called for protracted meetings. Several members spoke in tongues, including Mrs. MacArthur and perhaps he himself. He wrote several articles describing both the "blessings and the mischief of the movement."[27]

The Indianapolis Alliance branch had a different experience. G. N. Eldridge was away when a former city resident returned from California and encouraged the congregation to seek the tongues experience. Interested members called for "tarrying" meetings, but when Eldridge learned of the development, he telegraphed a deacon to bar the building to such gatherings.

Pentecostalism among Ohio Alliance people seemed to have a wider acceptance than elsewhere, and from that area the Alliance lost its largest number of branches and members. In January of 1907 Miss Ivey Campbell spoke to a group in Akron of her pentecostal experience while in Los Angeles.

W. A. Cramer, the Alliance superintendent in Cleveland, attended the meeting and became convinced of the rightness of the pentecostal message. He returned home to Cleveland and called some of his

*See "The Founder's Team" in the Appendix for more details.

people together to study the teaching. He related later that "the power of God fell on me...and the Holy Spirit soon began to speak through me in an utterance I had never learned."[28]

Miss Campbell went to Cleveland in the following month of February for a one-day meeting, but stayed four weeks. "Since that time," Cramer reported, "possibly fifty persons have received the baptism. Our Alliance branch is all on fire. Souls are being saved, believers sanctified, bodies healed, families are being united, debts paid, grudges settled and a general outgoing of love and fellowship is being manifested in a most beautiful manner."[29]

Speaking in tongues became so prominent in the Ohio region that Dr. Simpson sent Dr. Henry Wilson to see what was happening. Tozer wrote that the Episcopalian minister returned to New York with the report, "I am not able to approve the movement, though I am willing to concede that there is probably something of God in it somewhere."[30]

Dr. Simpson referred to the event in an editorial: "We have been delighted to hear from our good brother, Dr. Wilson, who has just returned from the Ohio conventions, that a deep spirit of revival appears to be resting upon the work and the workers in that district; and that our beloved people are being kept to a great extent from fanaticism and excess and are receiving all the fullness of blessing which the Lord is waiting to bestow without the counterfeit.

"May God give to all our people the spirit of entire openness to the Holy Ghost, and yet of spiritual sanity and practical holiness and wholesomeness."[31]

However, Dr. Simpson also warned of two dangers related to the pentecostal movement. In a *Living Truths* article he advised Christians not to be discouraged by counterfeits: "Just now there is much danger that the special gifts of the Holy Spirit shall be travestied to such an extent that rational Christians shall be turned away from the truly supernatural and divine manifestations of the power of God through the fear of the counterfeit.

"The counterfeit always implies the genuine and it is only as we recognize the true that we shall be able to discern the false and guard the honest seeker from its imposition. We must have the spirit of candor as well as the spirit of caution, and while detecting the spurious, not fail to recognize the true."[32]

He also warned of a second danger: "There is always danger to earnest souls who are seeking at any cost the best gifts of the Holy Spirit that they may be as open to the influence of wicked spirits as to the Holy Ghost.

"Satan is the great mimic, and loves to imitate God and counterfeit the highest and holiest spiritual manifestations; and his choicest victims are honest, earnest and unsuspecting souls. Let us therefore, not think that we are doubting God or questioning His leadings if we 'try the spirits' and 'prove all things.' "[33]

Personal Searchings

Dr. Simpson viewed the tongues issue not only as an administrative and theological matter but as a spiritual challenge as well. He, too, was of that choice group of "earnest souls" who seek God at any cost. As in the matters of sanctification, divine healing and baptism by immersion, so in the question of speaking in tongues.

His openness to God's Word and will had not deviated from the day when he vowed, "I felt that I dare not hold any truth in God's Word as a mere theory or teach to others what I had not personally proved."[34]

As the General Council of 1907 neared, he spent time in prayer and fasting, desiring a special anointing of God's Spirit so that "in view of the special movement of the Holy Spirit abroad today, that God would show His will about it."[35]

After council adjourned, he wrote some personal observations in his diary. "I noted first a quiet but real quickening in my own soul, and great blessing in the Council. God kept us united.

"At the close [perhaps referring to the all-night of prayer on Friday], He manifested Himself in some of the meetings in a very unusual way. There were several cases of the Gift of Tongues and other extraordinary manifestations. Some were certainly genuine, while others appeared to partake somewhat of the individual peculiarities and eccentricities of the subjects.

"So I saw not only the working of the Spirit, but also a very distinct human element, not always edifying or profitable. God led me to discern and hold quietly to the Divine order for the gifts of the Spirit in 1 Corinthians 12 and 14.

"At the same time I could not question the reality of the gifts. I was led to pray much about it and for God's highest will and glory in connection with it."[36]

In August of 1907, still seeking the will of God concerning tongues, Dr. Simpson returned to Old Orchard. At the close of the week, he entered to the place in the woods "where God healed me in August, 1881, and renewed my covenant of healing.

"At the same time I pressed upon Him a new claim for a mighty Baptism of the Holy Ghost in His complete pentecostal fullness embracing all the gifts and graces of the Spirit for my special need at this time and for the new conditions and needs of my life and work.

"He met me as I lay upon my face before Him with a distinct illumination. Then as the Presence began to fade and I cried out to Him to stay, He bade me believe and take it all by simple faith as I had taken my healing twenty-six years before. I did so and was enabled definitely to believe and claim it all and rest in Him."[37]

His diary over the next months records a sustained, intense searching through prayer and fasting for a deeper, fuller baptism of the Spirit in all His manifestations: on the lawn of his home at night...on the verandah late at night...on a train trip to Canada...even on his wedding anniversary.

Upon occasion God moved on Dr. Simpson with "a baptism of holy laughter"[38] or "a distinct sense of warmth, at times a penetrating fire,"[39] and a "mighty sense of rest, reality and joy."[40] But never an experience of speaking in tongues.

A new yet familiar note began appearing in his messages. In one published sermon based on chapter three of Philippians, he wrote: "There is a great deal of strain today after many things, temporal and social ambitions, success, fame and even extraordinary religious experiences. But Paul's supreme desire was to win Christ...what soberness, sanity, simplicity this will give to all our spiritual exercises and outreachings to make Jesus Himself the object of all our desires...Even the Holy Spirit is not to be desired above Jesus. His great ministry is to reveal Jesus."[41]

The diary entries ended abruptly on September 14, 1907. The next notation was dated October 6, 1912: "Five years have passed since these memoirs were written. Much has come and gone. God has been ever with me and wrought for me.

"No extraordinary manifestation of the Spirit in tongues or similar gifts has come. Many of my friends have received such manifestations, but mine has still been a life of fellowship and service.

"At all times my spirit has been open to God for anything He might be pleased to reveal or bestow. But He has met me still with the old touch and spiritual sense, and in distinct and marked answers to believing prayer in my practical life."[42]

For the founder and leader of the Alliance, the issue was finally clear. Through both his study of Scripture and his prolonged and sincere search for truth, he concluded that the gift of tongues was one manifestation of the Holy Spirit's infilling, but neither necessary nor the sole evidence of such an experience. He found himself led repeatedly by God back to an emphasis that formed the hallmark of his personal life and of the movement he founded: All for Jesus.

As editor of the official magazine, Dr. Simpson summed up the Alliance position in an April 1910 editorial: "The statement is made that the Alliance and its leaders are opposed to the manifestation of the Gift of Tongues in this age. This is wholly false.

"Our attitude has been often stated and is consistent and explicit. We fully recognize all the gifts of the Spirit, including 'divers kinds of tongues' as belonging to the Church in every age. And many of our most wise and honored workers both in the homeland and in the mission field have had this experience.

"But we are opposed to the teaching that this special gift is for all or is the evidence of the Baptism of the Holy Ghost. Nor can we receive or use to edification in our work and assemblies those who press these extreme and unscriptural views.

"We give and claim charity and liberty, that those who have not this experience shall recognize in the Lord those who have it and use it to edification. And that those who have it, shall equally recognize those who have not this special form of divine anointing, but have the Holy Ghost in such other gifts as He is pleased to bestow upon one and another 'severally as He will.'

"On this scriptural ground of truth, liberty and love, surely we can all meet, and no other is practicable without error, division or fanaticism."[43]

Years later someone, probably A. W. Tozer with his penchant for condensing many words into a few, summed up the Alliance position as "Seek not, forbid not."[44]

Refusal to endorse the position that all who receive the baptism of the Spirit must speak in tongues cost the Alliance dearly. Dr. William W. Menzies, an Assemblies of God historian, wrote: "Several great churches in the Alliance, and numerous outstanding ministers, reluctantly parted company with the parent body when the Pentecostal testimony was stifled by the Alliance leadership. Such 'come-outers' provided a substantial proportion of early Assemblies of God leadership."[45]

While the pentecostal testimony may have been "stifled" in some local branches, the official position was charitable and tolerant. Alliance leaders could not convince themselves concerning the exclusive emphasis on the gift of tongues; neither could they be so convinced by the advocates of this position. A parting of the way became inevitable and painful, especially for Dr. Simpson.

"I cannot refrain from recording the agony through which he passed," wrote Dr. MacKenzie, Dr. Simpson's friend for many years, "when so many of his most trusted and valued friends and workers withdrew from him because he did not go with them to the limit which was their ideal.

"He could not say of them, as did St. John, 'They went out from us, but they were not of us,' for they were. Their presence and prayers, their sympathy and service, had been a bulwark to him in times of stress and strain. But he had to let them go from him and trust God with the consummation, whatever that might be."[46]

During this hurt-filled period in Dr. Simpson's life, he was to lose yet another dear friend—perhaps the closest he ever had—due to death, not controversy.

Dr. Henry Wilson, the Episcopalian curate who had obtained leave from his bishop to serve with Dr. Simpson and the Alliance, had not been feeling well. He refused, however, to allow illness to keep him from going to Atlanta, Georgia, for a missionary convention. He preached in the Sunday services of February 9, 1908, but grew visibly weaker and weary.

If Dr. Wilson could have chosen the type of service to be his last on earth, he would have asked to be with children. Perhaps that was why God permitted his servant, who called himself "Big Baby Brother" when among the little ones, to speak on Tuesday to his favorite people, children, on his favorite topic, missions.

On Thursday morning, unable to arise from bed, he told his host the room was brilliant with a heavenly light, and there was an angelic host in the room. A few moments before midnight the angelic host departed, and with them, Dr. Henry Wilson.

Constitutional Council

The tongues controversy may have influenced the decision to draft a new constitution for the Alliance, but the pressure of growth and other changes played a part as well. By 1912 over 250 missionaries were serving overseas, and many local branches were acting increasingly like churches despite all declarations to the contrary.

Therefore the General Council of 1912 in Boone, Iowa, adopted a new constitution beginning with the preamble, "The C&MA, owing to providential developments, finds itself called to readjust itself to a larger fellowship...."

Chief architect of the constitution was Atlanta-based attorney Ulysses Lewis.* He had been one of many honorary vice-presidents from 1902 through 1911. When in 1912 the office of vice-president became functional, Lewis was elected as the first to hold that office. The 1912 constitution would determine the organizational shape of the Alliance for the next sixty years.

While the document largely reflected what was clearly accepted and practiced by 1912, it introduced a new and controversial article: the reversion clause.

It stated that property owned by local branches, Alliance schools and undenominational churches affiliated with the Alliance, when duly chartered by law, should contain a clause connecting it with the C&MA. In the event that such property should cease to be

*See "The Founder's Team" in the Apppendix for more details.

used as originally intended, "it shall revert to and become the property of the C&MA as incorporated under the laws of the State of New York."

The immediate purpose of the clause was perhaps to avoid further loss of property through defections to the pentecostal movement, but it did suggest that eventually the Alliance could become an ecclesiastical body. This prospect troubled many Alliance people, especially in Canada, who wanted the movement to remain true to its original declaration of a fraternal fellowship.

However, even the staunchest supporters of this role realized that Dr. Simpson would not live forever. When he, the towering founder and leader, was gone, what would hold the loose-knit Alliance together?

Like it or not, even more changes, crises and need of convictions would follow—and soon.

PART THREE

REDIRECTION

1912—1936

CHAPTER 8

Question of Succession

The measure of a movement is found in the durability of its beliefs, not the longevity of its founder.

1912—1919

Context of the Times

World War I convulsed Europe from 1914 to 1918 in one of those periodic outbursts of rivalry and brutality that have plagued the continent for centuries.

This one, however, outranked previous wars in the size of armies engaged in combat and in the variety of new weaponry with which to destroy each other. Airplanes, tanks, submarines and chemical gases joined the long-familiar rifles and cannons, to kill more than 8.5 million men in uniform.

Americans viewed the conflict with a detachment measured by the vast expanse of water between the Old World and the New. Neutrality later drowned in that same ocean when German submarines caused the loss of American lives and ships.

A broad spectrum of American churches opposed the war at first, but as the expanding conflict forced a choice, most denominations favored England, especially those like the Episcopalians and Methodists, with historical roots in the British Isles. The war effort became "The Great Crusade" to preserve Christian civilization.

Evangelist Billy Sunday, heir apparent of D. L. Moody, endorsed the war against "the Hun" with the same vigor used to battle Satan. He told audiences that if they could turn hell upside down they would find the words "Made in Germany" written there.

The war was not only good for American industry, it filled the churches. Church historian William Brown noted, "Never had the churches been better attended, never had so many members been more busily involved in the country's life and work, never had the general public's judgments of religion been so affirmative or their generosity with money more apparent."

The unleashed savagery of World War I shattered the heady optimism of European liberals that the world was getting better and better.

One liberal wrote of his disillusionment: "During the last three light-hearted decades, we have been smoking the opium pipe of evolution, telling the world how far it has risen, chiefly by its own force, from the depths in which it began, describing the speed by which it has mounted under our sage and dreamy eyes, and prophesying of its complete ascension in the near and sweet bye and bye. Recent events have broken the opium pipe and dispelled the delusion."

Unscarred by war on their soil, American liberals continued to puff the opium pipe of optimism in human nature for several more decades. It would take another war to shatter that pipe and their delusion.

The missionary enterprise of American Protestantism continued largely unhampered by the war since, excepting Palestine, the European conflict did not seriously extend to other areas. The most noticeable effect followed the armistice, when Germany lost colonial territories like Cameroon and Tanganyika in Africa. German missions had to pack up and leave with the ousted colonial regimes of the Kaiser.

The United States was still gearing up for the war effort when hostilities ceased. It left the nation at an extremely high psychological pitch, still seeking other causes to champion, other enemies to defeat.

Top leaders of mainline denominations joined forces to create the Interchurch World Movement, "a religious counterpart to the League of Nations," explained historian Brown. With a vision of "a united church uniting a divided world," they sought to rally American Protestants to a grand peacetime crusade. The crusade, however, soon floundered in expensive offices, lavish plans and lack of support.

People, it seemed, would rather fight a war than unite for peace.

Despite the Interchurch World Movement claim, churches were far from united. By 1919 battle lines between fundamentalists and liberals were clearly drawn—not between denominations, but between congregations within denominations.

The World Christian Fundamentals Association organized to war against the "Great Apostasy" of liberalism. The liberals airily dismissed their concerns as "noisy dogma versus sound reasoning."

Dr. Charles Blanchard, president of Wheaton College and an honorary vice-president of The Christian and Missionary Alliance, was one of the association's key organizers.

Dr. J. Gresham Machen of Princeton Seminary provided leadership for the conservatives and (on the issue of liberalism) their evangelical and fundamentalist allies. He claimed the controversy involved "two logically incompatible systems" and called for the ouster of liberals from church and campus posts of leadership. When the dust cleared, it was the antiliberals on the outside looking in.

In the melee of disputes and divisions, Christians of all labels found common cause in the war against liquor. The Anti-Saloon League of the nineteenth century drew much of its support from rural and small-town, middle-class Protestants.

By 1901 about one-quarter of the United States was legally "dry territory." Keyed up by their part in the world war, Protestants decided they could do better. They joined forces with other groups to push through ratification of the Eighteenth (Prohibition) Amendment so unpopular with nonchurchgoers.

The overall effect of Prohibition, the public feud between conservative and liberal churches, and the general loosening of morals in the war's aftermath pushed Protestants—especially evangelicals and fundamentalists—from the mainstream of national life for decades.

* * *

Alliance people in local branches and in mainline denominations joined wholeheartedly in "The Great Crusade" of Christianity against Germany. If their participation in other popular religious issues was muted and marginal, it was perhaps because they had other matters on their minds. They were preoccupied with the great cause of missions and the question of the movement's future as its founder aged and faded.

AT THE AGE of seventy in December, 1913, Dr. Simpson seemed as tireless as ever. He maintained a full schedule of preaching to congregations and conventions, of teaching at Nyack, of writing magazine articles and books, of leading the diverse and expanding movement he had founded.

Yet a certain tiredness was creeping over him. It was not only a physical exhaustion, though as Tozer pointed out, "There came into his eyes and upon his frame more than a suggestion of deep fatigue.

He had done five men's work, and he was feeling the weariness of five men."[1]

His weariness stemmed as well from the pummelling of his sensitive, emotional nature by too many crises: the defection of trusted associates to the tongues movement, the death of old and familiar friends like Henry Wilson, the waywardness of his sons and the gathering of storm clouds over Europe.

He lost yet another trusted colleague in the closing days of 1913. Josephus L. Pulis* had been associated with Dr. Simpson for more than thirty years. He was one of the original seven who met one cold November afternoon in Caledonian Hall for the first service of what would become the Alliance.

The Gospel Tabernacle became Pulis's universe of service: trustee, elder, leader of temperance services—someone Dr. Simpson could always count on to be there. Pulis would be missed by the church as an illustrious member, but Dr. Simpson lost an irreplaceable friend.

Always an impeccable dresser in previous years, Dr. Simpson, the grand old gentleman of the Alliance, preoccupied by many concerns, allowed his appearance to sag, though never to the point of sloppiness. His granddaughter allowed a glimpse of this when she recounted, "Grannie always followed Grandpa to his dressing room to superintend his wardrobe. Suddenly we would hear floating down from above, 'Bertie, that tie is a disgrace.'

"The reply was inaudible. Another admonition would follow from Mrs. Simpson. Then Grandpa's stricken tone: 'Maggie, Maggie, you insult me.' "[2]

The effect of Dr. Simpson's age on his role as leader of the movement was more sensed than stated. He had always led more by example than decree, and he intended it so, ever wary of ecclesiastical bureaucracy. Now his light touch on the wheel of leadership grew lighter still. That may have accounted for some of the reversals soon to follow, such as the educational crisis.

Leadership Sharing

Dr. Simpson had a gift for attracting high-caliber men and women as associates. The wisdom of his policy in role sharing became evident now, as qualified people picked up where their aging leader left off. The realization of his vision continued to unfold.

The 1912 constitution brought a reorganization of work that linked familiar names with new titles. The Board of Managers would now

*See "The Founder's Team" in the Appendix for more details.

appoint the heads of departments. David Crear, longtime treasurer, continued in that role as head of the finance department. Rev. A. E. Funk became the first foreign secretary and directed the foreign department. Rev. E. J. Richards* took over as home secretary and answered for the home department.

Dr. Robert H. Glover* was appointed deputation secretary and head of that department. Later in 1913 he succeeded Funk as foreign secretary, a position more suited to his abilities and experience. Toronto-born Glover had gone to China in 1897, about the same time as fellow Canadian Robert Jaffray, to open Kwangsi province to the Gospel.

The region had already repulsed efforts by two other missions and remained one of the most difficult and dangerous challenges to missionary work. Through much prayer and skillful tactics, the Alliance team established a beachhead and began to evangelize one village after another.

Both Glover and Jaffray were in Wuchow when the Boxer Rebellion broke out. Ignoring orders from the American embassy, they remained in the city until they were sure missionaries deeper in the province passed through Wuchow on the way to safety. By this time the Boxers were in Wuchow and plotting their death. The two men then escaped by river boat and rejoined their colleagues.

Men of stature like Dr. Glover began to assume responsibilities the aging Dr. Simpson could no longer carry. The work they had to oversee was summarized in the annual report of 1912. Alliance work overseas had grown to a staff of 259 missionaries in sixteen countries or fields.

The Alliance at home numbered 239 branches and affiliated churches located in thirty-five states and the Canadian provinces of Ontario, Manitoba and Alberta. Over half the American groups were in Pennsylvania (55), New York (30), Ohio (22), Washington (17) and California (12).

To direct this work in the United States and Canada, the names of only 182 workers appeared in the 1912 annual report. Of this total, 107 were ordained men and thirty-nine were women. By now the summer conventions numbered seven and, together with the city conventions during the winter, drew large crowds and generous offerings.

Effects of War

When World War I broke out, Alliance people in North America closed ranks with their governments in "The Great Crusade" to

*See "The Founder's Team" in the Appensix for more details.

win the war to end wars. In this they had the full support of Dr. Simpson, who by now was a naturalized American citizen and felt a strong loyalty to both countries.

He strongly backed the action of the Canadian government and later the American government in opposing Germany. In a sermon based on the passage in Genesis, chapter fourteen, he described Abram's battle against the confederate kings, and how it was approved in the court of heaven by the fact Abram received the blessing of Melchizedek, priest of the Most High God.

"Some were giving forth a very uncertain sound about that time, and others were clearly unpatriotic and wrong," remembered Dr. James M. Gray, "but when he spoke with the authority of the Bible he knew so well and the strong influence of a life hid with Christ in God, it brought boldness and steadiness to many."[3]

The war had little impact on overseas work. Only in Palestine were the two men and nine women advised to leave because of armed conflict between British and Turkish forces. Three single missionaries chose to remain: Misses Mary Butterfield, Mabel Best and Anna Gummoe. They would finally be forced to leave in May of 1917, but in the meantime they would make a deep impression on their neighbors, who referred to them as "the women who live next door to God."

In Congo (Zaire) by 1914 the high cost of thirty-seven missionary fatalities began to pay off when the Belgian colony emerged as the most responsive of the sixteen Alliance fields. Missionaries working with eighty-two Congolese church workers accounted for 322 baptisms, a church of over 1,100 members, and schools enrolling 2,500 children.[4]

Despite the outbreak of war—or perhaps because of it—the Alliance in North America had a good year of growth in 1914. Revival and conversions occurred in many areas. The Gospel Tabernacle in New York accounted for one hundred of the converts. The Missionary Training Institute reached a new high of 105 graduates.

In Canada, however, the war deeply affected the nation and its churches. Young men lined up in large numbers to join the army. At one point later in the war, the small town of Peterborough, with a population of 20,000 and an Alliance branch, would see within a twenty-month period 10 percent of its citizens don "the King's uniform." Other able-bodied men and women moved to the cities to join the labor force in the war industries. Churches in the smaller towns and cities suffered from a dearth of pastoral and lay leadership.

Despite the war conditions, Canadian Alliance people did their part in the spiritual offensive of the Great Commission. "Unless one has visited the Dominion, he can scarcely imagine the conditions," reported Dr. Simpson midway through the war. "The taking out of business pursuits of a half-million men, the War Tax, the special funds for various needs not covered by government taxes, have brought a severe financial strain. But the conventions are well attended and the missionary offering given with real joy."[5]

Alliance women did some mobilizing of their own. Mrs. Paul Rader and the sisters Cora and Ella Rudy had been concerned for some time about the lack of concerted prayer for missions by women. At the 1914 General Council, they called together the women attendees and formed women's missionary prayer groups. In time these would become the largest and strongest auxiliary of the Alliance in support of missions.

Good though the idea of women uniting for missions may have been in 1914, not until 1929 did the Board of Managers get around to granting formal approval, and then only after they found many prayer groups already active in local churches.

A somewhat similar situation arose in 1914 when General Council recommended that the Board of Managers "through the proper department recognize the rank of lady workers to be known as deaconesses with proper requirements and restrictions."[6] The designation of deaconess finally appeared in the 1978 edition of the Official Manual as a recognized category of Alliance ministry.

School Crises

The Alliance schools at Nyack became the first indirect casualties of the war years, as shortage of funds forced curtailment of various activities.

William C. Stevens,* dean of the Missionary Training Institute, and Dr. J. Hudson Ballard,* principal of the Wilson Academy (a private high school run by the Alliance) had been working to upgrade the Nyack schools with the explicit encouragement of Dr. Simpson. The official magazine took the position repeatedly from 1910 to 1912 that Nyack should become a multischool campus. The editors advocated a junior college, a liberal arts college "which would give us a hold upon the best minds of the country, and a three-year seminary for college graduates."[7]

In his 1911 report, Stevens concluded, "Finally, brethren, 'the Nyack Missionary University!' It is already at least the cloud of the size of a man's hand on the horizon."[8] And that vision would remain on the horizon for many years.

*See "The Founder's Team" in the Appendix for more details.

The dreams that both Ballard and Stevens shared for higher education were rejected by General Council in 1914. Not until the opening of the postgraduate Jaffray School of Missions in 1960 would the Alliance finally catch up with their vision and that of Dr. Simpson.

The reason given for the council action was a shortage of money. All the limited funds during the unsettled war years were needed for overseas outreach. The financial pressure was dramatized in 1914 when only eight new missionaries were sent overseas. More candidates were prepared to go, but lack of funds blocked the way. It was therefore not surprising that nothing could be diverted for educational needs.

However, opposition to higher education was already building. Alliance workers and lay people were well aware that the liberal movement had its source and support mainly in denominational universities and seminaries.

Following the action of General Council, Dr. Charles Blanchard, president of Wheaton College and a close friend of Dr. Simpson, proposed to the Board of Managers that his college be utilized by the Alliance as a finishing school for Nyack graduates. The board accepted his invitation.

Dr. Blanchard, a frequent speaker at Alliance conventions, offered a special privilege: The C&MA would be permitted to conduct missionary conventions on the college campus during the school year. This unique arrangement between Wheaton and the Alliance, extended to no other missionary society, would continue into the 1940s.

The 1914 action by General Council not only slowed down academic advance, it also precipitated the loss of two extremely valuable men. Stevens and Ballard both resigned their positions in the Nyack schools.

Stevens' resignation as dean of the institute ended almost thirteen years of ministry for which he was greatly qualified. Prior to his Nyack post, the Ohio-born son of a Presbyterian minister had organized the Gospel Tabernacle of Los Angeles. He had also worked the West Coast from Canada to Mexico as an Alliance superintendent.

To his college training, Stevens had added studies at Union Seminary in New York and two years of graduate studies in Germany. A classic linguist, he acquired skills in Latin, Greek and Hebrew in addition to German and French. He was offered many honorary degrees but refused them all, preferring rather to be addressed as "Pastor Stevens."

Dr. J. Hudson Ballard's resignation from Wilson Academy in 1914 after five years as principal was an even greater loss to the Alliance.

He had guided the school to accreditation by the strict New York State Board of Regents. At the same time, he earned a doctoral degree at Columbia University.

That was not all. Among his other activities while at Nyack, he preached regularly at the Gospel Tabernacle, served as assistant editor of *The Alliance Weekly,* taught at the institute and academy, and wrote over thirty articles. At the time of his resignation, he was the first education secretary of the Alliance and a member of the Board of Managers.

Had Dr. Ballard been an athlete in a later era, his number would have been retired when he left the team. He was a man no one could ever fully replace.

White Wolf Raid

Although the United States was only indirectly affected by the war in Europe during 1914, Alliance people were on a war footing in the spiritual world. They were dramatically reminded of this by events in China.

White Wolf Raiders, a bandit army of about 20,000 men, were terrorizing northwest China. They eventually arrived at the locked gates of Minchow, a city in which was located the headquarters of the Alliance Kansu Tibetan Border Mission.

Enraged by the city's refusal to unlock the gates, the bandits scaled the fifty-foot walls, forced open the gates and poured into the city. They shouted and shot, looted and burned, raped and killed in an orgy lasting several days. Over 1,000 people died, hundreds of young women disappeared and many parts of the city burned to the ground.

Raiders broke into the mission compound eight times. William Christie met them with traditional Chinese politeness, offering them tea and food, and matching wits with them. He was determined to shield the compound from the torch: his wife and little daughter Hazel, Anna Haupberg and Katherina MacKinnon were hiding in space between the walls.

Christie recounted, "During the daylight hours the bandits were given everything they asked for—animals, eatables, clothing, watches, etc. But after dark, when the seventh and eighth parties demanded women, I steadfastly refused and was threatened to death."[9]

Seeing that Christie would surely be killed, the young wife of a Chinese evangelist called out, "Here am I, take me!" The bandits released the missionary and dragged her off to their camp.

With the help of a Chinese friend, the missionaries fled on foot in the night and confusion. For two days they wandered for twenty miles through the countryside, dodging the searching White Wolf bandits. When the outlaws had plundered the area to the point of exhaustion and then withdrawn, the missionaries returned to Minchow and the smoldering rubble of their station. Grateful to escape with their lives and just the clothes on their backs, they began immediately to rebuild.

Another Loss

The Nyack schools suffered yet another reversal in 1915 with the death of Dr. George P. Pardington.* When only a boy ten years old, he had been beaten by a public school teacher and severely crippled.

He described his own condition: "I was twisted entirely out of shape, and when lying on the floor upon my back my body formed a complete arch, my head and heels only touching the floor."[10]

In 1881 he claimed by faith the Lord's healing. He gradually improved and by April 1885 he could testify: "I am well. My spine is straight. The old trouble is gone. I am perfectly healed. I have dedicated myself wholly to the Lord."[11]

The physical problem returned in later years, however, causing great pain and eventually deformity. But he refused to allow this handicap to end his ministry—or even his sense of humor.

After graduating from New York University and Drew Theological Seminary, he continued postgraduate studies until he earned his Ph.D. degree from New York University in 1898.

While a university student, he had become entangled in Higher Criticism attacks on the Bible and his faith suffered an eclipse. He credited the Friday afternoon meetings of Dr. Simpson in the Gospel Tabernacle with restoring him to full fellowship with the Lord.

Dr. Pardington spent the rest of his life teaching at the Missionary Training Institute. His concentrated textbook on systematic theology, *Outline Studies in Christian Doctrine,* gave little inkling of the humorous, intensely alive man who could convulse his students with hilarious laughter and disrupt other classes throughout the building.

Somewhere along the line, Dr. Pardington learned how to be a rifle sharpshooter. On one occasion he was guest speaker at a Bible conference in the Appalachians of North Carolina. A young camper named David Fant recalled that "chickens were abundant. When a daily supply for the table was needed, Dr. Pardington awed us with his rifle. He was a crack shot at something like fifty yards."[12]

The death of Dr. Pardington and the departure of Stevens and

*See "The Founder's Team" in the Appendix for more details.

Dr. Ballard, all within a short span of time, produced a school crisis at Nyack. Dr. Simpson had to enlist an unusual man bigger than the problems on the hillside. He found his solution in a Canadian from Peterborough, Ontario.

Walter Turnbull's* father had been drawn to the Alliance through Dr. Simpson's preaching. After attending the Missionary Training Institute, young Turnbull sailed for India as a missionary in 1903. His two brothers, John and Louis, also served with the Alliance in India.

Turnbull met and married an American missionary, Maude West, on the field. His wife fell sick and died while they were on furlough in 1909. Turnbull decided on further education and in three years earned a B.A. degree with high honors from McMaster University in Toronto.

While superintendent of a city mission in Vancouver, he was summoned by Dr. Simpson to take charge of Wilson Academy after Dr. Ballard's departure in 1914. When Dr. Pardington died the following year, Turnbull was also given the workload of dean at the institute.

Turnbull inherited a debt of $75,000 on the Nyack schools, mostly from construction projects, including a new administration building later called Pardington Hall. In six years he had the debt reduced to only $6,200, while at the same time enrollment grew to 353, of whom "about 190 came from Alliance branches and 160 from other circles."[13]

Call to Sacrifice

The war in Europe finally caught up with the United States in 1917. Newspapers, magazines and radios kept the public constantly aware of progress on the battlefield. In his annual address to General Council in 1917, Dr. Simpson related events in Europe to the spiritual warfare in which the Alliance was engaged.

"The world has been corroding through selfishness and God has permitted an awful baptism of sacrifice to awaken it to a new life," the Alliance founder said. "The story of heroic suffering and fortitude from the battlefields of France has thrilled the hearts of humanity.

"Surely, the followers of the Lamb should rise to a nobler sacrifice and heroism. May the Christ of Calvary touch us afresh with the spirit of His cross."[14]

That his son Howard was serving with the Canadian Army in France at the time perhaps made Dr. Simpson's reference to "an awful baptism of sacrifice" even more meaningful.

*See "The Founder's Team" in the Appendix for more details.

Dr. Simpson himself showed the way to "nobler sacrifice and heroism" by his example. The 1917 General Council address was to be his last, yet at age seventy-four he kept a strenuous pace throughout his last active year.

To those who in amazement asked how he could do it, Dr. Simpson had an unvarying reply: "There is no service which God expects of us for which He has not made the fullest provision in the infinite resources of His grace. We cannot dare too much if it be in dependence upon Him, for He has given us all His fullness, and sends no one warring upon his own charges."[15]

As if to prove it, his schedule in 1917 seemed as inexhaustible as it was exhausting. He attended all the summer conventions, filled many engagements outside his Alliance responsibilities, prepared and wrote a correspondence course commentary on one-third of the Bible, wrote pamphlets in connection with his other correspondence courses, wrote many letters, helped edit *The Alliance Weekly,* arranged and conducted the New York and Old Orchard conventions, and, as pastor, occupied the pulpit at the Gospel Tabernacle the Sundays he was in New York.

The Alliance fellowship responded to their leader's call for "nobler sacrifice and heroism" in a manner sure to please him: by enlarging the work overseas in the midst of a costly war year. Missionaries in Sierra Leone entered the vast French Sudan for the first time; twenty-five new workers went overseas; income rose by $55,000 to a total of over $258,000. And in spite of high taxes and soaring prices on the domestic scene, the missions department approved a 20 percent cost-of-living increase for missionaries on the field.

By 1917, after an entire generation of activity, the Alliance was looking more and more like a missionary denomination instead of a missionary movement. The annual report listed on the domestic front:

11 organized districts
34 states with Alliance branches or affiliated churches
270 Alliance evangelists and superintendents.[16]

The work overseas appeared even more fully developed:

16 fields in which the Alliance worked
97 central stations
335 outstations
118 organized churches
8,904 communicants
1,425 baptisms
2,827 inquirers
8,364 Sunday school children

5,570 primary school students
292 missionaries
599 national workers.[17]

With tireless consistency, Dr. Simpson reminded his listeners everywhere of the true nature and mission of the Alliance. In St. Paul, Minnesota, on his last deputational tour in December of 1917, according to the district superintendent, "he took occasion to emphasize in the strongest possible way the fact that the primary objective of the Alliance movement was not the teaching of special doctrines, but the salvation of souls and the reaching of the neglected classes from whom the conventional methods of modern churches were steadily creating a distressing gulf of cleavage and separation. He trusted that this should always be the primary ideal and aim of our work."[18]

Preparations for Departure

In January of 1918 Dr. Simpson, feeling the strain of unrelenting work and a persistent weakness, suffered a heart attack. It was no doubt a warning signal from his physical body that it was time to slow down. At age seventy-four he had no reason to complain.

After a vacation, his first real one in thirty years, he felt stronger, but his stride was broken. From then on he attended only five of seventy-one Board of Managers meetings. At the 1918 General Council, he deferred his usual role as chairman to vice-president Ulysses Lewis. Though he went to Old Orchard later in the year, he appeared in only a few meetings.

During its May sessions the Board of Managers took up a matter that had long concerned several members: the financial situation of the Simpsons.

From the day the Alliance founder relinquished his post and generous annual income of $5,000 as pastor of Thirteenth Street Presbyterian, he had refused to receive a salary either from the Gospel Tabernacle or from the Alliance national headquarters. Often he even refused traveling expenses to conventions.

Perhaps inspired in years past by George Mueller, the English layman who supported a huge orphanage by faith alone, he preferred to be self-supporting with God's help. He was thus freed of obligations to others and also able to dedicate to the work all the income that would have been his through a salary.

On one occasion, however, he acknowledged to an associate pastor "that it might be a very good school of faith for the pastor but that it was very bad discipline for the flock."[19]

The principle of faith no doubt generated some tensions between husband and wife in the Simpson household, especially when his resignation from Thirteenth Street Presbyterian precipitated an abrupt nosedive of salary from thousands of dollars to absolute zero.

Margaret Simpson recalled, "We had moved from the comfortable Manse on Thirty-second Street to a little four-room apartment [with five children]. One morning we had nothing for breakfast but oatmeal.

"Not being able to trust the Lord as my husband was doing, I went out and for the first time in my life ordered supplies for which I could not pay.

"For several days Mr. Simpson received very little money. Sometimes he would come in with a small piece of meat or some other necessity.

"One morning I received a letter from a lady in Philadelphia, whom I did not know, containing a check for one hundred and fifty dollars. I hurried over to the church office to have Mr. Simpson cash it at a neighborhood bank, and then made the rounds of the stores to pay the bills. That was the first and last time I ever bought anything for which I could not pay."[20]

Dr. Simpson's faith in the providential supply of his family's needs followed the principle of "faith with works" in the Epistle of James. Most of his income issued from his work outside the church. His manuscripts needed a printer, so he went into the printing business (the Alliance Press). His books needed a publisher and distributor, so he entered the publication business (the Christian Alliance Publishing Co.).

By 1918, however, he no longer owned the publishing business. Six years previously, realizing that his printed works were so closely associated with the Alliance that they were considered by the public to be the official voice of the movement, he turned the Christian Alliance Publishing Company over to the society.

His friend and longtime associate John Jaderquist was appointed the first publication secretary of the movement and given a mandate to make the publishing business a viable operation, something it had not achieved under its previous owner.

Ever mindful of the public and the need to put reading material in their hands, Dr. Simpson had designed his books to be as inexpensive as possible: small in size but with readable print, plain cover, limited number of pages became the standard format of Alliance publications—something of a forerunner of the popular paperback format years later. The savings in production costs were reflected in the low selling price of the books.

Jaderquist worked hard to walk the thin line between respecting

Dr. Simpson's concern for mass distribution of inexpensive books and the Board of Managers' desire that the publishing company pay its own way. Some of the measures he had to take made him unpopular with the Board of Managers and even troubled the former owner, but he did what he could so that the publishing company would not be a liability to the Alliance.

In addition to the printing press that Dr. Simpson still owned in 1918, he was the proprietor of other businesses involving properties, a realty agency, a development company and a restaurant. The various ventures shared a common trait: They were all encumbered with debt. Red ink on the bottom line was due mainly to his lack of time to oversee the enterprises. He had to depend on others with less ability or concern—or both—to manage his investments.

"There is no question that his business was the great burden that finally proved too heavy for him," admitted his sympathetic biographer. "He would have surrendered it in his later years; but while his own strength endured, he could see no way of deliverance.

"When he could no longer conduct it, he acknowledged to intimate associates that he had been mistaken in entering into business and that he should have kept himself free, as did the apostles, to give himself to 'prayer and the ministry of the word.' "[21]

That heavy burden was finally surrendered to the Board of Managers in May, 1918. Dr. Simpson provided his colleagues with a signed release enabling them to settle his business affairs. A committee was formed that included three of his oldest associates and supporters. With careful management and legal advice, and with "special supplementary gifts and pledges from friends,"[22] they were eventually able to satisfy all of Dr. Simpson's financial obligations.

Kindly and firmly, the Board of Managers overrode the founder's protests and pressed upon him an allowance modest enough in terms of his many years of unpaid service, yet adequate to care for the needs of the Simpson household.

One further kindness would come to the deserving Simpsons early the following year, this one from a layman, L. K. "Daddy" Brubaker.* While the Simpsons lodged elsewhere the opening months of 1919, this Pennsylvania Dutch farmer and his wife completely renovated their residence in Nyack, from roof to foundation—painting, papering, repairing, and all from the resources of their love and personal finances. For the Simpsons, it was like coming home to a new house.

During the same eventful meeting in May of 1918, the Board of Managers worked with the founder in the redistribution of his

*See "The Founder's Team" in the Appendix for more details.

various responsibilities. The correspondence school and courses they turned over to the Nyack schools. *The Alliance Weekly* they entrusted to Messrs. Glover, Jaderquist, Turnbull and Thompson, with Jaderquist continuing as associate editor. Glover and Jaderquist also handled most of the executive details between the frequent meetings of the board.

The business of reassigning responsibilities, softened by a deep sense of sadness, proceeded with a sense of dignity that often goes with history in the making. The board members knew they were presiding over the culmination of an era, and they did not take it lightly.

Passing Shadow

Whether it was the vulnerability of a mind grown weary from endless work, or a spirit reeling by the sudden lifting of pressures that long had called forth his best, something happened to Dr. Simpson for a period of several weeks.

Following the 1918 General Council, he entered a deep depression reminiscent of his earlier years. Never one to burden others with private struggles, he attempted to carry this one alone as well. But as the Light of his life grew clouded and the Friend of his soul seemed withdrawn, his close friends sensed what was happening.

For many crises of his life he had known the loneliness of a leader, but not this time. One by one, his friends would "drop by" or even come openly to converse with him along quiet paths or on the porch swing. They knelt with him in prayer at the close of day, gently urged him to sleep when the hour grew late, and kept a prayerful vigil throughout the menacing night hours that mocked his faith.

One day two of his friends, especially burdened to pray for his deliverance, knelt with him in the library. Alternately storming the ramparts of heaven and assailing the powers of darkness in Jesus' name, they petitioned God for his recovery.

Before they rose from their knees their beloved friend said, "Boys, I do not seem to be able to take quite all that you have asked. You seem to have outstripped me—but Jesus is so real."[23]

From that day forward, his biographer observed, no one ever heard Dr. Simpson speak again of the Enemy he had fought for so many years. The springtime of companionship with his Lord had returned so completely that all he could talk about was his wonderful Jesus.

Word must have reached him by then of yet another brother in ministry being called home. John Salmon, patriarch of the Canadian Alliance, had retired from active ministry late in 1911 with the ringing declaration, "I have preached what I believe, and I have believed ALL I have preached!"[24]

The Salmons had moved from Toronto to a small bungalow in Los Angeles near an Alliance fellowship, away from the cold Canadian winter and closer to their daughter in San Jose. Although retirement curtailed his ministry, he retained his position as an honorary vice-president of the Alliance, and was immediately appointed a field evangelist.

He preached in Alliance conventions and in services of other groups, but the thrilling highlight of his retirement ministry was a sixteen-month visit to the Far East, including six months in China. Though he spoke to many local congregations, his most effective ministry was counseling and encouraging missionaries of the Central China Conference of the C&MA.

In December of 1917 he wrote a farewell message to the Alliance family in *The Alliance Weekly:* "I consider it an honour to be connected with The Christian and Missionary Alliance, and have been ever since its formation years ago. Our fellowship together in the work of the Lord has been sweet. We have gone through many struggles at times, but have been sustained in our work of faith and labour of love."[25]

Six months later John Salmon suffered a massive stroke and, at the age of eighty-seven, he met face-to-face the Lord who had transformed him from a foul-mouthed sailor to a fearless preacher of God's amazing grace.

Regaining Momentum

The vacuum in leadership in the later years of the decade showed up clearly in a council report that only eight branches were added in 1917. It was time to regain the initiative, especially in view of the armistice halting World War I.

General Council recommended that each pastor or superintendent give one week out of six or seven for extension work. "The Forward Movement," initiated several years before, received new impetus as Paul Rader conducted Full Gospel Crusades in Toronto, New York and three other major cities.

District superintendents, already aware of the lag in growth, had taken the unprecedented step of meeting together in January, 1918. Participating in the conference was a young superintendent of the Central District who would be heard from a great deal in later years: H. M. Shuman. Not surprisingly, the meeting was held in

Pittsburgh, parish of the venerable E. D. Whiteside, of whom Shuman later said, "Probably he trained more home workers and missionaries than any other man in the Alliance."[26]

In a further effort to regain momentum and be prepared for significant changes in the near future, the 1918 General Council increased representation on the Board of Managers from fifteen to twenty-four members. One of the new appointees would himself become the subject of much discussion and debate in the question of succession. His name: Paul Rader.*

Question of Succession

Rader had already served with the Alliance for several years. His association with the movement dated back to 1912, when he ministered in Pittsburgh under the wise and watchful eyes of Whiteside. His preaching gifts had been quickly recognized, and invitations to speak came from all quarters.

Rader went to Chicago to conduct evangelistic meetings in November, 1914. Dr. Simpson arrived about the same time to preach in Moody Church. He invited the young evangelist to pray during the Sunday morning service.

Rader's prayer so impressed the congregation, which had no pastor at the time, that he was invited back for ten days of meetings in January, 1915. One month after the series, the congregation invited him to become pastor. And within another year Moody Church built a 5,000 seat tabernacle that Rader filled with people seeking God.

Dr. Simpson, always alert for workers on whom God's blessing rested, encouraged a wider role for Rader in the Alliance. By 1916 he had already been named an honorary vice-president and had led the "Forward Movement" for two years.

In special session during the 1918 General Council at Nyack, the Board of Managers included in its minutes an expression of "looking forward toward a closer affiliation to the work of our beloved brother, Rev. Paul Rader."

A way to do so was immediately suggested. With both Simpsons present, the board voted to sponsor a special eight-week evangelistic campaign beginning January 1, 1919. The group invited Rader "to assist in the planning and carrying forward such a movement."[27]

Rader accepted the invitation but requested he be given no official title. In the closing service of General Council on May 16, he preached a powerful message that drew many delegates to the altar for prayer.

*See "The Founder's Team in the Appendix for more details.

The following month Rader had lunch with Jaderquist and put the question directly to him: "Who is to be the next leader of the Alliance, you or I?" The longtime associate of Dr. Simpson denied any ambition in that direction, pointing out that as publication secretary he had been forced to make some unpopular decisions. He suggested there should be no successor, but rather an elected chairman "with heads of departments having the initiative."[28]

Rader told Jaderquist he believed the Alliance had fallen into a rut, but that he intended to open new missions and churches across the nation—either inside or outside the Alliance.

Once back in Chicago, he found so many demands on his time in his active and growing pastorate that he was unable to devote time to Alliance matters. His ambitious intentions to divide time between New York and Chicago proved impractical as the combined responsibilities required more hours than a day provided.

The exciting work of evangelism and pastoral activities in Moody Church proved a stronger attraction to him than seeming endless committee meetings of the Alliance. He returned to New York for only eight of the numerous Board of Managers sessions over the next year.

Meanwhile a deep division was developing within the Board of Managers over Rader's future role in the Alliance. The majority saw him as the obvious successor to Dr. Simpson and favored offering him the vice-presidency at the 1919 General Council. A minority held that he was too new to the Alliance and that he lacked administrative ability.

Attempting to resolve their differences and have clear leading from the Lord, the Board of Managers met in New York on February 24, 1919, for a night of prayer and then a scheduled consultation with the man from Chicago. Dr. Simpson occupied a room across the hall, unable to attend but joining with them in prayer.

Despite their best intentions, the board members could not agree on the nomination of Rader as vice-president. Neither could he express clear readiness to accept the responsibilities accompanying the office.

Following the session several board members and Rader met with Simpson across the hall. The Moody pastor would never forget the Alliance founder's impassioned prayer for the future of the Alliance. Coming away from the prayer room, Thompson related, "In his inner consciousness, whether he confessed it to himself or not, Paul Rader knew the mantle was falling on him."[29]

To the contrary, Jaderquist maintained this was never Dr. Simpson's intention. He would insist after the 1919 elections at General Council, "The sad fact is that Mr. Simpson felt the election of Mr.

Rader as a cruel blow."[30] Considering Rader's gift as an evangelist, Dr. Simpson may have wanted him as pastor of the Gospel Tabernacle in order to return the church to something of its former impact in earlier days on the city.

Correspondence in March and April of 1919 with men whom Rader highly respected made him uncertain about accepting the nomination. His beloved mentor E. D. Whiteside wrote, "Your vision of what God has for the Alliance is doubtless from Him, but the method you had in mind...was not God's method. You did not believe that God had appointed you leader...[or] you would have let Him bring it about instead of initiating it yourself."[31]

Dr. Glover's correspondence was even more pointed, "I find myself unable to share the feelings of most of my Board brethren that you are the one God would have to become at present the head of the Alliance movement. My reason is that I do not feel that you have had the necessary experience in real Alliance work, and that your strong qualities are not such as to fit you for an executive and administrative position like the presidency."[32]

Quoting these excerpts in a letter dated April 3, 1919 to the Board of Managers, Rader concluded, "You will please, then, let my name drop from your planning and your thinking as far as any leadership on my part is concerned."[33]

Subsequent meetings of the Board of Managers and expressions of support by the majority of members persuaded Rader to let his name stand for the nomination of vice-president.

Election and Promotion

The 1919 General Council met in Toccoa Falls, Georgia, during May. Absence of the founder, rendered too weak to travel due to a slight stroke, impressed the delegates that they stood at a crucial juncture in the progress of the Alliance.

Dr. Glover heightened their sense of solemn responsibility with his opening remarks. He reminded the delegates that the World Peace Conference in Paris was still grappling with postwar problems and that it was too early to anticipate "the ultimate terms of peace and the resultant world conditions."

"But this much seems certain," he emphasized, "that 1919 marks the dawn of a new era as distinct as the beginning of the Protestant Reformation or the inauguration of modern missions."[34]

Rader attended General Council and preached several times, but he returned to Chicago before the elections on Monday. The nominating committee submitted Rader's name for vice-president. Ulysses Lewis, who had formerly held the position, was nominated from the floor, but he declined. By an overwhelming voice vote, the council delegates elected Paul Rader as vice-president of The Christian and Missionary Alliance.

Dr. Simpson's promotion to the immediate presence of his Lord came with the same quiet grace and dignity with which he had lived and served his Master for fifty-four years.

On Tuesday of October 28, he spent the morning on his veranda conversing with a visitor from Jamaica. Then followed his last act, one he had always considered a high honor: praying for missionaries. He lapsed into a coma beyond recovery. Early Wednesday morning the tired body of God's chosen servant released its willing spirit with a serenity that must have been similar to the experience of Enoch, who "walked with God, and he was not for God took him."

Telegrams and memorials poured in from all over the world. Foremost leaders of the evangelical movement attended one or another of the four memorial services. They may not have agreed with Dr. Simpson on every point—nor he with them—but on the essentials they were united, and they loved him.

Rev. Henry W. Frost, director of the China Inland Mission, spoke for many: "Dr. Simpson belonged to the whole Church of Christ. His ministries overflowed boundaries and went out into every place."[35]

But the founder of a movement that spanned the globe was above all a man of vision, and vision looks to the future, not the past. Dr. J. Gregory Mantle's* parting tribute was therefore most appropriate. His sweeping glance took in the three hundred institute students who would form a double-column honor guard for the funeral procession at Nyack and later spread out to the four corners of earth. Then he cited the words inscribed on Sir Christopher Wren's tomb and applied them to Dr. Simpson: "So would I say of this man—'If you seek his monument, look around.' "[36]

End and Beginning

The passing of Dr. Simpson marked the end of an era, but a movement by its very nature must move ahead or collapse. The Alliance had its reference points in the example and writings of its founder, in the outstanding men who survived him and shared his vision.

But there were concerns and questions. Jaderquist spoke of a conversation with Dr. Simpson after the 1919 General Council: "Mr. Simpson begged me to do what I could to hold the brethren

*See "The Founder's Team" in the Appendix for more details.

steady. He said he feared they were in danger of getting away from the old standards of simplicity and sacrifice; that I had known the work almost from the beginning and he hoped I would do my utmost to stem the tide."[37]

Paul Rader, whose nomination to the vice-presidency had been strongly opposed by some very perceptive men, would now be president in Dr. Simpson's place.

Could he build on the vision entrusted to him?

CHAPTER 9

Troubled Transition

The secret of progress lies not in the absence of obstacles, but in keeping a right sense of direction.

1919—1926

Context of the Times

The decade of the 1920s was bracketed at either end by a major event with serious implications for the religious life of the nation: the Armistice and the Great Depression. The in-between years marked a steady decline in Protestantism for the average American.

The paper-thin peace in Europe quickly cooled the ardor of patriotism and lulled the nation into complacency. Referring to the churches' intense support of the war effort and their subsequent cooling off, one historian noted, '"The Great Crusade' ended its march on the lawn socials of normalcy."

And, as always, complacency proved more costly to the church than frontal attack by its enemies. All the denominational indexes that soared so high during the crises-filled war years—attendance, income, influence—now took a downward spiral that lasted throughout the decade.

Something more than the ranks of the faithful grew thin during the decade of normalcy. The Gospel was watered down in the name of relevance. Big business was considered good for both the church and the nation. Industry's themes of success, promotion and prosperity replaced evangelical emphases in many sermons.

One of the decade's most popular books, written by an advertising executive, placed Jesus Christ in the front ranks of the world's great business organizers. The author based his amazing thesis on an even more astonishing proof text: the boy Jesus' words in the temple, "Wist ye not that I must be about my Father's business?"

The Gospel likewise suffered at the hands of clergy who recast its claims in social terms. Salvation became release from poverty and oppression, the Kingdom of God translated into a social welfare state.

This Social Gospel, though popular with theologians and church officials, failed to stir the average person. As a result, the gap widened between institutional Protestantism and the marketplace of everyday life.

The 1920s did witness some significant religious developments. The initiative in movement shifted from evangelicals to ecumenicals as, midway through the decade, the Stockholm conference convened. Six hundred delegates from thirty-seven countries moved a big step closer to world-class status as they laid the foundations of an ecumenical approach to the world's social problems.

Fundamentalism and modernism continued to develop along mutually contradictory and hostile lines. The term *fundamentalism* came into popular usage during the 1920s to describe those ready "to do battle royal for the Fundamentals."

The essentials of fundamental faith emerged as something of a six-point checklist of doctrinal soundness: the inerrancy of Scripture; the virgin birth of Christ; His death a substitute sacrifice for sinners; His bodily resurrection and imminent return; and the historical accuracy of biblical miracles.

Modernists took a more generous view of human nature, believing in the historical process "by which the kingdoms of the world are becoming the kingdom of our Lord Jesus Christ." They also believed that since God was at work in nature and culture, these sources of truth needed consideration along with the written message of the Bible.

Fundamentalists in the major denominations gradually lost out, not because they presented their position poorly, but because denominational officials opted for tolerance and pluralism.

Modernism did not make a clean sweep of the churches. Denominations in the South held a steady, conservative course. Liberalism and modernism were to them merely Northern notions in the carpetbag of Yankee culture, which they had rejected since Civil War days.

In the public eye during the 1920s, the worst damage to the cause of biblical faith came more from monkeys than modernists. Although twenty states had enacted laws barring the teaching of Darwinism in public schools, the theory of evolution was gaining wide acceptance and undermining the credibility of Scripture.

A confrontation with educators came to public attention at the

1925 Scopes trial in Tennessee. The American Civil Liberties Union championed the evolutionist cause and hired famous trial lawyer Clarence Darrow to do battle with golden-tongued William Jennings Bryan of the creationist camp.

Bryan won the case in court but lost it in the media. A phalanx of reporters, headed by H. L. Mencken, a close friend of Darrow, came to town and turned the trial into a circus. They depicted fundamentalists as rubes and hicks with less intelligence than the monkeys from which they were allegedly evolved. This stereotype of Bible believers would persist for decades.

* * *

The doctrinal struggles of the 1920s increased the exodus of Alliance people from denominational churches to branch fellowships. The decade became what Dr. Simpson would have termed a "present distress," a time when Alliance people were justified in starting their own places of worship as they were "pushed out of their churches by false teaching and harsh prejudice and pressures."

But despite Dr. Simpson's admonition that such "local and independent churches should never be considered as Alliance churches in any technical sense," these groups of believers persisted in acting more and more like Alliance churches.

Once the question of succession was settled, they would move toward an identity in which the founder's wishes for a nondenominational movement would be more honored in the exception than the rule.

PAUL RADER,* now president of the Alliance, shared some striking similarities with his predecessor. Both he and Dr. Simpson wholeheartedly fulfilled the scriptural injunction, "Do the work of an evangelist."

In Louisville, Dr. Simpson had erected a large tabernacle-type church to reach the masses of people alienated from the formal church establishment. In Chicago, Rader influenced Moody Church to build a 5,000-seat tabernacle designed for a three-month evangelistic campaign in the city, but it served that purpose for ten years, three of which featured evangelistic meetings six nights a week.[1]

Both Simpson and Rader, powerful evangelists who could captivate massive audiences, also preached a message of deeper spiritual life and missions. Liberated from a deadening liberal theology like

*See "The Founder's Team" in the Appendix for details.

a revolutionary freed from prison, Rader embraced the Fourfold Gospel with a zeal born of personal discovery.

Rader, profoundly influenced by Simpson, placed him above others in esteem: "My outstanding impression of Dr. A. B. Simpson is that he was the foremost world man of our generation.

"Many great men of missionary vision have joined hands with others to spread the Gospel in the darkened lands," he explained. "Here is a man who, single-handed, started and carried forward a movement to 'the regions beyond.' He planted his workers in sixteen mission fields of the earth, and did it in twenty-five years."[2]

Critical Differences

Despite a sense of spiritual kinship with the Alliance founder, Rader differed from his predecessor in temperament and style, factors that would eventually cause serious problems.

Dr. Simpson, a congenial and cosmopolitan team leader, attracted support from a wide range of gifted men and women of differing backgrounds and views. Rader, a rugged individualist, preferred going it alone and ruling with an autocratic hand.

Dr. Simpson, whose sensitive and imaginative nature made him a poet, won the hearts of his hearers with his grace of speech. Rader, possessing a fiery, aggressive spirit that in previous days had found expression in prizefighting and broncobusting, overpowered his listeners with words like hammer blows.

The Moody Church pastor and Alliance founder differed on one other critical issue. For Dr. Simpson, the Alliance was his life; he served it with the strength of five men and the single-mindedness of one possessed of a vision. Rader divided his time between a church in Chicago and an elected office in New York. When forced to choose, Rader favored action rather than administration, crusades over committees.

The first indication of this problem came fast on the heels of Rader's succession to the presidency in 1919. He considered resigning from Moody Church, and then reconsidered. For more than two years, he would try to carry out the duties of two full-time posts, one as pastor and the other as president.

When Rader did turn his full attention to work for the Alliance, he achieved remarkable results. After only eight new branches formed in 1917 and General Council called for more attention to branches, Rader formed a fast-moving, high-powered team. In five weeks the team conducted conventions in five principal cities—New York, Toronto, Detroit, Syracuse and Cleveland—and initiated the opening of thirty new branches.

An Enlarged View

Rader's enthusiasm for overseas witness found reflection in the missionary program of Moody Church. In June of 1919 the church sponsored its fifth annual missions conference under Rader's leadership. The C&MA, along with thirteen other missions, took part in the conference. Pledges that year rose from $43,000 to $61,000 to support the church's own eighty-three missionaries and the work of various agencies.

Later in 1920 Rader and his wife set out on a seven-month deputation trip to seven Alliance fields, Europe and England. John Wanamaker, an outstanding Christian businessman in Philadelphia, gave Rader a letter of introduction to Prime Minister Lloyd George of England.

The Raders' send-off service in New York was moved to Calvary Baptist Church to accommodate the large attendance. Rev. John Roach Stratton, host pastor, welcomed Rader as one who, in the words of a published biography, was "not a man-made preacher, but . . . a prophet of God made such by the Holy Spirit."[3]

During the world tour, Rader spoke to a number of mass gatherings and counseled with numerous missionaries, but the most memorable personal experience of the trip happened in Shanghai. Upon his return to New York, he spoke in detail of the impact made on him by a brief after-breakfast meditation William Christie presented to missionaries in the Chinese port city.

Christie had read the passage in John 10 concerning Jesus, the Good Shepherd. Every time the Lord referred to Himself, Christie emphasized the pronoun: "*I* am the door . . . *I* am the Good Shepherd . . . *I* lay down my life for the sheep."

When Christie came to verse sixteen he read, "Other sheep *I* have which are not of this fold . . ." and he laid the Bible aside, looked around at the group and repeated with strong feeling, ". . . them also *I* must bring."

He paused, then quietly made a comment that burned into Rader's soul: "Brethren, no man can be a missionary. Jesus is the only Missionary. He can bring them. He says He must bring them. If He is abiding in His fullness in me, then I am carrying about China the great, the only Missionary. Only as I carry Him in His fullness, is my life a missionary life."

Deeply moved, Rader left the group. "I slipped quietly from the room to the closet of prayer—I wanted Him so much, the only living Missionary, to live in me. I must have it so for no man can be a missionary. This and only this is the answer to the question, 'What is our power?' "[4]

Personnel Imbalance

Rader reported to the Board of Managers some observations gathered during his world trip of Alliance fields. He voiced special concern about the number of women overseas living in pioneer hardship and dangerous situations. No doubt the recently concluded war contributed to the problem, but he urged that the imbalance not be permitted to continue.

The problem he raised had a familiar ring to old-timers. The annual report of 1914 recorded the following action: "That whereas there is an insistent cry for men in Palestine, South and Central China, India, the Congo and other fields, we recommend that men applicants be given precedence over women, excepting where the latter are needed to fill special posts of duty, or in cases of married couples, until the present demand for men has been more fully supplied."[5]

Apparently by 1921 women missionaries were still doing more than their part: of the 217 women missionaries, 123 were single, while men missionaries numbered 132. Rader's observation prompted at least one rather unusual admission by General Council: "That in view of the fact that it has been decided that single women cannot do as effective service on the field as married women, we confess our failure in not having made the question of their marriage to suitable, Spirit-filled men, who will promote and not prevent their missionary aspirations, the subject of sufficient and continuous prayer."[6]

Dr. Walter Turnbull, dean of the Missionary Training Institute, noted Rader's report and announced that no new woman applicants would be received except for those who qualified for the senior class by previous training. This action was expected to attract 300 young men applicants, and it did in fact bring about a higher ratio of men students—for about one year.[7]

The school also set up a "Thousand Men Fund" to provide financial assistance to men students, but fell far short of the ambitious goal.

Another pressing problem faced Alliance missions in 1921. Dr. Robert H. Glover, who had strongly opposed the progress of Rader to the presidency, resigned as foreign secretary midway through the year after completing some necessary overseas trips. His successor, Alfred C. Snead, must have appeared at the time to be a short-term solution for the vacated position. The Board of Managers designated him as acting secretary, and made him responsible for only seven fields at first.

A tall, delicate man with stooping frame and emaciated appearance, Snead had begun his ministry in 1905 as superintendent of the Alliance branch in Atlanta. Shortly after arriving in India two years later, he contracted tuberculosis and suffered frequent and severe crises.

A close colleague of Snead recalled, "During one twenty-four hour period he suffered four hemorrhages that seemed to drain the last lifeblood from his frail body. Then, in answer to believing prayer, his hemorrhages ceased, never to be repeated through all the years that followed."[8]

In a manner reminiscent of Dr. Simpson in earlier days, the new foreign secretary possessed an indomitable spirit that carried a frail frame through an arduous daily schedule for years.

Dr. Snead did not permit his physical frailty to stop him, any more than he allowed the impressive stature of his predecessor, Dr. Glover, to intimidate him. He took immediate control of the seven fields assigned to him and gradually received responsibility for other fields. By 1935, he would have full operational responsibility for the foreign department.

From then until his retirement twenty years later, "Dr. Snead reigned like a king on his throne."[9]

Domestic Adjustments

Alliance ministries in North America also required some close scrutiny and adjustments. Sweeping changes had taken place since 1881, when Dr. Simpson first envisioned "a great missionary movement that would reach the neglected fields of the world and utilize the neglected forces of the churches at home."[10]

Older lay movements, such as the tract and Bible societies, the colportage agencies, rescue missions and Sunday schools that had emerged in the middle and latter years of the nineteenth century, became regular features of society by 1920. Methodist holiness and pentecostal divisions had resulted in new denominations reemphasizing individual spiritual experience. Bible institutes, missionary agencies and independent churches were proliferating.[11]

The fundamentalist "come-out" (of liberal churches) movement, the prophetic conference movement[12]—all these movements, divisions, agencies and other factors required Alliance people to take another look at themselves and contemporary society and come up with new applications of Dr. Simpson's "neglected truths, neglected forces and neglected areas."

One aspect of the times had not changed between 1881 and 1920: the spiritual needs of a great number of people alienated from the institutional church—and their numbers were rapidly increasing as liberalism took over church after church. In one annual report of the 1920s, Alliance home secretary E. J. Richards pointed to over 50,000 empty churches and noted that 11,000 denominational ministers had resigned their pastorates the previous year and secured secular employment.[13]

How was the Alliance to respond to the spiritual needs of the 1920s when so many factors had changed since the 1880s?

Early in the Rader era, General Council approved district-level reorganization to achieve greater growth in a more coherent manner.[14] District superintendents, relieved of local branch duties, could now give themselves full time to oversight of their areas, establish new branches and recruit workers. Each was to receive support and counsel from a newly formed executive committee in his district.

Another response to the changing religious climate of the 1920s took the form of better training for home workers. General Council of 1920 recommended each district have its own two-year Bible school to train local superintendents. The spiritual leaders of many branches were outstanding laymen or women of the fellowship chosen by their peers, but they lacked formal training for ministry.

This council action influenced the opening of several district or regional schools: Simpson Bible Institute in Seattle, Washington, 1921; Boston Bible Training School, 1922; Whiteside Memorial Bible School in Pittsburgh, 1923; and Beulah Beach (Ohio) Bible Institute, 1925. In Canada, both the Canadian Bible Institute, Toronto, and the Great West Bible Institute, Alberta, began in 1924.

Tabernacle Strategy

These organizational and educational adjustments would help make the Alliance more effective, but Rader considered them inadequate. Convinced that the Alliance was "in a rut" at a crisis time demanding bold, sweeping measures, he believed the future lay in special teams and mass meetings in public halls, and the formation of tabernacles.

The tabernacle strategy involved hastily constructed and inexpensive buildings providing neutral ground for evangelizing great numbers of people untouched by or unattracted to the organized church. These spiritually neglected masses could find all they needed in the Fourfold Gospel and then be united in the great cause of world missions.

Rader received encouragement from E. J. Richards, who suggested to General Council in 1919 that tabernacles might be the wave of the future for the Alliance. He reported, "We have in mind one instance where a new town was entered, a lot leased and a tabernacle erected, seating about 300, at a cost of about $1,500. In the first month's meetings, scores were saved, and the first missionary offering amounted to over $1,300."[15]

Rader could have multiplied the instances as evidence that "tabernaclism" was an idea whose time had come. After returning from his deputational trip overseas, he conducted campaigns with remarkable results. He also encouraged others to organize campaign teams.

F. F. Bosworth and his wife formed a crusade team with his brother and wife, the B. B. Bosworths, all of them gifted musicians. One campaign took place in Pittsburgh, where a 3,000-seat tabernacle costing $13,000 witnessed the conversion of 4,800 people and the baptism of 250. After the campaign the organizers remodeled the tabernacle to seat 1,500, convincing many people to stay and become members.

Warren Collins, a layman from Fort Worth, Texas, formed a team with singer W. E. Odum. One campaign they conducted in Penn's Grove, New Jersey, resulted in hundreds of conversions and an attendance that kept growing until the tabernacle had to be enlarged to accommodate 1,500 people.

A military chaplain wanted to start an Alliance branch in the North Pacific District. A. L. Knudson, district superintendent, challenged him to enter the town of Bellingham, Washington. When cottage prayer meetings failed to spark interest, the chaplain rented a hall with seating capacity for 1,100 people. He engaged the Warren Collins party for a series of meetings that lasted five weeks.

During that time, 374 people were converted and many others claimed an experience of sanctification or healing. Before the five-week series ended, the group had incorporated as the Bellingham Gospel Tabernacle, purchased a building and installed a pastor.

However impressive the results of other campaign teams, Rader set the pace and standard. His brilliant preaching and powerful charisma attracted thousands wherever he went and turned every crusade into a triumph of the Gospel, though not necessarily an advance for the Alliance.

More convinced than ever of the effectiveness of the crusade-tabernacle combination, Rader resigned from Moody Church in late 1921. He then declined an urgent invitation to become senior pastor of the New York Gospel Tabernacle, citing his many responsibilities as president of the Alliance.

Even so, his presidential duties did not keep him from commissioning a 6,000-seat tabernacle not far from Moody Church in Chicago nine or ten months later. More people came to the opening service than the new Chicago Gospel Tabernacle could accommodate.

Conflicting Models

At about the same time, a Canadian pastor was emerging as one of the dominion's most remarkable church leaders. In 1918, Oswald J. Smith left the Presbyterian Church and over two years later became pastor of the Parkdale Tabernacle of the C&MA in Toronto, perhaps through the influence of his wife, who was a 1911 graduate of the Missionary Training Institute.[15]

Rev. A. W. Roffe, district superintendent, invited the Bosworth brothers for a campaign in Massey Hall, Toronto. Attendance numbering several thousand encouraged Smith and the congregation to follow up with a tent campaign featuring Paul Rader and the Cleveland Gospel Quintet, a remarkably gifted group of black singers from the Alliance branch in Cleveland. A series of such meetings culminated in 1922 with construction of a 2,000-seat tabernacle costing $90,000.

In his enthusiasm for tabernacle ministry, Smith had some caustic observations concerning the average church as he perceived it: "There are far too many. Some might well be abandoned. How often do we find a mere handful of people overfed and underworked, made up for the most part of women, self-satisfied and even anti-evangelistic!"[16]

As an alternative to the mainline denominations he proposed "the establishment of a number of large tabernacle centers in the big cities, to broadcast the truth at home and to form the basis of our foreign work . . . with strong executive heads in charge of each place."[17]

Smith later left the Alliance and founded the Metropolitan Tabernacle, eventually renamed the Peoples Church, a few miles from his former pastorate in Toronto. The tabernacle organization reflected his thinking of what such an assembly of believers should be.

Metropolitan Tabernacle had no formal membership, but a self-perpetuating governing board. It functioned as a center for mass evangelism, and Pastor Smith's messages were primarily evangelistic. The tabernacle avoided the functions of a regular church because, Smith asserted, "As soon as it seeks to become a church, it fails and the people leave. Ichabod ['the glory is departed'] is then its name."[18]

This type of tabernacle differed drastically from the New York Gospel Tabernacle. Dr. Simpson organized his group to function as a regular church with a congregational form of government. It had an executive board and elders elected annually by the members. Pastor Simpson preached Covenanter style: expository treatment of whole books of the Bible (the basis of his *Christ in the Bible* series). The Gospel Tabernacle observed the ordinances along with church discipline and maintained a balance of Christian worship, nurture, evangelism and missions.

Comparison of Smith's Metropolitan Tabernacle and Simpson's Gospel Tabernacle explained why Alliance leaders were becoming concerned with the new direction envisioned by Rader for the Alliance.

W. H. Chandler, a field evangelist, expressed the thought of many when he appealed to delegates of the 1921 General Council: "A precious heritage has been entrusted to us. Let us guard it with care and pass it on in its original form and flavor and fervency to those who follow us until Jesus comes."[19]

Growing Tensions

Regardless of Rader's conflicting views on church government, he stood without equal as the most articulate and persuasive proponent of the Fourfold Gospel in the Alliance.

The Alliance home secretary expressed regret in the annual report to General Council of 1922 that Rader could fill so few of the requests for mass campaigns that had come from at least one hundred cities. He noted that many shared the belief Rader should be free of all pastoral work in order to devote his full time and talent to evangelism and teaching the Fourfold Gospel.[20]

Turning aside this suggestion, Rader submitted to the Board of Managers a proposal for a "tabernacle commission" that in effect would reorganize the Alliance. The plan would establish tabernacles in all the large cities and have them under his direct supervision. The tabernacles would have committees or delegated commissions to program evangelistic and missionary activities. Branches already functioning in the area would come under the supervision of these committees.

The president also suggested in his proposal that the Alliance headquarters move to Chicago, or that at least an extension office be created and staffed by personnel qualified to hold mass meetings.

The Board of Managers agreed to study the possibility of an extension office in Chicago, but flatly refused to move headquarters or to phase out the local branch structure that formed the basic source of prayer, finances and candidates for Alliance missions.

As 1923 progressed, the divergence of views between Rader and other Alliance leaders became more pronounced. The proposed "tabernacle commission" would have dismantled the current Alliance structure—an intolerable thought to board members. The president's preoccupation with the Chicago Gospel Tabernacle formed another source of tension, because it kept him from many Alliance business and committee meetings that he should have conducted.

Rader's work in Chicago, despite all the good accomplished, added still another point to the growing evidence that his destiny was to act alone, not in a representative body. Though president of the Alliance, Rader had incorporated the tabernacle and other organizations independent of policies clearly set forth in the C&MA Manual.

At the root of these organizational tensions between the president and governing board of the Alliance lay a basic conflict of beliefs concerning the church. The Alliance tried to work with and in existing churches, while Rader considered them decadent and irrelevant.[21]

The Alliance worked hard to cultivate a nonpartisan image, foster an evangelical and cooperative spirit rather than a "come out from among them" attitude, and avoid attacks on denominations or other religious groups—even to the point of abstaining from the modernist-fundamentalist controversy, though the Alliance tolerated no compromise of basic biblical truths.

Under Rader's leadership, the Chicago Gospel Tabernacle followed the pattern of the "come out" movement and eventually became an unaffiliated church.

Rader's resignation was not questioned, just the timing and procedure. The Board of Managers resolved those details during the quarterly meeting of January, 1924, when it requested the president's resignation.

After doing so, Rader continued his ministry in the Chicago Gospel Tabernacle. He also organized a new missionary society incorporated as The Christian World Couriers.[22]

Despite their differences as workers, Rader and Alliance leaders continued friendly relations as brothers in Christ. By the time of General Council in 1924, all official relationships between Rader and the Alliance had been severed, but he attended and participated in its activities. As a parting expression of Christian grace and unity on both sides, Rader assisted in the concluding communion service led by his spiritual mentor, E. D. Whiteside.

Rader Era Gains

Rader's impact on the Alliance was as inevitable as his withdrawal. He had accepted the position of president determined to push, pull or otherwise lift the Alliance from what he perceived as a rut. He must have been satisfied on that point, for not since the founding years of the Simpson era had the movement seen so much action or growth.

During his tenure, mass meetings with attendance in the thousands and campaigns often lasting a month or more impacted Chicago, New York, Albany, Buffalo, Atlantic City, Baltimore, Boston, Pittsburgh, Philadelphia, Indianapolis, Dayton, Cleveland, Detroit, Louisville, Atlanta, Orlando, Miami, Houston, San Antonio, Dallas, Fort Worth, Tulsa, Oklahoma City, St. Louis, Birmingham, Winston-Salem, Durham, Toronto, Ottawa, Winnipeg, Calgary, Edmonton, Vancouver, and other cities.

The tabernacles and workers gained during this period presented curious contrasts.

In Toledo, Ohio, L. H. Ziemer, a former Lutheran pastor trained at Luther College and Seminary in Buffalo, New York, ministered to a congregation that met in the Toledo Gospel Tabernacle, a beautiful brick church with stained-glass windows.

Meanwhile, other branches met in severely plain structures called "glory barns."

Glenn Tingley, a former Methodist evangelist with no theological training, but ordained by the Alliance, went to Birmingham, Alabama. In six days he raised a wood-frame, tar-paper tabernacle seating 800 people.

He later went to Montgomery and built another Alliance tabernacle with capacity for 1,500 people. He continued his ministry in Birmingham, building a large congregation and producing one of the longest series of continuous radio programs in religious broadcasting.

In Tampa, Florida, a 1919 graduate of Nyack named John Minder envisioned a spiritual center where people would be trained in practical and spiritual leadership. By 1925 he had gathered a strong nucleus of support and built the Tampa Gospel Tabernacle with a seating capacity of 2,000.

Men like Billy Sunday, Gypsy Smith and Oswald Smith held campaigns in the Tampa tabernacle. Young men just starting in the ministry also worked out of the tabernacle. One of their number, Billy Graham, served as Minder's assistant while attending nearby Trinity College.

The Omaha Gospel Tabernacle dates back to the same Rader era. R. R. Brown* had been appointed superintendent of the Western District in 1920 and had transferred the district office to Omaha. In 1923 he started the tabernacle.

Brown found still another avenue of ministry in Omaha. Many

*See "The Founder's Team" in the Appendix for more details.

people considered radio, in its infancy, to be a passing fad. Not so Brown. He recognized the potential of radio and prepared for its arrival. When station WOW went on the air in Omaha, so did Pastor Brown. His broadcasts continued for forty years, at their height reaching an estimated audience of 500,000 listeners.

Personnel Losses

The Rader era registered losses as well as gains, primarily in some irreplaceable key men. Jaderquist, publications secretary and editorial member of *The Alliance Weekly,* had strongly resisted Rader's nomination for vice-president. After the death of Dr. Simpson, with whom he had worked for some twenty years, Jaderquist stayed until mid-1920 to help his successor at the publishing house get started. He then withdrew from Alliance ministry.

Dr. Robert H. Glover, foreign secretary, also openly objected to Rader's nomination and wrote him an honest and candid explanation why. Realizing that in good conscience he could not serve under the new president, Dr. Glover resigned in mid-1921.

Canadian clergyman Peter W. Philpott,* another early associate of Dr. Simpson and a member of the Board of Managers, opposed Rader for reasons similar to those of Dr. Glover and Jaderquist. Ironically, after Rader's departure from Moody Church, Dr. Philpott was called as pastor. He served the church for seven years, during which time he planned for construction of the present Moody Memorial Church.

Time eventually vindicated the men's perception concerning Rader's weakness in administrative ability. By then it was too late to retain these sorely needed men of ability.

In time, even the men who had favored Rader realized they were wrong. They opposed his actions and plans that would have taken the Alliance off course. They objected to his frequent absences at board meetings and eventually suggested to Rader that he leave office.

Narrowing Circle

The year 1924 saw the circle of Dr. Simpson's contemporaries reduced by two: his wife Margaret and his biographer A. E. Thompson.*

In her younger years as Simpson's wife, Margaret had opposed him on some key decisions and at times made his life difficult.

*See "The Founder's Team" in the Appendix for more details.

But once she caught up with his vision and became convinced he was a man sent from God, Dr. Simpson had no finer, more loyal and hardworking associate than his wife.

Shortly after the Alliance organized until her death at age eighty-two, Margaret Simpson served on the Board of Managers. Always alert to the interests of the C&MA, she was financial secretary.

She served on the foreign committee in the early days. She knew nearly all the missionaries as students on the hillside and, as superintendent of assignment of missionaries, she was considered an astute judge as to their fitness for candidacy.

At Margaret Simpson's funeral, E. J. Richards recalled that, as a newly appointed home secretary in 1912, he had called at her home and found her working on a large stack of correspondence. She told Richards that she had eight trunks filled with letters written to her by either missionaries from overseas or friends in the homeland.

When Richards asked if she answered them, she replied, "Every one."[23]

After her husband died, Tozer wrote that Margaret "lingered a few years to walk about and cherish memories and dream again of the hours she had never fully treasured while they were hers to enjoy. Not till he was gone did she know how much he had absorbed her life. She never quite lived again after he had left her.

"Often she would point out to some visiting friend the places about the home that had been made sacred by his presence . . . She never bothered to explain who 'he' might be. It never occurred to her that anyone could ask."[24]

Albert E. Thompson became identified as the biographer of Simpson when he completed *The Life of A. B. Simpson* one year after the founder's death. That distinction, however, was just part of a long and honorable ministry.

Like his former friend and associate, Thompson was born in Canada and raised in a Covenanter Presbyterian heritage. In his third year of study, he suffered a physical breakdown. He continued in poor health until coming in contact with John Salmon and experiencing a miraculous healing.

Thompson considered himself above all a missionary to Palestine though his ministry in the Holy Land was interrupted several times for other assignments. He served on the Board of Managers and on the faculty of the Missionary Training Institute. Busy and productive to the very end, he was asked by a friend if he ought not to rest awhile.

"No," he replied, "I've had enough of that. I want to wear out in the harness."

God granted him that wish on New Year's Day, 1924—the same day Mrs. Simpson died.

Senft Interlude

Vice-president Frederic H. Senft stepped into the presidency after Rader's resignation in January of 1924. As a bridge between a troubled period and more measured times, Senft filled a needed role.

A brief episode demonstrated the kind of leadership he brought to his position. A young and enthusiastic David J. Fant, Jr., fresh out of college, accepted an appointment to *The Alliance Weekly* staff. He presented himself to Senft, who was editor, with the words: "Here I am, your new assistant editor."

Giving the young man careful scrutiny through his iron-rimmed glasses, Senft responded in a deliberate, solemn tone: "No, not assistant editor—assistant to the editor."[25]

That same measured quality characterized his administration as president. He drew upon a long record of experience in Alliance ministry in his commitment to continuity of Dr. Simpson's vision.

Senft had opened branches in Altoona and Philadelphia. He became one of the first district superintendents in the movement. During his fifteen years of leadership, the Eastern District increased from two to sixty-three branches. A member of the Board of Managers since its first session in 1897, he had worked closely with the founder on many occasions.

The new president's enthusiasm for missions dated back to Bucknell College and Student Volunteer Movement days in Pennsylvania. He lived simply and sacrificially in order to return as much money as possible into the ministry.

He often encouraged others with the phrase, "Have faith in God," and lived according to that code himself. A young lady who lived in the Senft home recalled that no sentimentality was shown in running the home: "There was no arm of flesh to hold on to, no natural means to trust. It was no child's play. You either went all in or got out. It was really walk by faith, work by faith and go on, in the Master's name."[26]

When people placed jewelry in the offering for missions—which happened often—he tramped the streets tirelessly, going from one jeweler to another in search of the best price. Returning home weary but content on one occasion he explained, "You see, it is for missions, and the more I get the better it will be for the Lord's work."[27]

When confusion began to mount in Alliance circles because of new directions initiated by Rader, vice-president Senft joined with home secretary Richards to draft a "Suggestive Constitution for Affiliated Churches."

Drawing on Dr. Simpson's original constitution for the New York Gospel Tabernacle, the document was meant to help new churches emerging from tabernacle status understand how to relate to the Alliance. It provided a much needed step toward bringing some sense of common identity to a varied collection of individuals and groups calling themselves The Christian and Missionary Alliance.

Timely Interlude

Senft presided at the 1924 General Council held in Toronto, the first such meeting on Canadian soil. The report on overseas work gave some indication of the expanding work he was called upon to lead.

The Alliance now worked in eighteen mission fields. Fourteen thousand baptized members worshiped in 194 organized churches; the total did not include additional thousands related to unorganized "outstations." Fifty-six new missionaries had gone overseas during the previous year and another sixty-seven were preparing to go during the current year.

Foreign secretary Snead stressed the need for solid, unified support between the home and foreign ministries. Emphasizing the importance of the home base to missionary advance, Snead quoted the founder: "The greatest need and the greatest failure in the great missionary problem is the home base. Shall we be wholly true? Many of us cannot go. Shall we see that someone else goes, and by our prayers, sacrifices and standing behind him, share his recompense in the great day of the eternal harvest?"[28]

Following General Council in Toronto, Senft gave himself to the demands of leadership with the same steady qualities that had always characterized his work. The Alliance continued in an uninterrupted pattern of growth overseas, while the work in North America went into a holding pattern for several years.

One of his colleagues observed, "He served under others in the spirit of conservatism. He showed the same spirit of conservatism when he himself was in charge of Alliance branches. There was no danger of his running into extremes."[29]

Though not likely to produce dramatic results, Senft's style of leadership placed a much needed steadying hand on the reins of a movement shaken by a troubled transition.

Senft's administration came to an abrupt end on November 25, 1925, after he suffered a brief and fatal encounter with pneumonia. In a memorial service for the late president, Richards observed, "He touched the world from the smallest position to the highest that the Alliance could give, and left his imprint on every part."[30]

Senft's imprint on the highest office of the Alliance was of short duration, but it provided a timely interlude. His thoughtful, moderating influence during an unsettled period effectively drew the curtain on one era and prepared the Alliance for a new and promising one when the curtain reopened.

CHAPTER 10

Mixed Signals

"If the trumpet does not sound a clear call who will get ready for battle?"
—Apostle Paul

1926-1936

Context of the Times

"The physical signs of distress were everywhere," wrote journalist Cabell Phillips concerning the Great Depression.

"You encountered them with wearying monotony day after day: clusters of hungry men and women waiting like docile peasants for food handouts at the relief stations; the smokeless chimneys and rusting sheds of factories standing mute and empty behind their locked gates; the abandoned shops and stores, their doorways littered with trash, their grime-streaked windows staring vacantly upon half-empty streets; the drooping shoulders of a father, husband, brother or friend whose pride had been battered into lethargy and dejection by months of fruitless job hunting."

At the height—or depth—of the Great Depression, nearly 15 million jobless Americans fit Phillips' description as national income tumbled from $83 billion in 1929 to $40 billion in just three years.

The trauma of the times should have sparked a great spiritual awakening, as had happened during similar crises in American history. Some preachers had, in fact, heralded the economic crisis as a scourge that would drive the nation back to God.

But history did not repeat itself, and the hopeful preachers waited in vain for an awakening. Revival was as rare and scattered in the troubled thirties as the occasional healthy bank.

Why?

Spiritual depression had already fallen on Protestantism in the

1920s, leaving it unable to cope with its own problems, not to mention those of the nation.

By the late twenties the war spirit of the recent world war subsided swiftly and completely. In its place came a reaction against idealism and reform. Furthermore, the unpopular, church-backed Prohibition, and the public debate over doctrine diminished still more the stature of the church in public opinion.

A 1905 study showed that about 78 percent of Americans viewed traditional Christianity favorably and only 22 percent unfavorably. By 1930 opinions were nearly reversed: 67 percent were unfavorable.

During this period many mainline churches discontinued their midweek and Sunday evening services. Attendance in Sunday schools dropped below the 1916 level.

Another sensitive indicator of religious vitality, the missionary program, showed serious decline. In 1920 the Student Volunteer Movement reported that 2,700 students had volunteered for overseas service. By 1928 the number of candidates had shrunk to 252.

Much of the disarray in mainline churches grew out of their acceptance and then questioning of liberal theology. Too late they realized that in their liberality they had given away too many of their historical beliefs.

Even liberal spokesman Harry Emerson Fosdick preached a widely publicized sermon, "The Church Must Go Beyond Modernism." But by that time, harassed pastors were so busy trying to keep church doors open and pay bills that they had neither time nor energy to embark on a new adventure in redefining theology.

One aspect of liberalism, after some hesitation, began to assert itself again during the depression years: the Social Gospel. But even this religious activism was altered by sober realities. No longer did the churches believe they could to any great extent ease the widespread physical suffering. Many believed that only the federal government, with its resources and authority, could do what was needed. That meant backing Franklin D. Roosevelt and his New Deal—a horrible turn of events for Republican Protestants. Some denominational leaders not only urged the government to adopt a socialist policy, they chided the New Deal for not going far enough.

A national gathering of Methodist youth in 1934 circulated a pledge that began, "I surrender my life to Christ, I renounce the Capitalist system...."

Holiness and pentecostal denominations did not generally share in the Protestant decline. Their teaching emphasized the depravity

THE FOUNDER'S TEAM

Stephen Merritt

Henry Wilson

John Salmon

Carrie Judd-Montgomery

David Lelacheur

Old Orchard campgrounds in the early 1900s

ALLIANCE LEADERS AND WORKERS AT OLD ORCHARD, MAINE, IN AUGUST OF 1900

Standing, top row, left to right: G. L. Eldridge, Mrs. Eldridge, O.E. Mallory, F. E. Marsh, W. R. Newell, Henry Wilson, A. B. Simpson, W. E. Blackstone, Mrs. A. B. Simpson, Margaret Simpson, May Agnew, Mrs. Clark, Sarah Lindenberger, Ethel Green, Miss Warren. *Second row from the top:* C. N. Kinney, W. F. Meminger, A. E. Funk, David Lelacheur, S. C. Todd, Mr. Copley, James M. Kirk, D. W. Kerr, D. W. Myland. *Third row from the top:* William Christie, John Woodberry, M. Soderberg, Mr. Wang, Ms. Mallory, Lillian Reeves, Bessie White, Ms. Todd, Martin Ekvall, Mrs. W. W. Simpson, William W. Simpson, J. D. Bell. *Bottom row:* Mr. Prentice, Mrs. Prentice, William Franklin, Mrs. Wm. Franklin, Mrs. Moyser, Mrs. Martin Ekvall, Mrs. Mattie Simpson, Mrs. Draper, Emma Beere, Mrs. Jencks.

THE FOUNDER'S TEAM

J. Hudson Ballard

L. K. "Daddy" Brubaker

David Crear

Josephus L. Pulis

Frederic W. Farr

The business office in the Institute Building (Simpson Hall) of the Missionary Training Institute, circa 1920

J. Gregory Mantle (l.) and Kenneth MacKenzie

George P. Pardington

Albert E. Funk

May Agnew

William C. Stevens

Dr. Mantle speaking to men and women students (seated separately) in a chapel session of the Missionary Training Institute, 1920

THE FOUNDER'S TEAM

Front row, left to right: R. A. Forrest, Peter W. Philpott, H. M. Shuman, Paul Rader, G. Verner Brown, E. J. Richards, William Franklin, J. D. Williams. *Second row:* unknown, unknown, A. E. Funk. *Third row:* A. C. Snead, R. H. Glover, B. F. Armstrong, William T. MacArthur. *Fourth row:* David Mason, unidentified, Frederic H. Senft, Walter Turnbull, A. E. Thompson (Board of Managers, 1920)

THE FOUNDER'S TEAM

William H. Howland

E. D. "Daddy" Whiteside

John E. Jaderquist

Emma Beere

Ulysses Lewis

Walter A. Turnbull at his desk in the Missionary Training Institute, where he managed the day-to-day business of the school

Dr. R. R. Brown was honored in 1947, the twenty-fifth anniversary of his radio ministry. *Left to right:* Mayor Leeman of Omaha, Dr. Brown, Dr. H. M. Shuman.

William T. MacArthur

William Christie

OTHER NOTABLE LEADERS OF THE PAST

A. W. Tozer

V. Raymond Edman

R. G. LeTourneau

Alfred C. Snead

H. E. Nelson

of man and contained an invitation to a highly satisfying, personal salvation. This made sense to increasing numbers of individuals disillusioned both by the economic system and by the religious establishment, neither of which provided a soul-satisfying message of comfort.

During the 1926 - 1936 decade, for example, the Church of the Nazarene more than doubled to 136,000 members and the Assemblies of God increased threefold to 148,000. Radio evangelists, maneuvered out of free broadcast time by the Federal Council of Churches, broke into paid-time programming and proliferated rapidly. The most popular radio preacher was Charles E. Fuller, of "The Old Fashioned Revival Hour" originating in the Los Angeles area.

The continuing running battle between orthodox and liberal theologians proved costly in an unexpected manner. Evangelicals had distinguished themselves in an earlier era by their concern for social needs and problems. They believed that caring for orphans, the poor and the elderly flowed naturally from regenerated hearts transformed by the love of God.

However, as liberal denominations began to promote the Social Gospel as equivalent to the Gospel itself, social work fell into disrepute among evangelicals and fundamentalists. Theologians called this change of attitude "the Great Reversal."

When the defenders of historical biblical beliefs turned their big guns on liberal theology, "the Social Gospel was among the prime targets," wrote historian George M. Marsden. "In the barrage against the Social Gospel it was perhaps inevitable that the vestiges of their own progressive social attitudes would also become casualties."

While the mainline Protestant establishment suffered declining membership and influence, the Roman Catholic Church and the Jewish community were registering growth. H. L. Mencken, who had made fundamentalists look foolish in the Scopes trial, had a new line: "Every day a new Catholic church goes up; every day another Methodist or Presbyterian church is turned into a garage."

During the 1926 - 1936 period, Jewish congregations enjoyed a healthy increase of 13.7 percent. Roman Catholicism grew by 7 percent, mainly through immigration and biological growth.

While Jewish and Catholic religious communities obviously profited from their minority status, Protestants continued through the depression years to pay a heavy price for their historical role as the national religion. Linking the Gospel of Christ too closely to the American way of life that brought on the Great Depression forever changed the religious profile of America.

After the depression years, Protestantism no longer claimed to represent the religious life of the nation. It was but one of three religious communities and, in the eyes of many, last in line.

* * *

Alliance leaders recognized that the movement must make some response to the times that were changing so fast that the early twenties were barely recognizable by the late twenties.

But what should change, and what must remain?

Answers would not come easily to a movement that had been building for decades. If nothing else, the impending crisis would dramatize both the strength and weakness of the Alliance.

VICE-PRESIDENT Harry M. Shuman's election as president of the Alliance should have been assured when the incumbent, Frederic H. Senft, died. The constitution provided for an immediate transfer of title and functions, and most men would have considered the promotion a reasonable recognition of their abilities.

Not so Dr. Shuman.[1]

He wrote to the Board of Managers: "If you think it would be for the best interests of our Society for someone else to take this important office at this time, I will most cheerfully resign and will cooperate with any man who may be appointed."[2]

His willingness to step aside grew out of a deep respect for the office. He questioned his qualifications for the job. "It will require courtesy and courage, humility and force, tenderness and firmness. There will be needed fairness, impartiality, tact, a consistent following of clearly defined policies and a loyalty to our original vision and work.

"I do not feel that I am the man for this important place," he wrote.[3]

Those very qualities of fairness, impartiality, tact and loyalty to the work became the hallmarks of his lengthy tenure. They summarized a job description obvious in retrospect, one not drafted beforehand by a committee, but written in the lines of his life. The verdict of history, clarified by the passage of time, indicates that Dr. Shuman was the right man in the right job at the right time. A leader of lesser courtesy and courage, or of greater charisma and ambition, may well have found himself presiding over a movement splintered by strong-willed men of contrary convictions.

Basic Training

Born near Johnstown, Pennsylvania, in June of 1878, Dr. Shuman became aware early in life that God was shaping his future. "I recall that when I was four or five years of age I went into an old barn alone and tried to pray," he wrote. "When in my early teens, while riding on horseback going for a doctor for one of the family, I would pray for hours. I did not really know how to pray, but I wanted to pray."[4]

From his recollections emerges the profile of a precocious, highly sensitive and very private person. He learned how to read while still very young, but lost interest in the Bible, for it seemed to only condemn him. "I did not know the difference between the Law and the Gospel," he admitted.[5]

A few years later he had reason to feel guilty. Running around with some rough kids at school, he developed a habit of profanity that troubled him until he was converted in his late teens. His spiritual rebirth reflected how carefully he kept his inner thoughts and feelings to himself: "I did not go forward in the service, but when I reached home I knelt at my bedside and gave myself to the Lord."[6]

The pattern was repeated when he heard a sermon on full surrender to God and on the filling of the Holy Spirit. Again he did not go forward in the public service: "I opened my heart to the Lord while in my seat. The next day I seemed to be walking on air."[7]

Years later he enjoyed recounting how his friend, Rev. G. Verner Brown, had heard so much about sanctification he became confused. Finally convinced of his need for a deeper experience of God's grace, Brown prayed, "Lord, give me sanctification as You understand it." With obvious personal satisfaction, Dr. Shuman concluded, "That solved the problem for him as far as heart experience was concerned."[8]

Dr. Shuman's progress toward the presidency of the Alliance helped equip him for the widely varying functions of the office. He earned a teacher's certificate in 1898 and taught school. He attended a business college and worked a salesman's route for the Atlantic Refining Company. He received his basic training for ministry—as did so many others—under the vigilant tutelage of Rev. E. D. Whiteside of Pittsburgh.

Then, beginning in 1905, followed years of pastoral ministry, of teaching at the Lovejoy Institute in North Carolina, and of serving as superintendent of the Central District.

Completing Senft's term as president, he was elected in his own right in 1926. Nine successive terms and twenty-eight years later, at age seventy-six, he would not permit his name to stand for yet another term as president and chairman of the Board of Managers.

Dr. Shuman carried other portfolios as well. For many years he was president of the Missionary Training Institute. For twenty years he was editor of *The Alliance Weekly,* and for thirteen years he served as education secretary.

Dr. Nathan Bailey, a later president, recalled that Dr. Shuman was "an executive of rare ability and a parliamentarian without peer. Many delegates to the councils delighted to see him, dignified and unperturbed, bring logic and order out of sometimes muddled debate with a few words, and often with a dry comment that convulsed the whole body."[9]

He would soon need all the skills and humor at his command as he steered the Alliance through the troubled waters of racial minority involvement in the movement, the question of Alliance identity and the Great Depression.

Effective Black Ministries

For one who had enjoyed several years of teaching black students at Lovejoy Institute in North Carolina, Dr. Shuman would have been chagrined had he realized in 1926 what was happening. Alliance ministries by and among blacks crested during his first full year in office. Decades would follow before blacks once again had a meaningful role in the C&MA.

A few years before, Rev. A. E. Funk, national secretary for work among blacks, had proclaimed that the doors of opportunity for work among northern blacks were opening widely. He made a special plea for "a great conference of colored ministers to consider a plan in which extended authority could be granted to black leadership."[10]

Numerous black workers in the Alliance at the time were enjoying an effective ministry among their own people and earned the respect of their white colleagues. Two outstanding men were Rev. William Peter Robinson and Rev. E. M. Collette.

Robinson, born to slave parents in Virginia during the 1850s, moved to Pittsburgh around 1883 and was active in an African Methodist Episcopal Church for several years. However, following a deeper life commitment and an experience of divine healing as a result of Alliance teaching, he began to conduct home Bible studies.

These meetings resulted in the formation of Branch #2 of the Alliance in Pittsburgh during 1893. From that year until his death in 1911, Robinson pastored the multiracial congregation, where it was said, "many—white and colored—were saved, sanctified and healed to the honor and glory of God."

Collette was for over thirty-five years a licensed exhorter and then evangelist with the African Methodist Episcopal Church. His witness brought many people to the Lord, especially in the Greensboro and Raleigh districts of North Carolina.

Collette's experience of divine healing in 1898 had two startling results. First, his ministry now seemed to ignite revival wherever he went. Hundreds of people were converted and healed. Second, his church coworkers eyed him askance and whispered about the "strange doctrine" of healing he was preaching.

They sought to neutralize him by appointing him a conference evangelist, but the new assignment only opened to him even wider opportunities. In 1912, his license as evangelist was revoked and he found himself, like Dr. Simpson before him, "Christ's free servant."

From then until his death eleven years later, Collette had an itinerant evangelistic ministry of preaching salvation and healing, and became an influential leader for the Alliance among blacks. He encouraged numerous young people to enter the ministry and was directly responsible for starting the Alliance-affiliated Holy Tabernacle Church in Philadelphia.

Two black women not only founded one of the key Alliance fellowships in the black work, they encouraged the opening of branches in other states as well.

Mrs. Mattie A. Bowles started a weekly prayer meeting in her home shortly after arriving in Cleveland, Ohio, in 1889. Three years later, Mrs. Bell H. Smoot, a new Christian, began attending the meetings. The two women not only enjoyed a quick and enduring friendship, they became a powerful pair of Christian workers.

They began door-to-door visitation in 1893 and initiated what Mrs. Bowles described as rescue work among the poorer classes of the city. They rented a storefront for the group that gathered around them and by 1895 organized the second Alliance branch in Cleveland.

Bowles and Smoot then held conventions in five nearby cities and traveled to Kentucky and Tennessee to establish Alliance works. In 1903, Smoot encouraged black Alliance groups in Kansas and Nebraska as she traversed the nation to California.

By 1926, a black district encompassed some forty branches and affiliated churches in the East and Midwest. Rev. Edward Mark Burgess served as district superintendent and also as principal of the Pittsburgh (Pa.) Bible Training School. A second school for blacks, the Mary Mullen School, operated in Uree, North Carolina.

Best of all, the Cleveland Coloured Gospel Quintette was in full swing. Representing the finest in black gospel music and Alliance experience, the five singers were, in their own words, brought by

God "in a mysterious way...from different parts of the U.S.A. to Cleveland, Ohio, where they were saved one by one through the efforts of The Christian and Missionary Alliance."[11]

They had begun singing back in 1913 as a male quartet, but soon realized they needed another tenor. Their names were: Alexander Talbert, J. W. Parker, H. D. Hodges and Spurgeon R. Jones. One of the men heard Floyd H. Lacy sing at a wedding and decided he was their missing tenor. That Lacy was not a Christian, and that he belonged to a popular singing group known as the Musical Magpies, did not deter the quartet. They asked God to turn him around spiritually and then bring him their way, and God did. Lacy's professional singing experience and organizational talent quickly made him the group leader.

The quintet began singing first in their "Jerusalem," Branch #2 of the Alliance in Cleveland, and then gradually extended their radius of ministry until it reached 150 to 200 miles for weekend concerts. Their historian wrote, "Sometimes we would drive all night Saturday to reach our destination, sing all day Sunday, then drive all night Sunday, arriving home in time to go to our work on Monday morning."[12]

Paul Rader and the Bosworth brothers heard good reports of the quintet and invited them to sing in large campaigns in Pittsburgh, Toledo, Chicago and elsewhere.

The quintet's chance to go international came in 1922, when they traveled to Toronto with the noted black evangelist Dr. Charles S. Morris. The four-week campaign at the large Christie Street Tabernacle of the Alliance marked a decisive point. The men sensed God's call to full-time ministry: "One by one we threw up our hands and told the Lord we would give up our jobs, families, homes and everything to follow Him."[13]

Within days, Rev. A. W. Roffe, superintendent of the Canadian District, invited Dr. Morris and the quintet to conduct a three-month tour of Alliance branches in western Canada. The team provided a big boost to the Alliance work in the prairie provinces, where the work dated back to visits by Dr. Simpson. It had then been largely ignored until Roffe became district superintendent.[14]

The campaign in Calgary, for example, stirred the whole city with "a wonderful outpouring of grace upon the large crowds who flocked to the Victoria Pavilion," a facility seating 3,500 people.[15] The team drew the largest audiences in Winnipeg, where they conducted services for a month. "From reports given in the *Winnipeg Evening Tribune,*" reported *The Alliance Weekly,* "the city was greatly moved."[16]

An impressive Dominion convention followed in Toronto during

1923. This time the quintet was accompanied by Edward Burgess of Pittsburgh, who, in addition to his other abilities, was a powerful evangelist. The size and spirit of the gatherings indicated that perhaps the Alliance in Canada had at last turned a corner. The struggles experienced by John Salmon and William Fenton in getting the movement going in Canada were finally having their reward.[17]

By the time Dr. Shuman took office in 1926, the quintet belonged not just to the Alliance, but to the church at large, traveling throughout the United States and Canada. Beyond their knowledge, and perhaps even beyond their exuberant expectations, would lie campaigns in England, Ireland, Scotland, Wales and the Scandinavian nations. The tours, running as long as nine months, would draw immense crowds everywhere, turning hundreds to the Lord and even bringing the quintet before European royalty.

Three members of the quintet—H. D. Hodges, Spurgeon Jones and J. W. Parker—would later help a young pastor of Branch #2 in Cleveland, by then known as the Smoot Memorial Church, expand his ministry to international dimensions.

The three men formed an important part of the radio choir on Rev. Howard O. Jones' "Cleveland for Christ" radio broadcast sponsored by the church from 1952 to 1958. Jones had actually begun his radio ministry in 1946 with the "Hour of Freedom."

The ability of both choir and pastor prompted Radio ELWA in Monrovia, Liberia, to schedule the church's program as a regular feature of their Africa-wide service. In connection with this radio ministry, Jones conducted an evangelistic campaign in West Africa for over three months during 1957—the first campaign on such a scale in Africa by a black American evangelist.

The campaign attracted the attention of Billy Graham at the time when he wanted to integrate and enlarge his team of associate evangelists. Jones joined the Billy Graham Evangelistic Association in 1958 and for several years made Monrovia his base of operations in Africa.

Dr. Jones (he received an honorary doctorate from Huntington [Ind.] College in 1970) continued his ministry with the Alliance as an evangelist and as a member of various committees and groups, such as the C&MA Board of Managers and the President's Associates of Nyack College.

Declining Black Role

Alliance ministries among black people traced their roots to Dr. Simpson's years in Louisville. Disturbed by the prevalent practice of pew rentals and the still-lingering effects of segregation, he made sure the advertising of his church's evangelistic campaigns stressed the words, "free seats" for everyone.

Later in New York he counted among his friends Dr. Morris, the black evangelist who would later tour with the quintet. They conferred and prayed together concerning the needs of black people. Dr. Morris encouraged Dr. Simpson and the New York Gospel Tabernacle in their ministry to orphans, fallen women and slum dwellers during the 1880s, when evangelicals still considered social work an integral part of witness.

Relating black people to the Great Commission prompted Dr. Simpson to open the Lovejoy Institute in Mills Spring, North Carolina, during 1906. He envisioned a large role for the Bible school: "It not only contemplates the education and evangelization of the race here, but offers them a noble ambition and a national purpose, to evangelize their own people in Africa, and redeem the continent of their fathers for God."[18]

Five years later the Alliance accepted responsibility for the Boydton Institute in Virginia, a school founded in 1879 by Dr. Charles Cullis of Boston to prepare blacks for the gospel ministry.

Dr. Morris became principal of the Boydton Institute in 1920 and asked repeatedly for funds to underwrite the school's particular needs. "Our hope is that Boydton may yet do for the millions of colored people of the South what Nyack is so nobly doing for all," he reported, "but we have a somewhat peculiar condition to contend with in the South—a condition, not a theory.

"The public schools in the country are a farce, if not a tragedy. When pupils come here to study as preachers and missionaries, we have first to lay a foundation. They simply must be taught the three R's or we will not be able to help them much."[19]

Unfortunately for Dr. Morris and the role of black ministries in the Alliance, financial pleas for social work, such as the education of minorities, came at the wrong time. Even causes previously supported by the Alliance fell victim to the "Great Reversal," that excessive reaction of evangelicals to the Social Gospel.

By 1923, Dr. Morris parted company with the Alliance, and the Boydton Institute passed into the hands of a small holiness denomination. Both the Lovejoy Institute and the Mary Mullen School faced an uncertain future.

Although the three all-black schools did not produce the missionaries Dr. Simpson had hoped for, nine black Alliance workers did serve overseas between 1913 and 1937.

Miss Carrie Merriweather was the first of a number of blacks who graduated from Nyack and served in Sierra Leone. She landed in Africa in 1913 and in the early twenties was joined by six others:

Mrs. Eugene N. Thornely, Mr. and Mrs. Montrose A. Waite, Mr. and Mrs. Raymond H. Wilson and Miss Anita Bolden.

Bolden, whose married name later was Fitts, remembered those days of pioneer missions, when their work progressed slowly on a hut-to-hut, one-by-one basis. She recalled that the integrated missionary staff in Sierra Leone was too busy working to think about race relations.

She returned to the States in 1928 after five years of ministry. Malaria prevented her from returning to the field and she eventually married. Nonetheless, Mrs. Anita Bolden Fitts continued whenever possible to promote missions in the Alliance and in other church groups. At age eighty-eight during the C&MA centennial year, she was still doing what she could in a ministry that spanned nearly seventy years.

The integrated work of black and white Alliance missionaries, however, began to unravel in the 1930s. To some extent, consequences of the "Great Reversal," along with unresolved social and racial tensions, became part of the baggage both black and white missionaries carried overseas. The ensuing tensions persisted to the point that during Dr. Shuman's tenure the Board of Managers decided not to send or support black missionaries.[20]

This controversial decision hastened the decline of black involvement already precipitated by a conflict of priorities between black and white leaders. Mixed signals from the board room intensified the uncertainty of black Alliance people about their role in the movement. After all, if they were not accepted on an equal basis and could not fully participate in the Alliance's main purpose of existence, what was the use of even belonging?

Uncertain Identity

The uncertainty of black participation in the Alliance was only one casualty of mixed signals. An even larger debate swirled around the identity of the Alliance itself.

The issue probably did not attract much attention at the grassroots level, where pragmatism generally ruled. Branches (or affiliated churches or tabernacles or missions) and their local superintendents (or pastors or evangelists or lay leaders) gave little thought to the details of ecclesiology. They defined their own congregational needs and organized themselves to answer those needs, whether they identified themselves as a church or by another name.

Over the decades, therefore, the Alliance grew in a spontaneous, unplanned manner and to the untrained eye appeared as a conglomerate held together by an invisible hand. Its influence spread more widely and in more forms than its structure and method of operation could assimilate or consolidate.

In the late 1920s, however, an awareness emerged on the national level that such a policy of laissez-faire (every congregation chose the structure best suited to it) should not be allowed to continue. It deprived the Alliance of any coherent direction or combined impact on the nation.

General Councils of the late twenties and throughout the thirties therefore rang with impassioned pleas and hotly debated points of view. Were it not for the grace of God and the skills of chairman Shuman, some highly opinionated brethren might have brought discredit to the Alliance and their own ministries.

A widely respected district superintendent was asked to step down from office by the home secretary because he did not try to open new branches in his large district. One of his major contentions, with reason, was that a more structured Alliance identity would mean the loss of support from non-Alliance sources.

Debaters at General Council could support their differing positions as being historically faithful to the Alliance because the movement itself represented differing positions at different times. Development of the movement from Simpson to Shuman followed a zigzag course.

Dr. Simpson founded the Alliance to be a catalyst that would work primarily within existing churches. Through summer conventions and city campaigns, he sought to spur spiritually comatose congregations to a deeper life of faith in the Spirit and a resulting greater commitment to missions. He rejected the possibility of a C&MA denomination or even of a truly Alliance church. Branches were to be noncompetitive auxiliaries to existing churches.

Paul Rader planned to revitalize and redirect the Alliance through mass campaigns that incorporated the Fourfold Gospel and missionary emphasis. He expected to accomplish this by encouraging vibrant believers to come out of the decadent churches and join a tabernacle fellowship. Such tabernacles tended to become unaffiliated churches in every respect except name. He anticipated that the tabernacles would absorb branches already in existence.

Frederic Senft believed congregations should follow the pattern set by Dr. Simpson's Gospel Tabernacle in New York. He helped draft a suggested constitution for affiliated churches, hoping thereby that the tabernacles springing up in the Rader era would gravitate toward the Alliance and not be lost to other groups or denominations.

Dr. Shuman assumed office believing that the 1897 and 1912 constitutions should be treated as historical landmarks entrusted to the Alliance. He viewed the denominational churches, including the new evangelical ones, as still needing the Fourfold Gospel and missionary dimension that the Alliance promoted so well.

He discouraged the inclusion of unaffiliated churches because he considered the Alliance to be a nondenominational missionary society exclusive of institutional church forms and functions. Branches should be opened primarily to enlarge the support base at home for an expanded missionary operation.

Dr. Shuman told delegates to the 1929 General Council, "The work at home...should all be planned with a view to contributing in the largest possible way to the all-important work of the spread of the Gospel in the regions beyond."[21]

Irregular reporting of statistics from 1925 to 1929 reflected the confusion within the leadership as to the true identity of the Alliance. The report for 1925 showed thirty-six new branches, but no total report. The 1926 report concerning 248 church buildings and 96 parsonages must have disturbed anti-institutional delegates. The next year's statistics included 471 pastors and evangelists. Evangelistic campaigns in 1928 totaled 450, but the annual report made no mention of conversions or baptisms. The 1929 report cited 411 branches or churches, one less than reported in 1928.

The election in 1929 of Rev. G. Verner Brown as home secretary signaled an effort, however quiet and cautious, to bring more semblance of internal organization to the Alliance. Brown, sixty-two years of age when taking office, had known Dr. Simpson personally since 1897. He had pastored a local branch in Wilmington, Delaware, for ten years and then had become superintendent of the Eastern District from 1912 to 1929.

Ambivalence toward historical identity and lack of a united, contemporary mandate left many Alliance groups in uneasy relationship to one another and to the world around them. Like soldiers milling around for lack of a clear trumpet call to fall in and move out, the Alliance neared the traumatic Great Depression with scant preparation for providing a badly shaken nation with God's certain truth in a strong, united voice.

Impartial Depression

The Great Depression, ushered in by the stock market collapse in October of 1929, was nothing if not democratic. Everyone suffered, whether rich or poor, black or white, corporation or corner grocery store.

Mainline denominations suffered a decline in membership and

offerings. Even the holiness and pentecostal churches that had registered unusual growth in numbers were now filled with struggling, hurting victims of the financial fiasco.

While the Alliance did not rank with denominations that registered tumbling statistics, neither did it march with those of similar beliefs who enjoyed major gains.

The number of Alliance branches in 1930 dropped to ten below the 1928 level. Income showed a slight decrease from the previous year. For almost a decade, missionaries had been receiving full allowances, but for the first nine months of 1930, their living allowances were reduced by almost 18 percent.[22]

One of the first visible casualties of the depression years was the overextended education network of the Alliance. The 1920 General Council had recommended the opening of regional or sectional schools to train superintendents for the local branches. By 1925 four American and two Canadian schools were in operation, but already Alliance leaders were becoming aware that they had gone too far and too fast in organizing schools. The financial collapse in 1929 clinched the point.

General Council of 1928 requested the Board of Managers to take steps to reduce the number of Bible schools. But as one board representative to district conventions found out, "the local situation makes it very difficult to effect any radical changes after a school has once been established, and none of the district conferences were found ready to recommend the closing of their schools at this time."[23]

The Board of Managers then stepped in, and the ax fell again and again. Simpson Bible Institute in Seattle, Washington, closed in 1929, as did the Boston Training School and the two Canadian schools: Canadian Bible Institute in Toronto and Great West Bible Institute in Edmonton.

The Whiteside Memorial Bible School, formerly the Pittsburgh Bible Training School, closed as a district operation, but continued on a local basis until 1935. Beulah Beach Bible Institute struggled on until 1932 and then succumbed.

Only the schools at Nyack, New York; St. Paul, Minnesota; and Toccoa Falls, Georgia, survived the sweeping closures.

Eliminating both Canadian schools sent shock waves throughout the Dominion. The Toronto school was already a second attempt to launch a training center for eastern Canada and had moved into a new building only four years earlier. Closing this school was a particularly bitter pill for Torontonians to swallow.[24]

The Canadians, however, were not alone in suffering losses. Before the Great Depression ended, Alliance people on both sides of the border would have their fill of severe measures dictated by necessity.

Battered Offerings

Finances became another highly visible and critical function to be pummeled by the depression years. Yet amazingly, some churches in less industrialized areas increased their missionary giving to help offset losses in the big cities. Even the Alliance tabernacle in Buffalo, New York, gave almost twice as much for missions as for its own current expenses.

Alliance people in Toronto made a valiant effort to make up for losses elsewhere. The *Toronto Globe* reported in a feature article, "The Missionary Spirit," in May of 1931: "Adherents of The Christian and Missionary Alliance Tabernacle, Toronto, have furnished convincing and practical proof that the call of the foreign mission field still finds ready response.

"According to the announcement made on Sunday evening, the annual missionary offering amounted to approximately $20,000, an advance over the amount contributed last year.

"Admittedly, times just now are bad," continued the article, "and most organizations are prepared for a reduction in contributions, but this has not been the experience of The Christian and Missionary Alliance."[25]

The Toronto newspaper erred on one point. The Alliance also experienced a decline in receipts. Over a five-year period from 1928 to 1933, Alliance receipts for the General Fund fell 35.2 percent, from $629,222 to $407,589.

Rather than indicating a decline in missionary spirit, this record of giving evidenced a spirit of sacrifice. During the same period, the income of ninety-seven boards reporting to the Foreign Missions Conference in America fell a staggering 45.1 percent.[26]

Credit for softening the blow to foreign missions often belonged to the unsung hero of the local Alliance fellowship: the local superintendent (pastor). Since branches existed primarily for the support of missions, according to the prevailing policy, most pastors lived on freewill offerings.

During the depression years, some received less than $10 per week. The bare necessities of milk for babies and bread for meals had often to be prayed in. Cardboard liners stuffed into worn-out shoes lengthened their days and miles.

Rev. Samuel W. McGarvey, superintendent of the Eastern District, went to Clarion, Pennsylvania, in 1930 to dedicate a newly constructed Alliance meeting place. On arriving he noticed that the foundation consisted of concrete blocks laid without mortar on the frozen ground. The walls inspired an equal lack of enthusiasm: two-by-twelve uprights held together with raw sheeting and covered with black roofing tar paper.

The young pastor, serving his first branch, had desperately needed a building. He could hardly count on help from the struggling congregation that averaged twelve people in the morning service. To finance the tar paper chapel, he had personally borrowed $200 from his bride's parents and another $100 from the local bank. One end of the building was divided into three small rooms—a living room, kitchen and bedroom. The bathroom served both the churchgoers and the pastor's family.

Surveying the scene, the district superintendent remarked wryly, "There's nothing to worship here but God."[27]

Out of such starkly crude buildings and struggling branches, rivaling the hardships of many overseas missions stations, came the flow of support that fueled missionary advance during the lean years.

Retrenchment Rejected

Reporting to General Council in 1930, the home secretary expressed gratitude that most Alliance branches and churches had conducted "their program without serious retrenchment."[28]

Whether by design or coincidence, the foreign secretary picked up on the word "retrenchment" and issued a challenge. After commenting on missionary allowances being reduced another 2.5 percent during the past month, Dr. Snead pounced on the idea of pulling back.

"These facts of budget adjustment do not spell 'retrenchment,' but rather 'advance,' " he declared, "for we believe—and recent letters from the fields add confirmation—that not only will the marked advance of 1930 into new stations be maintained and further new areas entered in several fields this year; but also...there will be a healthy development in the native church."[29]

The overseas work had no plans to slow down, he implied, even if the home base proved unable to fulfill its commitment of support. Though not intended to reflect negatively on Alliance work in North America, the foreign secretary's emphasis on advance instead of retrenchment highlighted the contrast between Alliance work overseas and at home.

The foreign department knew its role and objectives, and was determined to get on with the job. That understanding of its mission had been reinforced by a strategic planning conference convened in 1926 to reaffirm historical goals and draft new guidelines to achieve them.

Participants of the conference included former field chairmen, furloughing missionaries, members of the Board of Managers and of Dr. Snead's staff. They scrutinized key issues, such as mission-church relationships, leadership training, pioneer evangelism and financial allocations.

The Alliance had adopted from the very beginning the policy of establishing overseas self-supporting, self-propagating and self-governing churches with trained local leadership. After a generation of missionary work, however, those objectives were not only receding, but entrenched methods were making overseas churches even more dependent on the mission.

The 1927 General Council adopted the findings of the strategy conference and gave them the force of official policy. With the intent of accelerating development of indigenous churches, the new legislation called for reduction of money spent on building projects, gradual withdrawal of subsidy for national workers and progressive transfer of authority to the national church.[30]

Dr. Snead had already witnessed what such a policy could achieve. In 1928, national workers supported by their own churches totaled 670, nearly half the total of indigenous personnel in Alliance mission fields. But of that number, 603 served in the Belgian Congo, the largest and fastest growing Alliance church overseas. The remaining 67 locally supported workers were scattered among the other eighteen Alliance mission fields.[31]

Convinced of the biblical rightness of Alliance overseas policy as reaffirmed in 1927, Dr. Snead launched one of the most memorable eras of Alliance missions. While agencies of other denominations and groups were reducing their overseas staffs by 25 percent and closing fields during the depression years, the Alliance took steps to enter four new countries.

During the 1928-1933 period, when hard times forced Alliance people to cut back their giving by 35.2 percent, the number of Alliance missionaries rose from 317 to 453—an increase of 30 percent. At the time, the new recruits knew that missionaries were receiving as little as 65 percent of a living-expenses allowance.[32]

The selfless pastor in Clarion, Pennsylvania, living in a tar paper building, had his counterpart in the missionary unsure of the amount of his next allowance and forced to live off the land, sometimes in a hostile environment.

Laos became an Alliance field of operations in 1929, the opening year of the depression, when the first missionary took up residence in Luang Prabang. The North Siam Mission of the Presbyterian Church had been doing some itinerant evangelism from time to time in the late 1800s, but transferred the area to the Alliance in the late 1920s.

Also in 1929, Alliance missionaries entered an unevangelized district of northeastern Thailand. When the American Presbyterians withdrew from the adjacent area of Korat five years later, they requested the Alliance to also take over their area.

In 1929 as well, Alliance missionaries penetrated the back country of Ivory Coast and made contact with the large and unevangelized Baoule tribe. They established their first station the following year.

During the height of the depression, Alliance missionaries from Congo surveyed South Gabon and discovered vast unreached areas. The Paris-based Evangelical Mission was asked about its plans, since the whole French colony was nominally its responsibility. After some delay, it permitted the first Alliance missionaries to enter Gabon in 1934.

Indonesian Opening

The spirit of Alliance missions during the depression years found powerful expression in Dr. Robert A. Jaffray. Cut from the same cloth as Dr. Simpson, he kept his eyes on the horizon and was always on the move toward it.

Already in his fifty-fourth year by 1927, and deeply committed to mission advance in South China and Vietnam, he sensed an inner leading toward the East Indies (later called Indonesia). Embarking on a survey trip of exotic islands like Borneo and crowded ports like Makassar, he asked repeatedly, "Is there anyone here who believes in Jesus Christ?" He received only blank stares and shrugs.

Though a veteran missionary of many years, he felt a spiritual chill creep over him. "While in Balik-papan," he wrote later, "deep depression of spirit and a feeling of discouragement, doubt and fear seemed to settle over my soul. It did not last long, but long enough to make me realize that I was on the enemy's territory. Yes, here is a place where the supreme rule of Satan has never been disputed."[33]

He reported the findings of his trip to the foreign department in New York and received a regretful reply that no funds were available to cover the huge expense of opening a new field. He then settled back with some sense of self-satisfaction that he had done his part.

His complacency was short-lived.

Though not a man given to dreams and visions, Dr. Jaffray had an experience so vivid and terrible while sleeping one night that he could not doubt its meaning. Human blood on his hands...running for his life...the Lord Jesus pursuing.

Upon awakening, he thought at once of the East Indies: "If I warn them not, if I preach not the Gospel to them, their blood is required at my hands."[34]

His biographer, A. W. Tozer, noted: "The New York Board heard again from Jaffray, and this time it was not a request. It was a declaration: He was going to Borneo. If they could not support him, he would go anyway. God was in this, and God would see him through. Back to Wuchow went a cable giving official permission to enter Borneo under the blessings of The Christian and Missionary Alliance."[35]

Permission and blessing, but no funds, no missionaries. The first lack he supplied from his own resources and help from some wealthy Chinese friends. The second lack he overcame by organizing a Chinese missionary society with two beloved colleagues, Pastor L. T. Chao and Leland Wang.

Within a year of Dr. Jaffray's survey trip to the islands in 1928, the first Chinese missionary was hard at work in Makassar.

Dr. Jaffray was in the East Indies when word came of the big crash on Wall Street, and with it a suggestion that he cut back on his expanding work in the islands.

His response was typically direct and immediate: "Do you ask, 'In view of the terrible economic depression of today dare we go forward in these new fields and commence new work?' Yea, rather, may we ask this—'Dare we in the face of the command of the Lord Jesus and in the face of the encouraging miracles He is working in our behalf, hesitate for one moment?' "[36]

Dr. Jaffray's response at age fifty-seven, plagued by diabetes and weakened by a heart condition, was to move from his residence of thirty-four years in Wuchow, South China, and make a new start in the Celebes port city of Makassar.

Clear Necessity

Would the account of Alliance work in North America during the depression years have been different if the home work had possessed as clear an understanding of its identity and goals as did the foreign work?

While other evangelical denominations and movements recorded growth—even doubled and tripled, the Alliance in the United States and Canada achieved little gain. At the same time, Alliance missions put together a string of strategies and achievements that became a standard for other missions.

Rev. Robert Ekvall spoke of the period in North America from 1925 to 1937 as characterized by "measured approach and carefully weighed decision; wise adjustment and careful, farsighted planning with a minimum of sudden change."[37]

This period of numerical stagnation may have been necessitated in part by the need for the Alliance to redefine and reorganize itself in a world radically different from the one inhabited by Dr. Simpson. Altering a corporate identity requires time and sensitivity toward honestly held but conflicting views.

No one was perhaps more qualified to do this than Dr. Shuman, the gentleman at the helm who epitomized his own high standards for the office of president.

The Alliance in North America, however, was soon to face new struggles and sacrifices that would make the depression years appear little more than a Sunday school exercise. It would need all the help possible, including that of minority groups which could bring so much enrichment. Holding to historical priorities, while adjusting to new methods generally approved, assumed even greater urgency in the 1930s.

Soon to be caught up in an international conflagration of unprecedented proportions, the Alliance could ill afford the continuing handicap of mixed signals.

PART FOUR

ACCELERATION

1937-1987

CHAPTER 11

The Crucible of Conflict

Suffering may not always be the making of a person, but it will bring to view what is already there.

1937-1954

Context of the Times

By 1937 the world scene was more bleak than President Franklin D. Roosevelt had ever known.

Militaristic Japan had finished the conquest of Manchuria and was extending its control into China. Fascist Italy had overpowered Ethiopia. Nazi Germany had taken over the demilitarized Rhineland. Civil war in Spain was turning yet another nation into an enemy of democracy.

The American president had to mask his alarm and move cautiously because he presided over a nation deeply divided over the issues of neutrality and intervention. A big part of the problem centered in a widespread pacifist movement with a religious backbone.

One of the leading liberal pulpiteers, Harry Emerson Fosdick, had vowed after World War I that he would never again support a war cause, and he spoke for millions of Protestants still reacting to the churches' enthusiastic "Great Crusade" against the Kaiser's Germany.

Some pacifists went so far as to question whether local police forces could be justified.

Denominational councils passed strong antiwar resolutions even though local churches were sharply divided on the issue. Interchurch groups such as the Fellowship of Reconciliation based in Nyack, New York, gained widespread support for pacifism, especially on university and seminary campuses.

Other voices grew strident in support of democratic causes, warning that Western civilization was at the crossroads. Church groups conservative in theology and politics tended to favor the government's taking a stronger stand against Hitler and Mussolini.

Arguments did not always rest on logic or biblical principles. Americans of German, Italian or Irish descent wanted to see England and France take a beating. Jews saw Hitler as evil personified. Anglo-Saxons generally supported the Allied cause, while Catholics sympathized with Franco's Spain and followed the Pope's contention that Communism was the world's worst enemy.

One church historian described Protestantism as pathetically divided and confused: "To put it bluntly, confusion over war and peace seemed more starkly extreme in the Protestant churches than in American society as a whole—and this is a damning comparison."

Confusion reigned among Protestants on more fronts than simply pacifism. The Social Gospel continued to appeal to church leaders, while the average churchgoers showed little concern. As the extreme hardships of the Great Depression began to ease, the proponents of social concern turned from relief activities to more socialist policies. The Fellowship of Socialist Christians was only one church group using terms such as "class struggle" and "class war."

A countermovement of conservatism rose up in the very denominations whose leaders pushed social activism the hardest. The Layman's Religious Movement, for example, flourished in the Methodist Church with the avowed purpose of counteracting socialism with Christian individualism.

Liberalism itself, fountainhead of social concerns, was challenged by a new school of thought: neo-orthodoxy. The movement had begun during World War I in a small parish on the Swiss border. Karl Barth, surveying the brutality of war and disintegration of social order, rejected the naive liberal theology that taught man was getting better and better day by day.

Neo-orthodoxy, also termed "reality theology," called for a return to belief in the wholly otherness of God, and in the sinfulness of man. Although these and other emphases indicated a return to biblical themes, thoughtful evangelicals rejected the new movement because its reservations about divine inspiration rendered the Bible a flawed book.

Fundamentalism itself was undergoing change as distinctives among the various groups came into sharper focus during the early 1940s. One camp continued to call itself fundamentalist and saw in the term a commitment to true Bible-believing Christianity; the group viewed itself as more opposed than others to any accommodation with liberal churches or compromise with truth.

Another group perceived fundamentalism as divisive, intolerant, anti-intellectual and unconcerned about social problems. Turning from the label of fundamentalism, they reached back into the 1800s and claimed the name of evangelical, a respected word synonymous with broad-based consensus on essential biblical doctrines and collective action among conservative Christians.

While fundamentalists and evangelicals were splitting, liberals were uniting. Some believe that formation of the League of Nations after World War I inspired the idea of a league of denominations as well.

Two major groups were converging on a common course in the late 1930s. The Faith and Order Movement stressed the need for churches to discuss theological issues and discover their shared faith. The Life and Work Movement believed that the way to achieve ecumenical unity was to work together on social issues.

The two world organizations met in 1938 in Utrecht and drafted a constitution that would create a single, worldwide council. The first assembly was to be held in 1941, but had to be postponed because of a crisis that enveloped the whole world in armed conflict. The meeting was finally held in Amsterdam in 1948, when the World Council of Churches formally organized.

Before that happened, fifty-seven nations plunged into the global inferno of World War II. It claimed 15,000,000 military personnel killed or missing, and perhaps twice that number of civilian lives.

The Japanese sneak attack on Pearl Harbor silenced the pacifist debate overnight among the American churches. Denominations rescinded their antiwar declarations, but there was no talk of a holy war reminiscent of World War I.

Under the pressures of war, the churches and federal government cooperated in some remarkable ways. In 1940, Washington announced that one chaplain would be provided for every 1,200 military service personnel. In the spring of 1941, Congress appropriated over $12,800,000 for the building of 604 chapels on military bases.

Denominations provided chaplains on a ratio based on their membership. The corps of chaplains trained by interdenominational staffs numbered more than 8,000. The Chaplains Association prepared a hymnal and other aids to worship funded by the government.

All of these cooperative church-state actions met with little or no protest.

Historian William Warren Sweet commented, "By pursuing this policy our government made clear its concern for the religious needs of all in the armed services.

"It further testifies to the fact that the . . . principle of the separation of church and state can be maintained, and at the same time the government may do much actively to further the cause of religion entirely apart from any sectarian participation."

* * *

Liberalism and the Social Gospel, with their logical offspring of pacifism and socialism, held little attraction for Alliance leaders and laypeople. Even the emerging split between fundamentalists and evangelicals evoked little response, though the Alliance would later join the latter group.

Still somewhat uncertain as to their position in the religious community, Alliance people generally viewed these theological and ecclesiastical controversies from a distance.

The gathering clouds of war, however, aroused their concern earlier than that of most conservative Christians, and for reasons far different from those of the liberals. While the East Indies and Indo-China, and even China and Japan, were viewed by many Americans as exotic fantasy lands, Alliance people knew them as real places inhabited by real people, because their missionaries worked in such places.

During the war years, The Christian and Missionary Alliance slowly organized in North America and worked overseas where possible. Alliance people impatiently awaited the day of peace, when they could surge ahead doing what they knew best how to do: represent Jesus Christ overseas where He was totally unknown or barely understood.

CELEBRATING its Jubilee year in 1937, the Alliance began looking ahead to the future with more anticipation than had been apparent in earlier years of the Great Depression. Though the decade of financial hardship still had two more years to run, jobs were becoming more available and money less scarce.

General Council in 1937 reflected this quickening mood by establishing a fiftieth anniversary Crusade Fund. Robert G. LeTourneau, an Alliance layman who built big machines and also thought big,[1] donated $6,000 to this extension fund. The Alliance nearly matched the gift with another $5,000.

Home secretary Brown explained the fund's goal: "This extension embraces in its plan the occupation of new strategic centers through the entire home field, as well as the incitation of established points."[2]

One of the 753 extension crusades during the year climaxed in a Minneapolis theater on May 10, 1937. Approximately 900 people attended and pledged $1,417.50 for missions. "When it is remembered," editorialized *The Alliance Weekly,* "that this was an extension effort, and that a large proportion of the givers were from other groups, the sympathetic value of the convention will be more fully realized."[3]

The number of branches and affiliated churches increased by 25, to 503 during 1937. Seventeen additions raised the unorganized groups to 253. Total membership, however, decreased by 754, to 34,721.

The dip in membership during 1937 despite all the Jubilee Crusade campaigns may have prompted a committee report of General Council in 1939 to observe, "The best extension method is to be found not in deliberate efforts to open new branches, but rather in the spontaneous spread of the work through a mighty surge of evangelism from within by the Holy Spirit; thus the development becomes automatic instead of mechanical."[4]

This best-method-is-no-method approach to extension seemed more a venting of frustration than a jubilation over the discovery of a new method. During the no-method year of 1938, membership averaged less than one new member per branch or affiliated church.

Camp Meeting Dynamics

Stalemate in growth, however, did not accurately reflect a certain vitality apparent when Alliance people got together, especially at camp meeting time. The movement had begun in a summer camp at Old Orchard, Maine, and the blessed habit spread until by 1938 almost every Alliance district had its own annual gathering.

Eastern District's Mahaffey Camp in western Pennsylvania during the mid 1930s conducted a ten-day program similar to other Alliance camps. The bargains alone gave campers something to shout about: a thirty-meal ticket for $8.00; a two-cot dormitory room for $2.50, or, if preferred, a commodious 12x12-foot tent with a wood floor for $3.00—not per day, but for all ten days of camp. These plain but adequate facilities could accommodate up to 3,000 people.

Some families insisted on a different level of comfort. They brought their own food, hauled their own trailer or raised their own tent. There was even an occasional cow or two for those who insisted on fresh milk for breakfast. The cool running stream nearby served as refrigerator.

Whatever their level of luxury, Alliance camp folk all shared a common interest: meetings under the big roof. There was little time for anything else. The vigorous schedule seemed intent on supercharging the saints with blessing that would last until camp the following year.

A typical day at Mahaffey meant:

6:00 A.M. - rising bell	1:15 P.M. - children's service
6:30 A.M. - prayer service	2:00 P.M. - prayer and praise
7:30 A.M. - breakfast	3:00 P.M. - Bible sermon
9:00 A.M. - youth service	4:15 P.M. - divine healing
10:00 A.M. - Bible study	5:30 P.M. - supper
11:00 A.M. - missionary message	6:45 P.M. - missionary reports
12:00 NOON - lunch	7:15 P.M. - song service
	8:00 P.M. - evangelistic service

The roster of speakers for the summer of 1938 at Mahaffey included representatives from a global swath of Alliance missions on which the sun never set: Dr. Robert A. Jaffray, Netherlands East Indies; Henry Wagoner, Chile; E. F. Stewart, Central China; N. M. Cressman, French Indo-China; and George Powell, French West Africa.

Among the Bible teachers and evangelists appeared such current favorites as Dr. Harry Shuman, William T. MacArthur, W. G. "Daddy" Weston, Thomas Williamson, May Decker and Harry L. Turner.

Choirs, orchestras, quartets and duets added to the music program topped by tenor soloist Ben Jenkins. Standing on tiptoes with his head thrown back, Jenkins let flow the songs of Simpson that had gripped him to the depths of his heart, songs like:

Fainting soldier of the Lord,
Hear His sweet inspiring word—
"I have conquered all thy foes,
I have suffered all thy woes;
Struggling soldier, trust in Me,
I have overcome for thee."

The baptismal service on the final Saturday afternoon at Mahaffey served as prelude to the climactic missionary rally on Sunday afternoon that drew crowds of 5,000 or more. Though the offering that July Sunday in 1938 was large, people still spoke of the missionary offering in 1930. In that year after the big crash on Wall Street, the pledge offering amounted to $140,000. A similar rally at Beulah Beach in Ohio netted $130,000 the same year.

No statistics or historical records, however, could convey the feeling that permeated an Alliance summer camp like Mahaffey in the summer of '38.

Rousing congregational singing startled echoes in the surrounding hills with refrains like, *"Oh Beulah land, sweet Beulah land, as on thy highest mount I stand"*... quietly coursing tears responded to truth made precious by masterful expositors...warm camaraderie viewed no one a stranger, only a friend not yet introduced... exuberant young people by the hundreds saw no obstacle to enjoyment in a camp program that offered only meetings.

It seemed almost contradictory that such people could enjoy their faith so enthusiastically, yet be unable to put together a thriving program of church growth that would attract others. Yet there was no doubting that what they had from the Lord was good and real.

Perhaps smaller in size but not in spirit, similar summer camps flourished in Old Orchard, Maine; Delta Lake, New York; Medicine Lake, Minnesota; Okoboji, Iowa; Camp Hebron, Massachusettes; Canby, Oregon; and Summit Grove, Pennsylvania.

Out of such spiritual training camps and supportive hometown fellowships came a generation of Alliance missionaries soon to be tested in ways mercifully not yet known.

Darkening Skies

Perhaps sensing the turbulent times that lay ahead, Dr. Snead pushed himself and his colleagues to insure that, whatever happened, churches overseas would be firmly rooted in the soil of local culture. That objective found him in the rugged mountains of Peru in October of 1937, anticipating a meeting with some 300 Quechua Indians.

He had not ridden a horse since his missionary days in India almost thirty years before, but the precipitous and narrow mountain trails permitted no other transportation. So, draping his skeletal six-foot frame over a saddle, he endured days of horseback riding.

Passing through one small town, he and his escort were confronted by an agitated Roman Catholic priest. The cleric threatened to incite the townspeople against them if they did not get out of town immediately. They spurred their horses onward.

Finally arriving at their destination of Pachas, Dr. Snead did not find the 300 Quechuas he had anticipated. Only fourteen men showed up—believers who had walked eleven days over 12,000-foot mountains to greet him. Seeing their strong desire to follow Christ, the lanky American felt fully rewarded for the discomfort and danger he had endured.[5]

Dr. Snead's leadership as foreign secretary during the depression decade helped the Alliance achieve solid gains overseas. The missionary force increased from 361 in 1929 to 469 ten years later; the total of national workers grew by 749 to an all-time high of 1,854. By 1939, overseas church membership had more than doubled, from 24,000 to 57,000, and the number of organized churches did indeed realize 100 percent growth, from 298 to 632.

Significantly, most of the growth centered in the Far East, where Japan was already on the march in both Manchuria and China.[6] It seems that God often moves mightily in areas soon to be plunged into great suffering.

Dr. Jaffray, always alert to international developments, had not the slightest doubt the world was moving rapidly toward another world war. During a brief furlough in 1938, he spoke often of the coming conflict. Concerned friends urged him to remain in North America, but he would not even entertain the thought.

"If I do not go back now," he said prophetically, "there is little likelihood that I can ever go back at all. I must return to the Far East. I want to die out there where my life has been."[7]

Other missionaries shared the same sense of urgency. Even while the Sino-Japanese conflict spread through Central China, Alliance missionaries to the south refused to leave and began to see results after years of sacrifice and fatalities. In 1941 more than 500 Chinese converts were baptized.

That same year in the Netherlands East Indies (now Indonesia), Rev. and Mrs. Herman Dixon and several national workers penetrated West Borneo (now Kalimantan) to evangelize hitherto unreached Dyak tribespeople. In ten months, some 1,500 Dyaks turned to Christ and 500 entered the waters of baptism.

Rev. Russell Deibler described the first of his eighteen-day trips into the Wissel Lakes area of New Guinea (now Irian Jaya) to evangelize tribes that had never ventured from their mountain villages. After a two-day trip upriver by canoe, he hired seven carriers and allotted to each one two fifty-pound tins, mostly food for the carriers.

Deibler himself traveled light: one change of clothing, a few blankets and no cot. He lived on a diet of rice, dried salted fish and green peas.

Each day the missionary and carriers crossed from one to five mountain ranges, constantly soaked by unrelenting rain and chilled by the high-altitude cold. The carriers cried aloud in their misery, while Deibler shivered silently. A previous expedition on the same trail had cost the lives of six carriers.

Once over the ranges and past the mountain streams, Deibler still faced hardship: The canoe carrying his personal belongings across a lake struck a rock and sank. Finally, at the end of the trek and across a long rattan suspension bridge, he met the Kapaukus and had his reward for the eighteen-day trek: Another of the lost tribes beyond the ranges heard of Jesus Christ for the first time.

Assembling Resources

The 1941 General Council elected Howard E. Nelson as home secretary. The decision would have considerable impact on the form and function of the Alliance in North America for years to come.

Nelson came to the office with perhaps more Alliance credentials than any other officer at the time. Another of "Daddy" Whiteside's boys, he grew up as part of the Pittsburgh Gospel Tabernacle family and began preaching at age fifteen. He graduated from both Wilson Academy and the Missionary Training Institute at Nyack and then joined Thomas Moseley in an itinerant tent ministry.

He settled down into the pastorate in Cleveland, Ohio, when he married. Then from 1926 to 1928 he served as assistant to W. E. Conley, who was superintendent of the Central District. Nelson succeeded Conley as superintendent and served in that post for thirteen years. Nelson's concern as both superintendent and then home secretary centered on extension. His somewhat jaunty style amused some, but people soon realized he was altogether serious about seeing the Alliance grow in North America. He viewed the pastoral and evangelistic responsibilities of the local fellowship fully as important as its missionary program.

He told General Council in 1942 he believed the Alliance was designed "to afford an ever-widening Christian and fraternal fellowship, and to secure for the worldwide missionary program an expanding measure of interest, prayer and practical support."[8]

The home secretary's first step to promote extension was to emphasize promotion itself: The Alliance had to start talking about itself if it wanted to attract people. The home department organized for the first time ever a bureau of promotion and publicity. Next followed an extension grant of $8,612, which Nelson used to help organize thirty-four new fellowships in 1942.

The stalemate in growth finally ended.

Nelson's department would increase the number of "churches and organized branches," as he called them, from 580 to 1,142 over the next eighteen years.[9] The home department would also add three new offices to help promote growth of the Alliance at home: the appointment of Mavis Anderson in 1952 as the first full-time Sunday school secretary; the selection of Rev. Weldon B. Blackford in 1954 as the first full-time national youth secretary; and the organization of a bureau of evangelism in the same year.

Nelson received backing in his efforts to upgrade Alliance home ministries from an old buddy: Thomas Moseley. After the two folded up their evangelistic tent and went separate ways, Moseley spent twenty-five fruitful years in the West China Mission along the Kansu-Tibetan border. To this record of service he added an undergraduate degree from Occidental College and a master's degree from the University of California. Wheaton College conferred an honorary doctorate on him in 1940, when he became the first full-time president of the Missionary Training Institute, a post previously held by presidents of the Alliance.

The two former tent campaigners agreed on the necessity of expanding and strengthening the curriculum at Nyack. This meant securing academic recognition from the New York State Department of Education, an objective the persistent Nyack president would achieve in 1944.

Breaking Storm

The world changed forever for the United States on December 7, 1941, when Japan attacked Pearl Harbor. Declaring war on the Axis powers of Japan, Germany and Italy, the nation assumed a role in world leadership it could never again renounce, as it had after World War I.

The war inflicted a terrible toll on the Alliance in terms of human lives and properties overseas. Japan overran ten of its twenty mission fields, imprisoned eighty missionary adults and forty-five children. Ten of the adults would either be killed or die as a result of the war.

The killing began in Borneo.

Rev. Fred C. Jackson knew he was a marked man. He had been flying a mission-owned amphibian plane for the Alliance, ferrying missionaries and supplies to remote parts of the island. After war came to Borneo, he could have flown to safety and been reunited with his wife, who was still in the States, but he felt his place was with other missionaries who could not escape.

Jackson volunteered to help the Dutch forces. He airlifted their sick and wounded to medical help on the coast, carried their mail and kept a lookout for the enemy. The Japanese would not forgive him for helping the Dutch. When Borneo fell to the invaders, Jackson hid his plane in the jungle and joined his friends, Rev. and Mrs. Andrew Sande, at the internment center in Long Berang. Jackson and the Sandes had all arrived in Borneo the previous year.

In the summer of 1942, the war ended for Jackson, the Sandes and their infant son, and approximately 120 other Americans and Europeans at Long Berang. The Japanese first murdered all the men, and then sometime later every one of the women and children.

Rev. John Willfinger, completing his fourth year as a missionary, was traveling deep in the interior of Borneo when the island came under Japanese occupation. Dyak Christians urged him to remain among them and promised to hide him from the enemy.

After praying for guidance, Willfinger wrote to a local Dyak official, who was also a Christian friend. "In this letter I inform you of my decision, which is the most difficult one of all my life.... If I hide, naturally the saints will be forced to lie and disobey orders, if they shelter me. I would be forced to drag them into sin."

He then pointed to the inconsistency he could not tolerate: "My intention upon leaving my country and family was only to make mankind righteous and not to bring them into sin, even though I pay for it with my life. In short, sir, because of Jesus Christ and His sheep, before I will do anything whatsoever that is not right, I will surely surrender myself."[10]

Willfinger walked out of the jungle in December of 1942 and gave himself up. He was executed on Christmas Eve, bayoneted repeatedly in the chest and spine.

Grace Dittmar was completing her second year of ministry in Sumatra when the invasion began. She escaped to Java and had the option of evacuating by plane or ship. She chose the steamer.

The plane she would have taken was shot down. Five of the eight ships crammed with refugees were sunk.

Dittmar arrived safely back in her hometown of Williamsport, Pennsylvania, but the harrowing experiences of the escape and voyage still claimed her life on December 7, 1942.

Just one day earlier, on the other side of the world, the war felled another Alliance worker. Mrs. Homera Homer-Dixon had spent fourteen fruitful years in French Indo-China.

Prison Horrors

The missionaries in Indo-China were interned in commodious barracks erected in Mytho by Vichy French officials collaborating with the Japanese. Conditions deteriorated rapidly when the internees came under direct Japanese supervision.

"Orders were given and countermanded; rules made and changed without warning or explanation," wrote Mrs. Lorna Grobb after the war. "Roll calls, held at the whim of the guards, became the order of the day. Japanese soldiers, usually drunk, ran berserk through the camp at all hours of the day and night."[11]

One momentary glimmer of joy lightened their suffering. The missionaries were startled to hear a gospel radio program coming from a radio in the guards' quarters. Somehow the Alliance church in Saigon had secured permission from the Japanese authorities to broadcast a half-hour service every Sunday afternoon.

Missionaries in the Philippines tried to evade the Japanese by going deep in the jungle fastness of Mindanao and setting up two secret self-sustaining camps. They got away with it for a year, but eventually the Japanese entered both camps and carried the missionaries off to internment centers.

Japanese treatment of prisoners in the Philippines seemed cruel, but restrained. "I have never been maltreated by our enemy in any form of physical cruelty," reported one internee of Manila's Santo Tomas Prison. "Our captors' mistreatment took the form of petty persecutions, building up false hopes of repatriation and proper food supplies—and then cutting down the food to starvation rations."[12]

While missionaries in the Philippines and elsewhere suffered in prison camps, local Christians in far greater numbers paid heavily for their faith and their friendship with the missionaries.

Rev. Florentino de Jesus, pastor of the Jolo Evangelical Church of the Alliance, lay in dungeon darkness and solitary confinement for days before knowing why the Japanese had arrested him. During interrogation alternating with torture, he learned the authorities suspected him of praying for an American victory, which he did, and of planning to smuggle plans of the airport to the enemy, which he did not.

"Tell the truth!" his jailers screamed as they beat him with a baseball bat. The only words to escape his lips until he collapsed were, "Jesus, Jesus."

Several days later the soldiers marched de Jesus out to a freshly dug grave. Forced to kneel and lean forward over the pit, he heard an officer warn him once again to tell the truth or die.

"I have told you the truth. I have no map," he insisted.

"Are you ready to die?" the officer asked.

"I am ready."

De Jesus felt the cold blade of a sword on his neck and then sensed the sword being raised above his exposed neck. It came whistling downward—and returned to the officer's scabbard.

The squad returned the pastor to his musty dungeon cell infested with vermin. During the forty-two days of solitary confinement, he probably wished at times the execution had taken place.[13]

Dr. Jaffray and his wife might well have escaped before the Netherlands East Indies fell to Japan, but he refused, saying, "I cannot leave while one missionary remains on the field."[14]

He moved the Makassar staff to a health resort several miles away at Benteng Tinggi. The Japanese left them unmolested until March, 1942, when they returned the men to an internment camp at Makassar. The women were kept at Benteng Tinggi and, for some reason, the commanding officer allowed Dr. Jaffray to remain with his wife and daughter. He enjoyed relative tranquillity and spent much time writing during that year.

Sometime in 1943 he was taken from his family and eventually landed at Pare-Pare on a farm converted into an internment camp. This prince of men thus took up his last residence on a farm originally built to raise pigs.

Willing Prisoner

Mabel Francis, like Dr. Jaffray, could have avoided imprisonment, but she had made Japan her home and under no condition would she leave—not even when the two countries she loved were at war with each other.

The diminutive Alliance missionary had set her heart on serving the Lord in Japan since she was a teenager in Tamworth, New Hampshire. She told how on one occasion she heard the voice of God speak in her heart, "You know that I love you."

"Yes," she answered, "I know that You love me."

"Then He spoke a word that changed my life," she testified. " 'Just as I love you,' He said, 'I love the people of Japan.' The call was so clear that I began at once to prepare."[15]

Miss Francis' outfit, even by 1909 standards, was meager: a small steamer trunk containing some cutlery, a few books and family mementos, a half-pound of cocoa and three cotton dresses. Her spiritual resources counted for much more, proving adequate for fifty-six years of ministry in Japan—twenty-five of them without a furlough.

When she arrived in Japan, Westerners were still oddities among the people and viewed with suspicion. That did not bother her because she planned to take as long as necessary to win their acceptance. She traveled by bike and preached when she could in and around Hiroshima until the people got used to her. Out of that tolerance grew respect, and out of respect, love.

Mabel's brother, Rev. Thomas Francis, joined her in 1913, and together they established twenty Alliance churches. Then her widowed sister, Anne Dievendorf, arrived in 1922. The two sisters' work would complement each other for the next forty years: Mabel, the evangelist, and Anne, the teacher.

The depression years brought a crisis for Mabel and Anne. The Alliance decided for several reasons to withdraw from Japan. She and the other missionaries received instructions in 1934 to return home for furlough and then possible reassignment to another Alliance field.

Mabel Francis could not shake the conviction that God had called her to Japan, not the Alliance mission. But dare she obey?

"I remember that I was frightened," she confessed. "I was still young at the time, and my future life seemed to be threatened if I stayed in Japan with no home church or organization or Board in back of me."

"I said to the Lord in my heart, 'But if I live to be seventy years old, everyone in America will forget that I exist, and I might starve right here.'

"And then the Lord said, 'If I let you live to be seventy....' "[16]

The two sisters stayed on as independent missionaries and continued their work with the Alliance pastors and churches. They saw their decision to stay vindicated by God's blessing on their ministry.

That decision also helped prepare them for another crisis in 1942, when they had opportunity to be repatriated to America. They again refused, even though it meant the stigma of being branded enemy aliens and suffering imprisonment.

Anne was arrested and interned immediately after Pearl Harbor, but Mabel lived under house arrest in Matsuyama for a year. Unable to circulate freely among the people, she prayed: "Lord, what shall I do?"

God answered by sending three very sick people. She decided, "If I can't have a preaching place, I'll have a hospital." She nursed the three until the police came to take her away nearly a year later.

The officer said to Mabel, "If we walk with you, it will make you ashamed, so we'll walk ahead and you follow." She remembered the painful parting with her friends: "They stood along the street weeping as I passed by. Some just stood by the side of their houses and, without making any other sign of emotion, signaled with a flutter of their fingers."[17]

Three years would pass before the two sisters, reunited in prison, would be free to return to Mabel's home in Matsuyama.

Redeploying Personnel

With so many Alliance fields in Asia closed by the war, attention turned to the two continents relatively free of conflict: South America and Black Africa.

Dr. Snead redirected some of the displaced Asia missionaries to these two areas and encouraged candidates to accept similar assignments. Thus, from 1942 to 1945, forty-two missionaries went to the five Alliance fields of South America—Argentina, Chile, Colombia, Ecuador and Peru. The three African fields—French West Africa, Gabon and Congo—received twenty-eight reinforcements in 1944 and 1945.

Though removed from military conflict, each of these fields contained its own dangers in spiritual and ideological warfare. The Roman Catholic Church, closely linked to the political establishment in most South American countries, openly resisted Protestant advance by every means possible.

Colombia missionary Rev. Leo C. Tennies reported that when he tried to rent a house in Salamina, the local priest first warned all the people not to enter the house. Then the priest condemned the homeowner so vehemently that he hurriedly canceled the rent agreement.

Later, when an evangelistic band of young men entered Pacora for the first time, the priest set up loudspeakers in the streets. The walls re-echoed with the warning that people should beware of these Protestant devils who were giving away vile literature and selling false Bibles.

Missionaries in Africa met with response to the Gospel, but trying to get to and from the continent posed grave risks. The ordeal of one small missionary group provided a remarkable saga of faith and determination.

A widowed Alliance missionary, Ethel Bell, and her two children, Mary and Robert, boarded a cargo ship in the West Africa port of Takoradi in September of 1942. Another missionary couple, Mr. and Mrs. Shaw, and their three children also booked passage on the New York-bound ship.

Two weeks into the South Atlantic, the ship was torpedoed by a German submarine. It sank in less than two minutes. The survivors struggled aboard three small rafts. The Bell family was intact, but only Shaw and two of his children managed to escape the sinking ship. Separated by the confusion, the Shaws were pulled aboard different rafts.

The three rafts tried staying roped together, but the danger of collision forced them to cut the ropes. Two of the rafts drifted out of sight, the mystery of their fate locked in the ocean's depths.

On the remaining ten-by-ten foot raft, nineteen people clung to life and hope for twenty days. Mrs. Bell, her two children and two of the Shaw children belonged to that saltwater-encrusted, oil-streaked cluster of huddled survivors. The sailors showed little interest in the missionary's religion at first, but as the days trickled into weeks, they began asking her to include them in her prayers.

Rations gave out on September 18. That same day the raft crossed the path of a convoy. An edgy American destroyer nearly blew it out of the water before realizing its jerry-rigged mast was not a submarine periscope.

One of the surviving sailors visited Mrs. Bell in the Barbados hospital where she was recuperating. He told her that her faith in action had made him a born-again believer. He left her with the words, "Mrs. Bell, there was a light over that raft."

"He was right," she wrote. "There was—the light of the eternal presence of God."[18]

Death and Deliverance

Japanese prison-camp conditions relentlessly wore down the internees until many could no longer survive.

Rev. C. Russell Deibler, the thirteen-year veteran who had braved the high ranges of New Guinea, succumbed to dysentery after a year in the stockade. Rev. Franklin Grobb, for fifteen years a pioneer missionary with his wife in Laos, suffered a severe attack of acute appendicitis in the Mytho internment camp. Japanese officials refused to authorize treatment until too late. He died of peritonitis on July 5, 1945.

Time was also running out for Dr. Jaffray in the internment camp at Pare-Pare. Food rations dropped below the starvation level. Sanitary conditions on the former pig farm became indescribable, guards terrorized their wretched wards and the rains seemed never to end.

"It is a solemn and awful thought," wrote A. W. Tozer, "that this man whom the continents and islands could not contain is now contracted to the pitiful and narrow confines of a wretched Japanese prison cot, and dying of starvation."[19]

As life ebbed from his wasted body, Dr. Jaffray perhaps remembered saying during his last furlough, "I must return to the Far East. I want to die out there where my life has been."[20] On the night of July 29, 1945, his desire became reality.

Just two weeks later, the guns fell silent and Japan bowed low in defeat. The war was over, but for the Alliance in the East Indies one more tragedy remained.

Rev. William Presswood and his wife Ruth were reunited after their separate prison ordeals. Both seemed to recover rapidly from their long internment. They declined repatriation to the States and plunged back into the ministry he had begun in 1930 and she had joined in 1941.

Returning from a survey trip to interior Borneo in January of 1946, they were thrown into the rapids when their canoe capsized. The rapid current swept them some 300 yards downstream, mostly underwater, before they could be rescued.

Presswood's near drowning may have triggered the attack of pneumonia several days later. Still weakened by his prolonged internment, he could not fight off the illness. So the war, though past, reached forward into time and claimed its last Alliance missionary, one of the finest the islands had known.

New Initiatives

World War II ended as abruptly—with a terrifying mushroom cloud over Hiroshima and Nagasaki—as it had started with oily black clouds over Pearl Harbor. The belligerent nations would be a long time making the transition from war to peace, but not so the Alliance.

Dr. Shuman and his colleagues had begun planning early in the conflict for the postwar era. Dr. Shuman wrote in 1943, "The foreign department and the Board of Managers of the Society have been giving careful thought to this question of a post-war missionary program. If the Lord tarries, it is believed that there will be very unusual opportunities for evangelism in all mission lands, and we shall be prepared...."[21]

As the president enumerated details of the anticipated costly transition, he also gave an indication of how deeply the war had affected the Alliance by 1943:

— The 80 missionaries and 45 children interned by the Japanese in the Far East must be returned to North America when the war ended.

— The 136 adults and 65 children in other areas of Asia and Africa should be furloughed after difficult years of service beyond the normal limits of time.

— The Alliance suffered a total loss of equipment, houses and furnishings, vehicles and boats on mission stations overrun and looted by Japanese forces.

— At the outbreak of hostilities, $38,000 in funds was lost in transit.

To this list of losses by 1943, Dr. Shuman added the encouraging note that 137 missionaries and their 85 children stood ready to resume their overseas ministries when the war ended.

He estimated the total cost of a sweeping revitalization of the missionary program would be $520,565. Of that total, over $228,300 had already been put in reserve for the first wave of renewed missionary advance.[22]

Some missionaries started moving back to their fields as soon as peace was secured in 1945. The following year, another 126 workers joined them. In addition to experienced personnel returning to their fields, Dr. Snead announced that the Alliance purposed by God's help to appoint an additional 250 new recruits for the war-stricken areas between 1945 and 1950.

A few veteran missionaries did not have far to go. They were the internees who elected to stay in Asia and resume work immediately.

Rev. E. F. Gulbranson, missionary to the Philippines, spent most of the war years with 3,700 other civilian internees in the Santo Tomas Prison in Manila. They were rescued in February of 1945 by a blazing column of American armor that blasted a 100-mile corridor through enemy lines to liberate them. American authorities learned later that the Japanese prison guard had planned to execute all the prisoners later that same day.

Waiting to be flown back to the States, Gulbranson had second thoughts about going home: "I knew that once I had reached the States, it would be impossible to return within six or eight months without a 1-A priority, which would not be issued to an evangelical missionary."[23]

He stepped out of the waiting line, took his name off the list of repatriates and returned to Zamboanga as soon as it was liberated. Flying over the city in a military transport plane, he glimpsed the Ebenezer Bible Institute for the first time in three years.

"Praise God for His goodness!" he whispered excitedly to himself. "It's still standing!" So was the church and its people. Gulbranson lost no time in getting back to work.

Rev. and Mrs. W. H. Oldfield led the vanguard of returning missionaries to China. They arrived by ship at Shanghai in February of 1946 and pushed on immediately to Wuchow, site of the mission headquarters and home for many years to the Jaffray family. The Oldfields' experience paralleled that of others returning to their areas.

"We entered a land of wreck and ruin," he reported. "The fine buildings of our fair city of Wuchow were piles of broken brick and tangled timbers. Churches and missionary residences had been looted and destroyed, and there was nothing but bare walls and broken brick."[24]

The Oldfields hurriedly distributed the supplies they had brought in steel drums. Relief funds helped secure some of the food and medications long denied to the Chinese Christians. Only three years later, Alliance missionaries would be forced to leave again, this time because of Communist control of China.

In Japan, Mabel Francis and Anne Dievendorf once again faced a choice of returning to the States or remaining in Japan. Mabel had reached age sixty-four and had spent the last thirty-six years in Japan with only two furloughs. American occupation authorities suggested they go home to America and recuperate from their wartime ordeal.

The two feisty little women would not hear of it. They walked out of the internment camp straight back to a ministry of love among the Japanese people they had adopted as their own.

Mabel began visiting wounded Japanese soldiers in the hospitals, dividing among them the chocolate bars and other supplies given her by American GIs. "You have lost the war," she told the men, "but God has something for you yet."[25]

High-ranking government officials of Matsuyama welcomed Mabel back to their city with formality that barely masked their deep emotion. She and her sister received invitations to speak everywhere. They told the discouraged and devastated people that the Bible said they should honor their parents and the emperor, but they must go beyond that and believe in Jesus Christ. Hundreds did, and thousands more heard the Gospel for the first time.

Years later, in 1962, Mabel would receive from the Emperor of Japan himself membership in the exclusive Fifth Order of the Sacred Treasure. She was the first person in Japanese history to receive the highest civilian honor while still living.

The citation expressed remarkable appreciation for her contribution "to the welfare of the Japanese people in their distress and confusion at the time of their defeat" and for "the long years spent in leading hundreds of Japanese to the knowledge of God, to peace of heart and mind."[26]

Independence Atmosphere

If Western missionaries and colonial officials returned to their familiar haunts in Asia after the war expecting to pick up where they had left off, they experienced a rude shock. Populations from French Indo-China to Netherlands East Indies that had just endured cruel years of Japanese occupation had no intention of meekly submitting again to European domination.[27]

Colonialism would no longer be tolerated in the major territories of Asia. Neither would missionary paternalism.

The Alliance policy of encouraging strong indigenous churches proved not only biblically sound, but politically wise in the postwar independence atmosphere.

In the East Indies, for example, people movements before the war produced many converts and churches in a remarkably short time. Rev. Walter H. Post returned in 1945 concerned that the rapid growth might have produced a superficial church that could not stand under persecution.

His fears proved groundless: "We found there had been no mass falling away in any part of the field. Practically every church had remained intact. Very few individuals or villages had returned to their old heathen customs or former religion.

"About one half of the native workers continued their ministry although they had to support themselves, often under very difficult conditions. In several fields we found villages near the Christians, which were formerly indifferent, asking for teachers and showing responsiveness to the Gospel."[28]

Several other fields with thriving indigenous churches registered similar growth during the war years, when missionaries were either few in number or absent altogether: Congo, parts of French Indo-China and the Philippines. However, in most of the Alliance mission fields, numbering twenty-one by 1950, the total of pastors supported by local congregations had slipped from 67 percent in 1935 to 48 percent in fifteen years and the situation showed no prospects of improvement.

A special committee appointed by the Board of Managers concluded that indigenous policies adopted in 1927 were being either consistently ignored or inconsistently applied.[29] The committee issued a strongly worded report that in essence said the only acceptable bottom line of missions activity was a church of believers who could stand on their own—baptized, sanctified and united in helping others know the same Lord and Savior. Anything less amounted to failure.[30]

New Missionary Generation

While the first wave of veteran and new missionaries spread out to overseas fields after the war, a second wave of recruits marched off to Alliance schools: former servicemen and women, many of whom had found a new set of values when fighting for their country.

Brigadier General Luther D. Miller, Chief of Army Chaplains, noted that more young men and women attended church, read their Bibles and earnestly prayed while in the armed services than at any time in the history of the country.[31]

In a program termed the "G.I. Bill of Rights," the United States government provided financial aid to veterans for higher education. Postsecondary schools, such as Bible institutes, that wanted to accept students under this program had to qualify as accredited institutions. This development helped produce a stronger theological program balanced by a basic general education. The Missionary Training Institute, already accredited by the state, went a step further and added a fourth year of study. Other Alliance schools soon followed.[32]

Because war has a way of reducing faith to its essentials, many Christians in uniform discovered they had more in common with one another than their denominational orientations had indicated. The postwar years therefore saw an increased willingness among former servicemen and women, including those in Alliance ministries, to cooperate with other evangelical groups.

This acceptance of other believers regardless of their church label, an Alliance principle beginning with Dr. Simpson himself, found contemporary expression in the C&MA's writer laureate, A. W. Tozer: "Sectarianism is one of the most noxious ills that can afflict any church or denomination. And remember that denominations and churches are only what their members are. That we love our church and cherish it is most natural and desirable, but never should we allow a feeling of exclusiveness to enter."[33]

Alliance congregations in North America found this wider evangelical fellowship through cooperating with organizations like Youth for Christ, the Billy Graham Evangelistic Association and Child Evangelism.

Interaction overseas became even more important and specialized. Alliance mission leaders had an established policy not to diversify unnecessarily, but to cooperate when possible with paramission groups on a contractual basis.

Missionary radio offered such an opportunity, especially since several major organizations had something of an Alliance background. Trans World Radio grew out of a vision shared by Rev. Ralph Freed, an Alliance missionary in the Middle East for twenty-one years, and his son, Paul. HCJB, the powerful "Voice of the Andes" in Quito, Ecuador, was cofounded by Rev. Reuben Larson, an Alliance missionary in Ecuador, and Clarence Jones, director of radio programming for Paul Rader in Chicago. ELWA in Monrovia, Liberia, came into existence through the persistence and sacrifice of William Watkins, son of longtime Alliance missionaries in Guinea.[34]

As these missionary radio stations went on the air, joined by FEBC in Manila, Alliance missions in the various geographic areas utilized their facilities. By the 1980s, the participation of Alliance national churches and missions would grow to over 400 gospel broadcasts per week at an annual cost of over a half-million dollars.

Mission Aviation Fellowship, founded by Christian exservicemen, became another specialized paramission agency used by the Alliance. Years before MAF got off the ground, however, Dr. Jaffray realized the potential of aircraft for his field and made airborne missions part of his strategy.

He began requesting funds in 1936 to purchase a plane, but in the depression years income could hardly cope with missionary allowances, let alone a plane. He would not be put off. Several years later a sizable amount came to Dr. Jaffray through a family inheritance. With this and with help from some donors, he enabled the Alliance in 1939 to buy its first missionary aircraft: a single-engine Beechcraft biplane with floats.

The five-seater aircraft cut exhausting travel to the interior of Borneo from weeks on rivers and paths to hours by air. It had the exciting effect of multiplying the capacity of the mission without adding personnel. The happy arrangement came to a tragic end when the Japanese destroyed the plane and executed its pilot, Fred Jackson, in 1942.

Revived use of aircraft for missionary work in Indonesia resulted indirectly from the crash in 1945 of an Army cargo plane in New Guinea. When the survivors stumbled out of the interior, they confirmed reports of a Stone Age people hidden in the romantically named "Valley of Shangri-La" behind the towering ranges.

Rev. Einar Mickelson set his heart on evangelizing this unreached people. Dutch colonial officials kept delaying permission to enter the valley because they designated it uncontrolled and therefore unsafe. They finally relented in 1952.

Two unsuccessful attempts by land to reach the area, known locally as the Baliem Valley, convinced Mickelson and his colleagues that penetration must be achieved by air. A twin-motor seaplane purchased by the Alliance lifted the advance missionary party over the 14,000-foot mountain ranges and deposited them on an uncharted river in the valley. At that very hour, Alliance prayer groups around the world were fasting and interceding for the success of their mission.

Mickelson and his colleague, Rev. Lloyd Van Stone, took with them a Kapauku tribal couple with a child to demonstrate their peaceful intentions. They clambered ashore and cautiously faced the intense scrutiny of Dani cannibal warriors, not knowing whether the conclusion would be life or death. After a suspense-filled moment, when it seemed to them as if the whole world held its breath, the Danis stepped forward in peace.

Clarence W. Hall described the Baliem Valley venture in *Reader's Digest.* He observed, "Of all the breeds of brave and gallant men, these are the most heroic—and the most unaware of their heroism."[35]

One of those heroes, Al Lewis, was flying the seaplane on a supply run to the Baliem when it slammed into one of the fog-shrouded peaks surrounding the valley. The Dutch government named that area "Lewis Top" in memory of the pilot.

Completed Agenda

In 1926, Harry M. Shuman had debated whether to let his name stand for election as president of the Alliance. As he waited prayerfully for divine guidance, the portion of a verse came to him: "the Most High is sovereign over the kingdoms of men" (Daniel 4:17).

Through the crushing decade of the Great Depression and the harrowing years of World War II, he held to that promise of the Most High as he carefully guided the Alliance through the folly and fury of mankind at its worst.

The 1954 General Council wanted to elect him again as president, but he refused. At age seventy-six, after twenty-eight years as president, he knew enough was enough. The grateful assembly of delegates unanimously elected him president-emeritus.

In his gentlemanly and unspectacular way, and with the help of the Most High, Dr. Shuman had presided over drastic changes in the Alliance.

When he took office in 1926, an indecisive Alliance stood confused by mixed signals about its character and destiny. When he retired, the future of the Alliance as a missionary church had been basically determined.

When he became president, the Alliance had 391 missionaries and a $677,000 budget. When he stepped down in 1954, a $2.5 million budget supported 720 missionaries.

Thirteen years later, Dr. Shuman would again sense when enough was enough. With the same simplicity and attention to detail that had characterized his administration, he and his wife together would make all the plans necessary for the final promotion—including hymns to be sung and people to participate in the memorial service.

Then, with the quiet confidence of a good administrator whose agenda had been completed, he would await the final adjournment, the date being set for February 8, 1967, by the Most High.

CHAPTER 12

Converging Lines

The more some things change the more they become the same.

1955-1975

Context of the Times

Some decades have a style all their own, a certain character that may be reduced to a word. The thirty years after World War II had that certain quality: the respectable 1950s, the raucous 1960s, the reflective 1970s.

The Respectable Fifties

A nation of decent people found its hero in General Dwight D. Eisenhower. The landslide victories that swept him into the White House seemed to safeguard the respectable values that summed up a decent nation. "It's like America come home," sighed one elated voter.

One of the values President Eisenhower championed was faith in God—whatever His name. "Our government makes no sense," he declared, "unless it is founded on a deeply felt religious faith—and I don't care what it is."

Congress agreed and added the words, "under God," to the Pledge of Allegiance.

Perhaps reflecting their foxhole encounters with God, exservicemen and women made sure religion figured in their postwar life and in the "Baby Boom," that 50 percent increase in the birth rate between 1948 and 1953. Sunday school attendance soared from 24.6 million (1945) to 38.6 million (1956). Church membership took a corresponding jump from 49 percent of the population in 1940 to a peak of 62 percent in 1956.

Interest in church, unfortunately, seemed in some quarters to have more to do with being American than Christian. Sociologist Will Herberg observed, "The typical American has developed a remarkable capacity for being serious about religion without taking religion seriously."

If respectability implies acceptance, pentecostals were joining the in-crowd during the 1950s. Upward mobility and greater prosperity brought many pentecostals into the middle class. Television programs by Oral Roberts beamed the movement into homes across the nation. The Full Gospel Business Men carried the pentecostal message to a whole new network of professional and businessmen.

Other evangelicals improved their image in the fifties. Organizations such as the National Association of Evangelicals joined with electronic media programs like "The Old Fashioned Revival Hour," and found support in quality periodicals like *Christianity Today.* Together they moved evangelicals into the mainstream of American life with a gospel message tuned to the times.

Evangelicalism found its finest expression in Billy Graham, a young evangelist whose striking appearance and articulate abilities did not, by the grace of God, obscure his apparent humility and transparent sincerity.

Through the skillful use of organizational techniques and mass media, he did more to gain a worldwide hearing for the Gospel than any other religious speaker in his or any previous generation. And through his willingness to "fellowship with all born-again believers," he exerted a major influence in uniting Christians in both evangelism and evangelicalism.

The Raucous Sixties

In sharp contrast to the previous decade, little seemed to go right in the sixties. In 1961, a clumsy attempt to overthrow Castro went down in the waters of the Bay of Pigs, while in the same year the Berlin Wall went up in Germany.

The Vietnam War began.

President Kennedy's assassination in 1963, followed by a similar fate for his brother and for Martin Luther King in 1968, left the nation stunned and frightened. Exclaimed John McCormack, the aged Speaker of the House of Representatives, "My God! My God! What are we coming to?"

The "Baby Boom Generation" did not help matters. "By the mid-1960s," wrote historians Thomas Askew and Peter Spellman, "these babies had grown into a virtual army with unchanneled energy; idealistic, restless, searching, unacquainted with suffering, and accustomed to the spoils of a highly materialistic and television-oriented culture."

Neither did religion a la mainline denominations help a troubled nation. The World Council of Churches met in Uppsala, Sweden, and swung from a "faith and order" emphasis to a "life and work" platform that often espoused radical causes.

Social activists in the National Council of Churches seemed to think that setting the nation straight was all up to them—and well they might, as radical theologians proclaimed "God is dead." They did not mean He was nonexistent, just irrelevant—which was just as devastating to a nation stumbling through race riots, political assassinations, an unpopular war and youthful disenchantment.

The Roman Catholic Church sensed a need for change and jumped into the whirlpool by convening the Second Vatican Council in 1962. Out of three years of deliberation came a new sense of freedom with widely divergent interpretations.

Moderate Catholics saw a green light to read the Bible for themselves, celebrate the Mass in their mother tongue and dialog with Protestants—even sing hymns like "A Mighty Fortress Is Our God." Activist priests and nuns in the church thought they found support for a radical new theology of liberation that labeled Christ a revolutionary whose Gospel advocated the violent overthrow of oppressive regimes.

Vatican II's quiet admonition and the Pope's sharp insistence on not tampering with the birth process produced the "disaster of American Catholicism," according to sociologist Andrew Greeley.

In the disastrous years between 1965 and 1975, the number of Catholic seminarians tumbled from 49,000 to 17,000; attendance at weekly Mass dropped from 71 percent of the faithful to 50 percent. The number of nuns declined by one-quarter; defections from the priesthood became commonplace.

The raucous sixties had their good points as well as their bad.

The winds of change forced an irrevocable transformation of the political map. Nationalism rose in revolt against a century of Western colonial domination and wrested vast areas from its control. From 1950 to 1975, Africa alone gave birth to forty-two sovereign states.

Demise of the Western colonial system splashed over Christian missions in the emerging nations like a bucket of ice-cold water—refreshing, but not altogether enjoyed. Missionaries were no longer leaders, but partners and guests. National churches were now free to realize their own potential, with the inevitable risks and responsibilities.

Confusing liberation with maturation—or seizing the opportunity to downplay a missions program emptied of biblical imperative—

mainline denominations lost interest in missions. Between 1958 and 1971, the number of missionaries in America's six largest church bodies declined from 4,548 to 3,160. Conservative groups and faith missions sensed new opportunities and increased their overseas commitments.

Winds of change also swept over the American political and social landscape, carrying away some ugly vestiges of the past. The day of reckoning for segregation began when a few blacks, at great personal risk, sat in the "whites only" section of a bus or restaurant.

The civil rights movement grew to a confrontation in Selma and Birmingham, Alabama. The culmination came in the massive 1963 march on Washington when Martin Luther King delivered his "I Have a Dream" speech.

The Jesus People attempted in their own way to confront organized religion. To the extent that these long-haired young rebels of conscience supported a return to basic New Testament life-style and an openness to the Holy Spirit, they brought a refreshing renewal to local churches.

The Jesus People found a certain renewal already at work in mainline churches. In 1960, an Episcopalian rector confessed to his 2,000-member congregation in Van Nuys, California, that he had spoken in tongues.

He was not alone. The charismatic movement, an interfaith spiritual revival usually accompanied by speaking in tongues, spread through mainline denominations with startling rapidity. Unlike the earlier pentecostal movement, which resulted in new denominations, the charismatic movement remained largely a renewal factor within established churches.

Charismatic renewal swept through the Catholic Church with even greater force. The flashpoint occurred in 1967, when four members of the Duquesne University faculty attended a small Protestant charismatic prayer meeting.

Just seven years later, 35,000 Roman Catholics gathered for the eighth charismatic conference on the campus of Notre Dame University.

The Reflective Seventies

Even in the late 1960s, some observers of the national scene detected a drift away from political and social activism on the part of college students. Young people became more reflective, searching for inner meaning and reality.

Inter-Varsity Christian Fellowship was ready for this trend and drew 12,000 college students to "Urbana 70." Two years later, Campus Crusade mounted "Explo 72" that attracted 75,000 (mostly youth) to Dallas, Texas.

Christians, unfortunately, did not offer the only solution to a nation staggered by the chaotic sixties. The "pursuit of a private heaven" for many people took the form of occult practices—a mixture of astrology, spiritism, witchcraft and drug-induced experiments.

Like carpetbaggers from the East, Indian gurus arrived in numbers with their various schemes to fill seeking minds and to empty fat purses. The saffron-robed disciples of Hare Krishna gyrated in the streets of New York and thirteen-year-old Maharaj Ji flew to the West Coast to add more converts to his reported 3 million followers.

Then came Key 73.

The national evangelistic campaign was supported by 140 denominations and directly or indirectly involved 100 million Christians of every persuasion.

Roman Catholic bishops gave Key 73 their blessing and over forty dioceses participated. This ecumenical aspect kept many evangelical groups from joining the campaign.

Lack of finances proved a blessing in disguise as Key 73 had to shift from the anticipated use of mass media to programs in the local church. Every conceivable form of outreach had its day: home Bible studies and community-wide campaigns, fairground booths and Christian art festivals, telephone surveys and youth rallies.

Scripture distribution campaigns proved the most popular method. By the end of 1973 some 40 million copies of Luke-Acts had been distributed.

Carl F. H. Henry, whose editorial in *Christianity Today* originally sparked the campaign, wrote at the end of 1973: "There is every reason for Key 73 participants to look and labor toward a significant bicentennial climax in 1976."

* * *

The zigzag decades from 1950 through 1970 witnessed a basic change in the mind-set of movers and shakers in Alliance circles of North America: They realized they had a message needed at home as well as overseas.

These key men and women formed part of a larger evangelical coalition that was penetrating the mainstream of national life as an articulate alternative to its secular emptiness.

At the same time, something of a phenomenon was taking place within the Alliance itself.

Generally speaking, the vision, experience and teaching of denominational or independent sending agencies in the West flowed overseas to create national churches of similar appearance and character. The Alliance, however, experienced something of a reverse flow.

Leaders with overseas experience and principles such as evangelism-in-depth, church growth, theological education by extension and key-city projects began to impact on the sending churches in North America. The awareness grew that the Alliance should be producing the same kind of evangelism-minded, self-propagating churches at home that it was planting overseas.

As the lines of thought and activity in North America and overseas began to converge, a consensus also emerged: The Alliance was in fact a missionary church.

DR. HARRY L. TURNER, former missionary and then president of the Alliance since 1954, reflected the reverse flow taking place when he addressed General Council in 1960.

"Rightly or wrongly, the days are past when we are only a fellowship," he told the council delegates. "Today we are a church. We must tell the world what we believe and why we believe it. We are not ashamed of our badge.

"We want our colleges, our pastors, our missionaries, our members to courageously and intelligently say, 'This is it.' Then and only then will our Tomorrow be strong in its God-entrusted foundation....

"We thank God also for all that has been done in the past by the various means employed in the homeland," he continued, "but it is not enough—not nearly enough. The time has come to act in a daring manner."[1]

Hidden behind a meticulous and professorial appearance, Dr. Turner himself possessed a daring manner that flared at times not always to his credit. Although born into wealth and prestige in Campbellford, Ontario, at age nineteen he chose the fast track. Three years of hard living brought him to tuberculosis and the end of the line in 1908.

Turner stopped at the home of an atheist friend—the one friend he had left—on his way to a sanatorium. While there he literally cried out to God for mercy. God not only performed within him the instant miracle of the new birth, but also the lesser miracle of immediate and total deliverance from tuberculosis.

Four years later, while studying for the ministry, he struggled with what he called an "intense hunger to know the Holy Spirit." After reading articles in *The Alliance Weekly* concerning the deeper life, he shut himself in his room for days and sought the Spirit's fullness. God answered the young man's prayer in such a manner that thereafter he referred to the experience as "the high mark of my Christian life."[2]

The Alliance Weekly also pointed him toward Dr. Simpson, who was speaking at a missionary convention in Toronto. Their discussion led to Turner's ministry with the Alliance, first as pastor and then as missionary to Argentina.

After a gap of several years, he returned to service in a variety of activities that included teaching and college administration, the offices of district superintendent and vice-president of the Alliance. Delegates to the 1954 General Council in Chicago elected him as the fifth president of the C&MA, a position he would hold for six years.

Administrative responsibilities often have a way of taking a person, who was effective as a public speaker, and turning him into a pulpit drone. Dr. Turner (he received honorary doctorates from John Brown University and Houghton College in 1955) escaped that affliction, perhaps because he delighted above all in speaking about the Holy Spirit. Students who heard him speak at the Missionary Training Institute in the 1950s not only remembered him as a captivating speaker, but decades later they could still remember what he had said.

The Turner tenure, however, produced more than memorable messages. Some key men joined his administrative team and introduced policies that propelled the Alliance along new ways that would have drawn applause from the founder.

Church Growth Initiative

The summer vacation that Rev. Louis L. King spent in the resort center of Landour, Mussoorie, India, produced perhaps the most profitable work-oriented experience he would ever have on vacation. He and his family had joined about 500 other missionaries who annually spent a month in the cool hills of Landour above the steaming, congested flats of India in the rainy season.

By long-standing agreement, one of the four weeks of rest and recreation at Landour featured a missionary conference with speakers drawn from the vacationers themselves. Dr. Donald McGavran addressed the missionaries in the summer of 1950.

A graduate of Yale Divinity School, affiliated with a liberal denomination, and an educator by profession, the wiry, bespectacled little man with impish eyes nevertheless thought, talked and taught evangelism. Even more startling, he espoused a radical new approach to evangelism.

Rejecting the slow and methodical one-by-one approach almost universally practiced, he spoke of "people movements" and "bridges of God." He urged the missionaries to look for existing cultural and social infrastructures through which the Gospel could travel to win whole families and even communities to God.

To his application of theology and sociology to evangelism, Dr. McGavran added a third element: expectation. He was once asked why some denominations were growing, while others in the same area remained static. "There's no mystery," he explained. "What do [the successful churches] have in common? They all expect to grow, and then are going out and doing it."[3]

"McGavran was beginning a movement, but for many years he would not have a single disciple," noted one writer.[4] He was wrong.

"After listening to McGavran for an hour or so, I became a convert," recalled Louis L. King concerning the Landour conference in 1950. He returned to his ministry with a changed attitude toward evangelism and from then on carefully followed everything that Dr. McGavran did and wrote.

The working relationship between the two men assumed greater importance when King returned home in 1953 and became regional director for Asia and Europe. Aggressive evangelism, including people's movements, and targeted church growth became major emphases he urged upon Alliance missionaries in India, Hong Kong, Taiwan, Japan, Thailand, Indo-China, the Philippines and Indonesia.

In 1953 also, Rev. George Constance, missionary to South America, was appointed as regional director for South America, Africa and the Middle East.

Growth Handicaps

Before dramatic growth could be achieved, however, a stumbling block had to be removed from a number of the society's mission fields: a stifling, pervasive attitude of paternalism in some missionaries—including some of the most successful and influential.

The problem was not new. As early as 1926 a blue-ribbon panel of missionaries and administrators had determined that far too much money from North America went overseas for support of pastors and churches that should be on their own. General Council of 1927 heartily endorsed the three-fold policy of self-support, self-government and self-propagation for national churches issuing from missionary work.

Except for Congo, Vietnam and parts of Indonesia—significantly, the fastest growing Alliance mission fields—the policy of nationalizing the work met with lukewarm enthusiasm or outright rejection for about twenty-five years. Many missionaries sincerely believed that unless they kept tight control of the national church, it was sure to go wrong.

This brand of missionary colonialism drew fire from a committee formed by the Board of Managers in 1952 to study the progress of indigenous policy in the overseas work. Noting that the number of self-supporting workers overseas had actually decreased during the previous fifteen years, the committee report had some stinging observations to make concerning some then-current missionary methods.

It was common practice, the committee observed, "to go into an area with plenty of money, erect church buildings, build a Bible school, employ workers who would carry out explicitly all the instructions of the foreign missionary and through his efforts and through the efforts of his employees evangelize, get converts, bring them together, build more churches, and get more workers to do the job. This is the quickest and easiest way for the missionary to carry on his program in any field."[5]

The method did produce results. By 1952 the overseas work of the Alliance claimed 973 organized churches and 89,828 members led by 2,410 workers.

The committee report nevertheless pointed out that such growth would continue only on two conditions: if more and more money came from North America, and if missionaries continued to work in the country. The winds of change and rising tides of nationalism made the future of both conditions very tenuous.

When the report came to the attention of General Council in 1955, the delegates acted decisively. They ordered that steps be taken immediately to bring all Alliance mission fields into compliance with the indigenous church policy.

Armed with action by both General Council and Board of Managers, the foreign department reorganized, increased its administrative staff to five persons and moved to implement the indigenous policy under its new foreign secretary, Louis L. King.

"Our policy is to be one of persuasion, not coercion," ruled the incoming missionary leader. That meant changing the mind-set of both missionaries and national church leaders.

Persuading some missionaries that the indigenous policy was right and necessary would not be easy. A missionary by definition believes deeply and tenaciously in the rightness of his or her cause.

"Not a few spiritual crises occurred," noted the foreign secretary. "Some thought and even propagated that compliance with the council-mandated requirement was a terrible setback—a certain wrecking of the work that had been built up at such sacrifice of human life and costly endeavor. Some argued that, because of political upsets and triple-digit inflation, the time was not propitious for eliminating pastors' subsidies. Attempts were made to scuttle the policy."[6]

The foreign department proceeded on its intended course by organizing sessions for furloughing missionaries several days before General Council. The precouncil conferences presented the case for indigenous principles and backed them with firsthand experiences of missionaries who witnessed some of the amazing results when overseas churches were set free of mission control to grow in the Spirit.

Foreign secretary King and his associates also had to promote nationalization among overseas church leaders, many of whom were deeply aware of their lack of training and resources.

The first test of implementing the indigenous policy came in 1955, while King was still regional director. The initial Southeast Asia Conference brought together seventeen national church leaders and twelve mission chairmen from ten countries. The nine-day conference in Bangkok, Thailand, focused on only one topic: the church—self-supporting, self-governing, self-propagating. Within a year, 251 overseas churches had voluntarily gone off mission subsidy.

The second Asia Conference moved to Saigon in 1958. By this time, national leaders had had time to test the indigenous church policy and found that it worked. They displayed more frankness and freedom in speaking. Outstanding church leaders like Le-Van Thai of Vietnam, R. P. Chavan of India, Philip Teng of Hong Kong and Florentino de Jesus, Sr., of the Philippines spoke with confidence of their growing churches.

When one Asian delegate spoke of seeking more foreign funds, another participant rebuked him indirectly by reflecting on a passage in the Book of Acts. "Why was the Apostle Paul forbidden to go into Bithynia and Asia?" he asked. His conclusion: "If Paul had been allowed to come to the Far East, maybe Christianity would have died there. [God] knows our Oriental impediments. We are quite slow...a bit self-centered...supernationalists. I'm afraid Christianity would have been buried in the Orient in oblivion."[7]

Regional conferences in Africa and South America reported similar results of growth once the church assumed responsibility for its own growth and development. By 1960 the foreign secretary could report a remarkable turnaround in the overseas work: "All overseas pastors everywhere were entirely dependent upon national sources for financial support."[8]

Did the new indigenous policy hinder growth of the national church? From 1955 to 1960, organized and unorganized churches grew from 1,051 to 1,426; church membership jumped from 49,000 to 80,000. Self-supporting churches and groups increased from 562 to 1,219.[9]

New Homeland Mind-set

While Louis King was shaking up the foreign department and giving its far-flung ministries a new sense of direction and impetus, Leslie W. Pippert took over as home secretary and began pursuing similar energetic policies in North America.

He arrived at the top post in the home department after serving five pastorates in the Midwest from 1934 to 1952, followed by superintending the Northwest District for seven years. Promotion to the head office at "260" in New York City meant nothing to him unless he could achieve some sorely needed improvements, he told a friend.

"He could never be satisfied simply to be the administrator of an inward-looking group of people whose interest in missions was sometimes an excuse for their lack of soulwinning in the local church," wrote Dr. Bernard S. King, who knew him well.[10]

The article continued, "If some would say that he worked too hard or drove himself too fast or was too impatient, no matter. Leslie Pippert was persuaded that God had given him certain responsibilities, and he was uncompromisingly faithful to his trust."[11]

Those "certain responsibilities" could be summed up as Evangelism and Extension—both spelled with a big "E". He built on the ground-breaking work of his predecessor, H. E. Nelson, by directing all the activities of the home department toward visible and viable results in the form of thriving churches.

In his initial report to General Council he included, for the first time ever, statistics on recorded baptisms in North American churches—thereby serving notice on homeland pastors that numbers did indeed count, and he would be watching them. Several years later, he enlarged on the importance of preserving gains when he voiced concern that the number of professed conversions exceeded recorded baptisms by a ratio of three to one.[12]

Pippert considered evangelism a key element of every pastoral ministry worthy of the name, but he held pastors equally responsible to disciple converts until they became active members of the church.

This insistence on commitment after conversion must have rattled church windows across the country, because many Alliance pastors perpetuated a traditional nonchalance toward membership. Some churches in the 1960s still had no active membership list. One report estimated that the Alliance had half again as many active adherents as members.[13]

The home secretary did not sit in his office and fire off directives to the constituency. He took his campaign on the road to the 1,555 official workers and 1,174 churches in 1960.

Six years before the trend-setting Berlin Congress on Evangelism in 1966, Pippert had already crisscrossed the continent to hold evangelism conferences for Alliance workers. Two years before the congress in Berlin he had seen to it that every district conducted its own congress on evangelism. Even before attending that Berlin convocation, he had scheduled a similar Evangelism Congress in Atlanta for Alliance pastors, evangelists and district officers in North America.

With relentless drive, Bernard King noted, the home secretary "succeeded in getting a responsible element of homeland leaders to face the need of evangelism, to meet the scriptural imperative, and to convey to their districts and churches a sense of spiritual direction."[14]

Alliance Men

Home secretary Pippert's tenure marked the beginning of organized laymen participation in church growth.

The concept of Alliance Men took place in a setting many laymen could relate to: a fishing trip. Three men were relaxing in a lakefront cabin between fishing forays on Lake Erie in 1951. Vern and Irvin Sir Louis, of Akron, Ohio, and Frank Meyer of Hamburg, New York, found their small talk about fishing turn to serious discussion about fishing for men.

They reached a conclusion: "Surely the men of every church should be willing to take a more active role in the witnessing outreach of the local congregation. Then they pledged together to be willing to follow the Lord's leading in making their convictions known to other laymen."[15]

One year later, the Board of Managers approved the proposal for an organization known as Laymen's Crusade for Missionary Action, and on July 29, 1953, the forerunner of Alliance Men was organized as a nonprofit New York organization. John Wright, of Detroit, became the first president.

In the years that followed, Alliance Men supported their local churches in many ways, such as house-to-house visitation, extension projects, special Heritage Week activities and stewardship seminars.

A disaster struck in 1976 and brought Alliance Men closer together as a national organization. A killer earthquake in Guatemala claimed more than 20,000 lives and leveled hundreds of buildings. Two-thirds of the thirty-two Alliance churches in Guatemala were either totally destroyed or heavily damaged.

The disaster prompted the start of another Alliance Men activity that involved members of different churches in the same project. They became known as construction missionaries.

Walter Meloon, a small-craft manufacturer and president of the laymen's organization, called on men with building skills to help the Guatemalan Alliance community recover from the earthquake. The response was immediate and encouraging. Volunteer work crews, each numbering thirty to forty men, were soon at work in the Central American nation on a rotation schedule every two weeks.

From that time forward, construction teams would become an important aspect of laymen activities. By 1985, Alliance Men groups would be meeting in 645 locations and claim a membership of 8,600 men.

Wide-angle Presidency

When Dr. Turner retired as president in 1960, General Council elected Dr. Nathan Bailey, the vice-president, to succeed him.

The choice suited Alliance churches on both sides of the northern border. Born and reared in Wilmington, Delaware, the young Nyack graduate, class of '31, served his first pastorate in Matoon, Illinois, and then spent the next twenty-six years of ministry in Canada as pastor and then district superintendent.

Dr. Bailey's extended stay in Canada foreshadowed a wide range of interests and activities during his six terms in office. He would travel literally millions of miles to both domestic and foreign destinations to keep in touch with the expanding Alliance world.

He certainly traveled more extensively than any of the five previous presidents of the Alliance. He probably also participated in more affiliated organizations than his predecessors. Over the next eighteen years, Dr. Bailey would play a leading role in the National Association of Evangelicals, the World Relief Commission and the Alliance World Fellowship.

Although interested in every operation of the society, he ranked education and training of Alliance workers a top priority. Comments to General Council reflect this concern: "God expects us to understand the meaning of our generation, the meaning of our age, and like David to serve our own generation by the will of God.

"Many people are an anachronism," he continued. "They are out of joint with their times. They belong either to the past or to the future—more often they should have lived a hundred years ago.

"We cannot hold back the changes which come in human relationships and the varying cultures of nations from generation to generation. We must speak to our times or lose our opportunities for contact and witness by our very inability to minister."[16]

Alliance higher education received a big boost in 1960 with the election of the first full-time education secretary, Dr. Gilbert Johnson, a faculty member at Nyack. One of the first major problems facing him was the exodus of Alliance young people to non-Alliance schools and then into various denominations.[17]

The year 1960 provided another milestone in Alliance higher education. Jaffray School of Missions opened on the Nyack campus under the sponsorship of the foreign department. The new school, reflecting Dr. McGavran's church growth principles, offered a curriculum that integrated theology, missiology and sociology on a seminary level.

Jaffray's limited attraction to missionaries and overseas candidates kept enrollment low at first. Then heightened expectations of congregations in North America prompted an enlarging of the school's curriculum and in 1974 it became the Alliance School of Theology and Missions, forerunner of the Alliance Theological Seminary.

Meanwhile, General Council of 1967 authorized the college in Canada to develop its own graduate school in keeping with the Canadian educational system. Canadian Theological Seminary began operations in 1970 at Regina, Saskatchewan.

The colleges as well updated and expanded their curricula to keep pace with the changing demands of higher education.

Nyack College and Simpson College became designated as liberal arts colleges, while St. Paul Bible College, Toccoa Falls College (associated), and Canadian Bible College remained Bible colleges, but added a broader base of general education.

LeTourneau College, though completely independent, provided another source of higher education for many Alliance youth.

"Conscience of Evangelicalism"

While the Alliance worked hard at building up some institutions, God saw fit to close another—a one-man institution who left the whole church wiser and richer.

Aiden Wilson Tozer never traversed an ocean or visited a mission field. He never attended college—not even high school. Yet when Dr. Tozer collapsed on Sunday morning of May 12, 1963, and died early Monday, the comment heard most frequently in tribute resembled that of a leading minister in Toronto: "He belongs to all of us. He belongs to the whole church of God."[18]

A. W. Tozer began life as the third of six children in the home of a working man in western Pennsylvania. He himself left school after the eighth grade to take a blue-collar job with Goodyear Rubber in Akron, Ohio. When God converted Tozer in 1915, shortly before his eighteenth birthday, He also quickened his mind and made him an avid, lifelong student.

Evangelist Leonard Ravenhill said, "Men like him are not college bred but Spirit taught."[19]

"During his early Christian years," recalled Rev. Raymond McAfee, "he read widely in everything and some of his early mentors feared for him. But he pressed on and surpassed them all. He often likened himself to a hungry bee gathering nectar from any flower."[20]

His addiction to words and ideas led naturally to his honing of writing skills until his pen became a ready servant of God—ready to slash like Toledo steel or caress like a downy feather.

Dr. Tozer—he "earned" honorary doctorates from Wheaton College and Houghton College—wrote as he preached, and preached as he wrote. The two ministries were tightly interwoven. His longest ministry in a church ran from 1928 to 1957 in the Southside Alliance Church in Chicago. He became editor of *The Alliance Weekly* in 1950 and continued in that post until his death.

His nasal-tinged voice would have won no elocution contest, but audiences quickly forgot that as they were trapped, overpowered and carried along by the force and clarity of his thoughts. Listening to Tozer was something like gripping a bare high-voltage wire.

Although the pulpit needs of one parish for twenty-nine years forced him to prepare new sermons constantly, he had his favorite "traveling sermons." During one summer convention he told Louis King he had preached one sermon on Proverbs 16:31 thirty-one times. "The next evening he again preached it with enormous effect upon the large audience," Dr. King recalled.[21]

What Dr. Tozer practiced, he also recommended to others. "When he invited me at age twenty-three to fill his pulpit on a Sunday," Dr. King continued, "he requested that I not preach a new sermon, but to repeat one I knew had been blessed of God."[22]

Dr. Tozer's writings carried his message to an audience far wider than his voice could ever reach. His editorials and articles in *The Alliance Weekly* quickly doubled the magazine's circulation and created an international readership. *Christianity Today, His,* and many other publications sought his articles.

Editor H. F. Stevenson wrote from London, "We knew him only by report and through his writings, but by these he made a profound impact. His survey of the contemporary scene was as relevant to Britain as to his own country, so that his books and articles were read avidly here also."[23]

Dr. Tozer personally authored eight books and edited another on devotional verse. The books, like his messages and articles, evidenced the Spirit's gift of perception, a piercing analysis of what went on in the world, and what God thought about it. Dr. Warren Wiersbe called him "the conscience of evangelicalism."

In that unsought-for role, Dr. Tozer often had to take evangelical Christianity to the woodshed, but he did so because of a deep and abiding love for the church. Viewing the proliferation of parachurch agencies—an estimated 130 in the United States by 1960—he spoke up in defense of the church.

"The highest expression of the will of God in this age is the Church which He purchased with His own blood," he wrote in an editorial. "Any religious activity to be scripturally valid must be part of the Church.

"Let it be clearly stated that there can be no service acceptable to God in this age that does not center in and spring out of the Church. Bible schools, tract societies, Christian businessmen's committees, seminaries, and the many independent groups working at one or another phase of religion need to check themselves reverently and courageously, for they have no true significance outside of or apart from the Church."[24]

Though Dr. Tozer drew praise that made him seem bigger than life, he was thoroughly human. His tongue and pen could sometimes be sharp beyond redemptive value, yet his apology could be as quick as his wit when he offended unnecessarily.

What made him a man like his fellows was an incessant sense of humor. "This was given Dr. Tozer in abundant supply," recalled his close associate and friend McAfee, "and he had to bodily strangle about 95 percent of it or he would be undone by its uprising.

"I could always tell by the content of humor in his preaching how tired he was. If the audience was convulsed by his discourse, he was tired: his guard was down and humor sneaked through.... But it must be carefully noted that he was never a clown, nor did he ever allow sacred things to become involved in his pleasantries."[25]

McAfee, like others who knew Dr. Tozer well, acknowledged "he was far from flawless, but it was not hard to look past his flaws when you knew he was a worshiper—one whose heart was fixed on God continually, who wanted to know Him more than he wanted any other thing in life. His work and ministry, his preaching and writing, his personal and public life all revolved around five words, 'I fell down to worship' " (Revelation 22:8).[26]

Following this very human prophet's heavenward ascent, some people kept waiting to see on whom his mantle would fall. Anyone with the slightest flair for expression would be foolishly hailed by his admirers, "We've found another Tozer!"

Evangelist Ravenhill was closer to the truth, "I fear we shall not see another Tozer."[27]

Zaire: Church Under Trial

The Alliance achieved total nationalization of its overseas churches in a remarkably short time of five years—just in time to meet many newly emerging nations with an indigenous national church already autonomous.

The decade of the sixties marked the beginning of social and political upheavals that would rage for years in the group of developing nations known as the Third World. Local problems, regional nationalism and Big Power politics combined to subject several Alliance churches to the worst trial by fire they had yet known.

The Alliance church in Zaire, formerly the Belgian Congo, led off in 1960 with internal conflicts that for a time split the dynamic church of 39,000 baptized members.

The apparent problem centered in the church's 10,000-student parochial school system operated by the mission and financed jointly by mission subsidies and student tuition. During the colonial era, the mission had steadfastly refused to bring the schools into the government's subsidy program because of its suspicions toward the Roman Catholic-controlled Ministry of Education.

After independence in 1960, certain clergy and lay leaders demanded immediate government support for their schools. Flooded with problems of its own, the new regime refused, claiming the schools were not certified for subsidy.

The angry leaders then turned on the mission, holding it responsible for the lack of subsidy and demanding that the mission pay the total bill to keep the schools open. When mission leaders responded that they could not assume such a staggering financial burden, the stage was set for years of trouble.

The school issue, however, was only a surface issue that masked a deeper problem. A group of politically ambitious young men—many of whom were not members—looked upon the Alliance church's tens of thousands of members and followers as a power base to launch them into political orbit.

The clique tried through various ways to take over leadership of the church. Many church leaders, led by Rev. Kuvuna ku Konde Mwela, opposed their efforts. Years after the schools were duly recognized and subsidized by the government, this power struggle continued. The church was split, people beaten and recriminations generously traded by opposing parties.

Mediation in 1968 by church leaders from other areas of Zaire and a moving of God's Spirit in reconciliation brought the badly splintered church together again in a miraculous fashion.

One critical point of agreement gave some meaning and value

to the years of suffering. The reunited church leaders unanimously agreed that the church was a spiritual body, not a political party; as such, it must be led by those whom God called and ordained, and in whom God's Spirit ruled.

Once that was settled, the Zaire church resumed its winning ways, more than doubling within a decade.

Indonesia: Church Under Threat

A different kind of problem had been brewing in Indonesia since 1960. The Communist Party and its auxiliary Indonesian Peasant Brigade had grown rapidly under President Sukarno's "guided democracy." Within five years, the Communists gained virtual control of many villages and districts. The order went out from headquarters that on October first they would seize control of the country.

The armed cadres failed in their first strike to liquidate all the opposition generals. The army rallied, put down the uprising and then, reinforced by an enraged Muslim population, embarked on a rampage of slaughter that left more than 100,000 Communists dead.

Field orders seized from the rebels revealed that during the first ten days of the coup all religious leaders, Christian and Muslim, were to be eliminated. At that time the Alliance missionary staff totaled 115 men and women. The Indonesian Alliance Church of 68,000 baptized members was led by thousands of ordained and lay church leaders. The Alliance was only one of many missions and churches in Indonesia on October 1, 1960.

Had not God overruled, the planned annihilation would have been one of the worst disasters in church history.

Instead, the Indonesian people, stunned by the treachery of the Communists and horrified by the savagery of the Muslims, turned to the Christians' God by the tens of thousands. Thus the wrath of man was made to praise the Lord.

Guinea: Church Under Pressure

In Guinea, West Africa, the political winds of change blew over Catholic and Protestant missions with hurricane force. A government decree dated May 1, 1967, ordered all foreign missions out of the country within thirty days.

President Sekou Toure's expressed intention was to speed up africanization of the churches in his country. His real purpose was apparently to clip the wings of the Roman Catholic Church, which played an active political role in Guinea but took orders from Rome.

To be seen as impartial, the government applied the eviction notice to all foreign missions.

The government's stated intention worked in favor of the Alliance, though this development was certainly not foreseen by the Marxist-Islamic regime.

The national church president and mission chairman met with President Sekou Toure to inform him that the Evangelical Protestant (Alliance) Church had been africanized and recognized as such by the government three years before its own africanization campaign. Since the church already exercised full autonomy, the delegation suggested that Alliance missionaries could be permitted to remain and work in the country.

The government relented to a degree. Twenty-six of the forty Alliance missionaries received permission to remain and work in three designated areas. For everyone else—Catholic or Protestant—the deadline remained in force.

If the religious community was shocked by the expulsion order, the regime was in for a suprise of its own. The African Christians needed several years to adjust to the new reality, then their churches began to grow at an unprecedented rate.

The Alliance church in Guinea reported 45 organized churches, another 99 unorganized congegations and 1,473 baptized members in 1965. Within fifteen years the number of churches would triple, unorganized groups quadruple and baptized membership increase to nearly 4,000.

Vietnam: Church Under the Gun

Until 1975, the oldest living Vietnamese could not remember a time when his country was free of foreign domination. Younger Vietnamese could not remember a time when they were not at war.

For nearly a century before World War II, the French governed Vietnam. Then came the Japanese occupation forces until 1945. The French tried to return the country to colonial status after the war and met with armed resistence. The thirty-year war began.

President Eisenhower sent several hundred military "advisers" to democratic South Vietnam in 1960 to help turn back aggression from Communist North Vietnam and its surrogates in the South, the Viet Cong. Although American involvement eventually grew to a half-million soldiers, South Vietnam collapsed fifteen years later.

The Evangelical (Alliance) Church of Vietnam, the country's largest Protestant denomination, experienced growth and blessing during the decades of war. By 1961, the church counted 319 congregations with over 32,800 members. The Vietnam mission had 134 missionaries, making it the largest maintained by North American Alliance churches.

Church and mission leaders had hoped that their long record of humane ministry and nonpolitical involvement would win them neutrality in the conflict between North and South. The events of May 30, 1962, shattered that hope.

The mission-operated leprosarium near Banmethuot treated approximately 1,800 patients on a regular basis. A modern hospital, nursery for children, dormitories for men and women patients, six quarantined villages and other facilities had helped many thousands of lepers since the center opened in 1949. The staff assumed that the Viet Cong would not risk the wrath of local tribespeople by attacking a medical center that had generated enormous goodwill. They were wrong.

The Viet Cong swept through the hospital complex, carrying away at gunpoint Dr. Ardel Vietti, a medical doctor; Archie Mitchell, the hospital director; and Dan Gerber, a Mennonite staff worker. The three were never again heard from, their fate locked in the jungle fastness.

Banmethuot returned to the news in January, 1968, during the Tet offensive. The Viet Cong overran the mission, scattering grenades and gunfire in every direction. Missionaries Carolyn Griswold, Ruth Wilting, N. Robert Ziemer, Ruth and C. Edward Thompson died in the attack or shortly after. Leon Griswold, a volunteer layman and father of Carolyn, also perished in the raid.

Alliance missionary Betty Olsen and Wycliffe translator Hank Blood met with a worse fate. Together with an American development worker, Mike Benge, they were taken prisoner and hustled off into the jungles. Betty and Hank did not make it. Abused, humiliated and driven to exhaustion, they died along the trail.

Only Mike Benge survived the ordeal of forced marches and eventually arrived at the notorious "Hanoi Hilton" prison camp in North Vietnam. Released five years later, he told how Betty and Hank had refused to hate their captors and died praying for them. Their faith made a believer out of Benge, the tough ex-Marine and survivor of the Hanoi Hilton.

Vietnamese and tribes Christians suffered unnumbered heavy losses in the Tet offensive and throughout the long war, but the church kept growing. By 1975, the church included 510 organized churches and about 54,000 baptized believers. Two hundred seventy-six students were studying at the Nhatrang Bible Institute and another 900 followed courses in the theological education by extension series. Outstanding men like church president Doan Van Mieng gave the church wise and firm leadership.

When collapse of the South Vietnamese government became certain in early 1975, over 130 Alliance missionaries in Vietnam, Cambodia and Laos were either reassigned to other Alliance fields or brought home on early furlough. A few missionaries remained in Saigon until the last possible moment to help arrange escape for church leaders who would be marked for punishment by the victorious invaders. Church president Doan Van Mieng and about 500 pastors chose to remain and face with their people whatever lay ahead.

The uncertainty of that future ended within a year of the war: Communist officials ordered pastors to get jobs and help "rebuild the country"...confiscated the Nhatrang campus and ended all formal theological training...scheduled compulsory activities to compete with Sunday services...consigned key Christians to re-education camps.

The shooting stopped in Indo-China, but for Christians in Vietnam, Laos and Cambodia, the war continued. Theirs was to be a future under the authority of relentless antagonists who won a military war after thirty years, and were equally determined to win the ideological one—even if it took another generation.

Christians in Indo-China were no strangers to fear, but one of their concerns had nothing to do with a hostile regime: the possibility of being forgotten by fellow believers in free countries. In the bits of information trickling out of Vietnam and its neighbor states appeared a recurrent plea: "Pray for us."

Integrated Growth

While Alliance missions registered gains and losses through the turbulent years of 1960 to 1975, the North American work steadily increased. Home secretary Pippert maintained a steady pressure on the churches to grow and multiply. The number of churches during the 1960s increased from 1,174 to 1,401, while inclusive membership rose from 117,179 to 155,537.

Dr. McGavran's Institute of Church Growth settled permanently at Fuller School of World Mission and began to impact on churches in North America with lessons and experiences gathered from around the world. The school promoted a philosophy of mission free from the artificial divisions of "home" and "foreign" work.

Dr. McGavran and his associate, Dr. Peter Wagner, insisted that any church worthy of the name must participate in "an enterprise devoted to proclaiming the Good News of Jesus Christ, and to persuading men to become His disciples and dependable members of His church."[28]

This dual emphasis summed up Pippert's own philosophy of

St. Paul (Minn.) Bible and Training Home, birthplace of St. Paul Bible College

Above, second graduating class of St. Paul Bible Institute, 1917. Harold Freligh, far left, became faculty member in 1919. *Right,* Rev. and Mrs. J. D. Williams started St. Paul Bible College in their home. He was president, 1916-1925.

Mrs. Williams and her Greek class, 1924. She was a very popular Bible teacher.

The original administration and classroom building of Simpson Bible Institute, when the campus was still in Seattle, Washington

W. W. Newberry founded Simpson Bible Institute in 1921 in Seattle

Dr. and Mrs. R. A. Forrest founded Toccoa Falls Bible Institute in 1906 and received from the Alliance through Dr. Simpson $1,000 to launch the school.

Dormitory tents for students were "winterized"

Beautiful Haddock Inn contained dining room, chapel, lecture hall and student living quarters

Some Alliance-supported Swedish missionaries and American Board (Baptist) missiona

A close-up of the convoy pictured above

Missionaries, including Harry Taylor (see arrow), interned in Bilibio Prison, Manila, during World War II, receive their first mail from home

aped the 1900 Boxer Rebellion in China by convoy through Mongolia into Siberia

A bombed-out mission residence at Banmethuot forms the background for American soldiers pausing to honor martyred missionaries at the bunker site where they died

Dr. R. A. Jaffray with Chinese associate,
Leland Wong, circa 1936

Mabel Francis received key to the city of Matsuyama from the mayor

The 1975 inaugural meeting of the Alliance World Fellowship in Nyack, New York

PRESIDENTS OF THE CHRISTIAN AND MISSIONARY ALLIANCE

Albert B. Simpson
1887-1917

Paul Rader
1917-1924

Frederic F. Senft
1924-1925

Harry M. Shuman
1925-1954

Harry L. Turner
1954-1960

Nathan Bailey
1960-1978

Louis L. King
1978-1987

Melvin P. Sylvester
First president, Canadian C&MA, 1980

linking evangelism to church growth as a growing and dynamic force in the Alliance churches of North America.

The home department received indispensable support from the finance department. While spiritual vision and solid planning are prime requisites for church growth, adequate funding must follow close behind.

Dr. Bernard S. King, treasurer from 1952 to 1976, was especially gifted in financial planning and management. With a banker's mind and a pastor's heart—he had followed Pippert as pastor of the Alliance church in Lyle, Minnesota—he established the Church Extension Loan Fund in 1960. Within eight years the fund's assets grew to $5 million as it helped churches and related institutions finance their building programs.

As the conviction spread in Alliance circles that evangelism and church growth should be as much a priority at home as overseas, some churches discovered different ways that could be achieved.

Vern Sir Louis, an insurance broker in Akron, Ohio, found one way to integrate witness and fellowship. He conducted low-key, layman-oriented home Bible studies with an evangelistic message. As people were converted and friends contacted friends, the Bible studies grew in size and multiplied. At one overcrowded meeting in Stow, near Akron, people asked, "Why can't we have a church in this area to train our children in God's Word?"

A church was born in those home Bible studies and grew to become a large church and center for training people interested in evangelism. Over six thousand people attended seminars at Stow during the sixties and then returned to their churches inspired to start their own home Bible study groups.

The Circle Drive Alliance Church in Saskatoon, Saskatchewan, discovered another way to reach out and grow: revival.

Lou and Ralph Sutera, members of the First Alliance Church in Mansfield, Ohio, were conducting a series of meetings in the Ebenezer Baptist Church of Saskatoon in October of 1971, when revival came. Attendance outgrew the church and moved to the Alliance church by invitation of the pastor, Rev. Walter Boldt.

As Alliance people and others joined in the spiritual renewal, the services had to move again, this time to a 1,800-seat auditorium. Repentance, confession and a deep cleansing by the Holy Spirit began to characterize meetings that spread through midwestern Canada, parts of Ohio and Michigan, and even overseas to the Netherlands.

The Circle Drive Alliance Church had been carrying a $173,000 debt on an inadequate church building that could only seat 700 people. The revival gave them a new set of goals. Under Pastor

Boldt's leadership, they cleared the debt and built a new $3.1 million complex on twenty acres adjacent to a major highway.

In one decade, the church registered 1,295 conversions and saw 50 young people go into training for ministry. Giving rose from $370,000 to over $1.8 million. Missionary giving increased from $65,000 to $175,000.

Alliance Key 73

The culminating big push by home secretary Pippert came in 1973. A national-level campaign of evangelism called Key 73 mobilized many denominations in a yearlong effort of "proclaiming the Gospel and converting souls."[29] The ecumenical character of Key 73 kept the Alliance from participating in the national campaign, but the concept and timeliness were too good to ignore. The solution: Alliance Key 73.

Pippert enlisted the help of Rev. and Mrs. Willys Braun, who had successfully coordinated large evangelistic campaigns in Zaire. Although preparation began in 1971, and the Brauns produced reams of material and seemed tireless in promoting the campaign, it was still gaining acceptance and picking up speed by 1973, when it should have been in full operation.

Key 73 experienced a similar lag as some of the largest denominations, like the Southern Baptist Convention, did not actually get into full gear until 1974. Assemblies of God president Dr. Thomas Zimmerman, executive committee chairman of the denominational effort, could have been speaking for the Alliance when he concluded, "Key 73 was just the churches getting organized to begin their work."[30]

Pippert did not live to see the conclusion of Alliance Key 73. The hard-driving home secretary was felled by a heart attack midway through the year and midstream in his ministry. Many of the tributes praised his leadership in bringing an emphasis on evangelism and church growth to the Alliance. But the most telling tribute would come later, when General Council of 1978 set a startling goal of doubling in size within ten years.

As one of that host of heavenly onlookers, did Leslie W. Pippert give another of his tight smiles and a curt nod of approval?

Status Change

Concern for evangelism and care of the believers would have been familiar emphases to Dr. Simpson, had he returned to survey the Alliance of 1970, but its organization would have been unrecognizable. The movement he had founded was now a denomination in everything but name.

Change from a simple to a complex structure seems an inevitable part of growth, as do the stresses generated by an organization that does not keep up with changes produced by growth.

Like a family growing up in a house no longer suited to its needs, the five departments at the international headquarters on Forty-fourth Street in New York were getting in one another's way. The home department acted like a church and the foreign department like a mission, the finance department tried to keep both happy, while *The Alliance Witness* and the executive departments attempted to get along with everyone.

The time had come for a move to larger quarters and, more importantly, for a reorganization from top to bottom, from the board room to the local church.

The move toward a more formal church structure had already been given impetus by a doctrinal statement approved in 1965. Rather than a formulation of new theological positions hammered out by intense debate and exhaustive research, it represented a summary of beliefs long held.

The 1928 doctrinal statement, an important document used in preparation of the later statement, was used in all Alliance Bible schools and had to be signed annually by each of the teaching staffs. Framers of the statement simply took the nine articles of the Christian Fundamentals Association and attached to them the distinctive Alliance testimony embodied in the Fourfold Gospel.

The 1965 statement of faith enlarged the scope and significance of earlier doctrinal formulas by including Alliance churches and members as well. It became the first such statement formally adopted by General Council and facilitated the reorganization to take place in the 1970s.

The 1970 General Council appointed a reorganization committee to study every aspect of Alliance operation theologically, philosophically and practically. The committee was then to draft a balanced plan for the division of responsibilities among the departments.

After years of study and debate in committee sessions and on council floor, the committee put together a workable plan. It redefined and regrouped primary activities and support functions. The plan also clearly defined executive roles and provided necessary checks and balances.

The 1974 General Council's approval of the reorganized structure gave the Alliance a new and official identity. *Eternity* magazine noted the significance of the action under the title, "C&M Alliance Converts to Denominational Status."

The report read in part, "After 87 years as a para-denominational organization dedicated to missionary activity, The Christian and Missionary Alliance has officially recognized what many people have known for years: the Alliance is a denomination. By a vote of 834 to 98, delegates to the Alliance's General Council meeting in Atlanta (Georgia) adopted a new constitution and by-laws making the Alliance a denomination."[31]

That same year the Alliance headquarters, which from the beginning had been located near Times Square in New York City, moved up the Hudson River to Nyack.

Converging Lines

Like a parent learning from the child, the Alliance in North America looked at overseas churches planted by its own missionary efforts and saw what should be done at home. The Alliance profited from an unusual reverse flow of lessons and examples from the mission field to the sending churches.

But the transformation might not have come to pass, had not the Spirit of evangelism worked through men such as H. E. Nelson, Leslie Pippert, and those who followed them in the Division of Church Ministries.

Pastors and churches began to realize their work was very much like that of the missionaries they sent abroad: winning people to Jesus Christ and establishing them in a local church.

The problem with converging lines, however, is the possibility of obscuring certain distinctive strands that must always be kept in view.

Could the Alliance make the adjustment from a movement to a denomination without losing its distinctive missionary character?

CHAPTER 13

This One Thing

Some organizations, like people, can only do one thing at a time, and do it well.

1975-1987

Context of the Times

History of the last quarter of the twentieth century will record that the most intensely religious among Americans also became the most vocal and active in public issues.

After years of self-imposed exile from the mainstream of national life following the Prohibition fiasco and the Scopes trial, Bible-believing Christians dramatically reentered the forum of public debate and corridors of political power.

People who took religion seriously could no longer be taken lightly. A Gallup poll in 1976 indicated that 34 percent of all adult Americans claimed a "born-again" experience—some 50 million people. Four out of ten believed that "the Bible is to be taken literally word for word."

More than any other single event or idea, the Supreme Court's ruling on abortion in 1973 (*Rowe v. Wade*) aroused religious conservatives like a jostled hornet's nest. The court's decision overrode the laws of all fifty states by permitting abortion on demand.

What stirred many hitherto passive God-fearing citizens was the Supreme Court's deliberate and total exclusion of Judeo-Christian values in its ruling. Personal preference and even convenience were judged more important than sacredness of life.

Catholics and Protestants began to realize that a moral consensus no longer united the nation. Francis Schaeffer was right: America was beyond the post-Christian era of indifference—its official institutions were openly attacking basic Christian values.

Rev. Jerry Falwell's Moral Majority was only one of numerous religio-political action groups determined to return morality to government and society.

"The New Right" coalition of conservative religious citizens played an important role in the election of both Jimmy Carter and Ronald Reagan to the presidency. They mounted an assault on "secular humanism" that had displaced even noncommital references to Christianity in school textbooks. They picketed and boycotted stores selling pornographic literature until by 1986 more than 20,000 stores stopped carrying products like *Playboy* magazine.

The "Electric Church" played a key role in the resurgence of evangelical visibility. Robert Schuller's "Hour of Power" drew an audience of 2,667,000 in 1983. Jimmy Swaggart, Oral Roberts and Rex Humbard were not far behind.

The entire religious TV audience in the 1980s was variously rated between 10 and 22 million viewers. Billy Graham's special telecasts were believed to reach up to half the nation.

The alliance of these and other programmers in the National Religious Broadcasters association made it a religious and political factor to be considered. Presidents, politicians and would-be contenders treated the association with care, if not respect.

Mainline denominations accused "televangelists" of stealing their members and income. Respected researchers George Gerbner and George Gallup did not still the "bucks and bodies" debate, even though their extensive study indicated that "Pray TV" tended to make viewers attend church more often and put more money in the offering plate.

Whatever the problem, mainline denominations were on the downward trend. Of the ten largest Protestant bodies in the United States during the seventies, seven suffered an average loss of one member in ten. All the declining denominations emphasized social action, almost to the total exclusion of evangelism.

Canadian church attendance slipped even more: from 60 percent of the population in 1957 to 35 percent in 1982. The United Church of Canada membership dipped from 1,062,000 in 1966 to 900,000 in 1982.

Denominational losses at home adversely affected missionary efforts. Missionaries supported by member groups of the National Council of Churches decreased by one-half in numbers between 1962 and 1979.

Overall, however, Protestant career missionaries rose sharply to approximately 40,000 in 1986. Another 20,000 served in "short-term abroad" programs ranging from two months to two years in length.

The increase came mostly from evangelical sending agencies. Evangelical Foreign Missions Association members, for example, increased their missionaries on the field by 63 percent during the 1960s and 1970s.

North American support of Protestant foreign missions in 1984 was believed to top one billion dollars.

The biggest story in overseas missions actually took place overseas. A 1986 estimate put the total of Third World missionaries at 20,000, and some missiologists expected it to reach 100,000 by the end of the century. Korean churches alone were planning to have 10,000 missionaries abroad by the year 2000.

The combined force of foreign missionaries and local church leaders oversaw remarkable growth in the 1980s. An average of 16,400 Africans became Christians every day in 1984, totaling nearly six million a year.

Churches in East and South Asia added 360,000 and 447,000 new members respectively during 1984. Christians in mainland China increased to an estimated 25 to 30 million, many of whom met in thousands of house churches.

In contrast, European and North American churches together were losing about 2.8 million people each year to nominalism and unbelief. No wonder Billy Graham stated that the center of Christianity was moving eastward.

Despite impressive numbers overseas, Christianity still remained a minority faith, numbering in 1982 only 1.5 billion professing believers of every description in a world population of 4.7 billion. The percentage of Christians in 1984 ranked less than its peak of 34 percent in 1900.

Part of the problem lay in a lopsided placement of missionaries whose primary task was to win converts.

Missiologist Ralph Winter gathered statistics showing 95 percent of the North American missionary force was working with churches in the developing countries, while only 5 percent worked in areas without established churches, such as Muslim countries.

Evangelicals both in North America and overseas were faced with increasing competition from Roman Catholics and false cults in the last quarter of the century.

Ever since Karol Wojtyla became Pope John Paul II in 1979, he worked hard to reestablish the Roman Catholic Church as an active world force. By 1984 his efforts began to pay off as he traveled farther and more frequently than any previous Pope to put his personal imprint on the church.

Even an assassination attempt in Rome did not deter John Paul II from "bathing in the masses," as he put it. Everywhere he carried the message of a church supreme, drawing its strength from ancient dogma, and proclaiming a message essentially sacred and spiritual.

This conservative stance brought the Pope into conflict with radicals who preached a revolutionary Christ and a theology of violent liberation. The Pope's position also infused new life into many Catholic endeavors, especially missionary work.

The Church of Jesus Christ, Latter Day Saints (more commonly known as the Mormon church) also emerged with an energetic missionary program in the last quarter of the century. It not only competed with evangelical efforts, but attempted to subvert new converts in overseas churches.

When Spencer W. Kimball became president of the Mormons in 1973, he inaugurated the most dynamic missionary period in Mormon history. From 1974 to 1981, the overseas force jumped from 17,000 to 30,000 young men and women.

Largely through their missionary program, Mormons doubled in size between 1950 and 1964, to over two million. They doubled again by 1984, reaching a total of five million members.

Jehovah's Witnesses grew even faster than Mormons during the 1970s—a startling 45 percent worldwide. Career missionaries serving in 200 countries baptized nearly 162,000 converts in 1983. Even lay members were expected to donate time each month to outreach. The rapid growth of Jehovah Witnesses was a direct result of a calculated number of hours spent in evangelistic work—an average 2,000 to 3,000 hours of work for each baptized convert.

Competition abroad and moral decline at home were hallmarks of the century's last quarter. Would evangelicals be able to meet these challenges successfully?

Certainly—if they avoided the mistake of some mainline denominations that tried so hard to be culturally relevant they lost spiritual power and a distinctive Christian message.

* * *

The Alliance entered 1975 in a stance clearly different from that of the previous eighty-eight years of existence.

Now a denomination, it would come to stand as squarely committed to church growth at home as it did overseas. No longer would confusion arise from the paradox of promoting the opening of new churches on the mission field while downplaying the same activity at home. Leaders of the North American work could now promote church extension and development—even evangelism—with an expectation of support not always assured previously.

THE THREE-QUARTER MARK of the century bore special significance for Alliance missions.

Fifteen years had passed since 1960, when all remaining Alliance national churches had emerged as fully autonomous entities. Now they were all co-equal with North American churches who had founded them through missionary work.

At the same time, the dust and din of newly acquired independence had settled down. Normalcy of sorts had returned to many Third World nations where Alliance missions and churches worked.

New Dangers

In place of political unrest or civil strife that had threatened the work of the Gospel in the pre-independence era, new and more subtle dangers arose. Beginning in the 1950s and stretching into the 1970s, many younger churches found themselves serenaded by new siren songs that would in effect have lured them to grief like ships drawn to the reefs by false signals.

Regional associations emerged in the sixties, presenting themselves as the new wave of the future for Christianity in developing countries. They promised to lead young national churches to greater fulfillment than that possible through continued cooperation with the foreign missions that had founded them.

The East Asia Christian Council of Churches, the All Africa Conference of Churches and other regional groupings claimed to be the ecumenical movement of Protestantism with a "world mission." While declaring themselves independent of theological controversies that divided Western churches, they were privately funded by the World Council of Churches.

These organizations promoted a comprehensive new agenda for overseas churches, one that would replace the so-called outdated views of has-been Western missions. The new plan called for political activism to replace proclamation of the Gospel, for social programs to replace church planting, for government programs to improve society from without, instead of spiritual rebirth to transform society from within.[1]

Such ecumenical efforts to subvert leaders of young evangelical churches overseas carried added allures of financial aid, attractive salaries and scholarships abroad. Alliance church leaders in Vietnam, Ivory Coast and Guinea seemed especially targeted for such attention in the 1960s and 1970s.

However, once this assistance was accepted by unsuspecting national church leaders, it could lead eventually to spiritual sterility and severed relations with their founding missions.

One way to combat these overtures to Alliance overseas churches would be the creation of a worldwide fellowship. In such a gathering, national leaders could encourage and counsel one another as members of the same family—which indeed they were. Dr. Snead laid the groundwork for such a fellowship. His successor, Louis King, further advanced the idea, beginning with regional conferences on each continent that would eventually lead to a world fellowship.

Another reason for such an Alliance grouping became apparent in 1975: the need to promote evangelism as a top priority. While all Alliance overseas churches were growing by certain standards, populations around them were increasing so much faster that the churches were actually losing ground.

Alliance World Fellowship

In a certain "fullness of time," the Alliance in North America scheduled what proved to be the inaugural meeting of the Alliance World Fellowship, May 26-29, 1975, at Nyack after General Council.[2]

The conference lived up to its billing. Seventy-four representatives from thirty-four nations drew up a constitution that spelled out clearly the formation of a consultative fellowship. Its primary purpose was for mutual encouragement and edification in fulfilling the Great Commission of their one Lord.[3]

The constitution provided for a conference every four years, led by an eight-member committee representing six geographical areas. In addition to its ten-point statement of purpose, the constitution also incorporated the eleven-point statement of faith adopted by North American Alliance churches in 1965.[4]

The Alliance World Fellowship began in 1975 with a community of 5,845 organized local churches around the world. It would have subsequent meetings in Hong Kong, 1979, and in Lima, Peru, 1983. By that time, organized churches in the fellowship would have nearly doubled to 10,238.

North American churches and their overseas counterparts shared more than just a quadrennial meeting for mutual support. Bonding their fellowship, like an inner seam strengthening the garment, was a series of unusual church-mission agreements.

These formal documents, generally in effect for five years, pioneered a new method of cooperation between sending and receiving churches. The first such agreement took place in December of 1965 between mission and church leaders in Zaire. The practice gradually expanded until similar agreements became the working document in each country where an Alliance mission and a national church worked together.

The church-mission agreement operated on a basic premise that both parties were full and equal partners in the ministry of the Gospel. Each had separate, defined responsibilities, while together they shared other activities. The church, for example, chose its own leaders and managed its own finances. The mission had sole responsibility for educating missionary children. By the same agreement, church and mission workers jointly entered new areas to evangelize and plant churches.

A clause in the church-mission agreement scheduled specific times for leaders of both groups to meet and evaluate their progress or resolve problems that might arise. The whole procedure served to dissipate tensions and improve working relationships.

The Alliance World Fellowship contained still another common bond. Several of the overseas churches supported missionary programs of their own.

Japan had led off in 1959, with the first missionary to go overseas from an Alliance overseas church, and the very first Alliance missionary to Brazil. Miss Mutsuko Ninomiya went to Brazil to work among both immigrant Japanese and the Brazilians.

The Alliance Church Union of Hong Kong commissioned its first missionary in 1963. In twenty years this foreign missionary society grew to thirty workers in nine countries—including the United States and Canada.

CAMACOP, the Alliance church in the Philippines, began organizing its foreign department in 1963 and sent its first missionary couple to Sumatra, Indonesia, five years later. In time, Argentina, India and Peru also organized missionary work. By 1986, these six overseas churches had fielded a total of thirty-seven missionaries.

Thailand showed what different national churches working together could accomplish. Former missionaries to Thailand returned for a visit after eight years' absence. They were surprised to see Third World Alliance missionaries.

They met Beth Limare, an Alliance missionary from the Philippines, who was studying the Thai language. She already knew five other languages, and perhaps that was what helped her to begin conversing in Thai after just two weeks of study.

In Korat, they also met Edward and Amy Ng, supported by the C&MA Church Union in Hong Kong in their ministry among the overseas Chinese in Thailand. Later they talked with Miss Vaneda Suwatchalapinum, the first missionary sent to Thailand by Hong Kong Alliance churches.

Another young couple from Hong Kong, the Yungs, had completed language study and was preparing to replace Miss Suwatchalapinum when she left on furlough.

The former missionaries saw encouraging growth in Thailand,

but they said, "The greatest satisfaction of all was seeing the completion of missions—the sending out of missionaries by Third World churches."[5]

CAMA Services

Formation of the Alliance World Fellowship in 1975 stirred feelings of joy mixed with grief.

Just a few months before, Communist forces had triumphed in Indo-China. Alliance churches in Vietnam, Laos and Cambodia suddenly found themselves under hostile domination. Christians joined the thousands upon thousands who created a refugee crisis by a massive exodus from the three countries.

The decision to leave their homeland, culture, relatives and friends for an unknown destination was not easily made. But had the refugees known what awaited them—months and perhaps years of restricted activities in prison-like camps, humiliation of surrendering the determination of their future into the hands of alien agencies and unseen authorities, the gnawing fear of not knowing what would happen or when—had they anticipated these sufferings, the refugees might have debated even longer before deciding to flee their homelands.

Yet they fled by the hundreds of thousands, voting with their feet a massive rejection of the Communist system. Many crossed into Thailand over mine-infested footpaths. Those who left by boat for Malaysia, Indonesia, or even Hong Kong, had other dangers to face: storms at sea in creaky old crafts crammed with people, and the threat of pirate ships whose crews plundered, raped and murdered without mercy.

The Alliance had already set up a refugee and relief agency in 1972 to aid war victims inside Indo-China. CAMA Services (the initials stand for the full Alliance name) helped to resettle displaced persons, provide "survival kits" to those who lost everything, even organize medical services. Dr. Dean F. Kroh, a veteran medical missionary for years in Zaire, headed a medical team in a Cambodian hospital. CAMA Services operated only in areas where the Alliance had work, and incorporated a strong spiritual ministry in its activities.

These humanitarian projects ended abruptly with the fall of Indo-China. CAMA Services immediately transferred its operations outside the three-nation area. Refugee workers, including former Indo-China missionaries, spread out to camps strung along the Thai border. Other workers did what they could to help the thousands of confused, vulnerable and desperately needy refugees who found refuge in the United States, Canada and France.

By 1978, the nonprofit relief agency expanded its ministry to include the war-battered population of Lebanon and famine victims in Africa. CAMA Services was itself something of an alliance in character. Over 90 percent of its operating funds in 1978 came from agencies outside the Alliance, including ZOA (Committee for Helping Southeast Asia, a group of Christian business people in the Netherlands), and TEAR (The Evangelical Alliance Relief) Fund in Holland and England.

By the mid-1980s, CAMA Services would be operating on a half-million dollar budget and still working in Thailand, Lebanon and sub-Saharan Africa among thousands of people seemingly enmeshed in an endless cycle of tragedy. Its funds would still come largely from the same European agencies with whom it had worked so well for years, plus a few new ones, like Samaritan's Purse.

Centennial Advance

The 1978 General Council in Birmingham, Alabama, demonstrated in a remarkable manner what a few delegates with vision can accomplish for the good of the entire denomination.

The Committee on the President's Report and General Legislation began its statement in the usual fashion. It expressed gratitude for the eighteen years of presidential leadership by Dr. Nathan Bailey as he arrived at the end of his tenure.

Then committee members put their searchlight on 50,000 reported conversions worldwide and analyzed the total in a disturbing fashion: "During 1977 our Society averaged, per church in North America, less than 12 conversions, just under 4 baptisms, and not quite 3 new members. Overseas, the 'per church' averages were 4.7 conversions and 2.5 baptisms."

The report noted in a laconic tone, "Our 'per church' average leaves much to be desired."

Committee members did not leave it at that. They proceeded to suggest to General Council a remarkable solution for this underachievement by recommending "that Council adopt as a goal, to be reached by our 100th anniversary, the doubling of our North American constituency, with a comparable increase in personnel, general fund income and overseas ministry."[6]

The goal seemed so unrealistic and extravagant it left many delegates dubious about adopting the recommendation. But after debate and prayer, the mood of General Council shifted from "Can we?" to "Why not?" Delegates accepted the challenge and the Board of Managers later set the official dates from April 1, 1979, through March 31, 1987—eight years in which to achieve an across-the-board doubling of the Alliance![7]

General Council delegates took another step in 1978 that would make the Centennial Advance more likely to succeed. They elected Dr. Louis L. King as the seventh president of The Christian and Missionary Alliance.

The "reverse flow" of Alliance missions impacting on home churches again became apparent. Although Dr. King entered pastoral ministry in 1938 after graduation from the Missionary Training Institute, most of his service related to overseas work.

The King family was actually enroute to India in 1941, when the Japanese bombed Pearl Harbor. Waiting to resume their interrupted passage to India, he pastored churches in Westmont, Illinois, and Lincoln, Nebraska.

Louis King's pastoral ministry during the war years included a strong emphasis on evangelism. "I believe," he said repeatedly, "that the Apostle Paul was referring to pastors when he wrote to Timothy, 'Do the work of an evangelist.' Evangelism is an essential part of pastoral ministry."

Evangelism continued as one of his prime concerns during six years of missionary work in India. It assumed even greater importance after he met Dr. McGavran, whom *Christianity Today* called "the Father of Church Growth."[8] Targeted goals of growth became a permanent part of his strategy.

Later, as regional director for the Far East and then as vice-president of the Division of Overseas Ministries, Dr. King urged both missionaries and national church leaders to give a large place in their work to evangelism. He preached, counseled and insisted that the church's primary function in the world is to bring people to a saving knowledge of Jesus Christ. Every other program that competed with or delayed that singular imperative must be discarded or turned over to others for action.

Now this man, totally committed to evangelism and comfortable with the strategy of targeted growth, became leader of the Alliance at the precise moment the churches of North America went on record to say it was time to set goals for growth and meet them.

Timing of the decision and choice of the leader were apparently providential, not coincidental.

Another change in leadership took place in 1978. Dr. Keith M. Bailey, successor to the late Leslie Pippert, moved from the Division of Church Ministries to the editorial office of Christian Publications, Inc. But before he left, he got the doubling campaign off to a strong start with "Project 10,000." The plan, prepared under his supervision and carried out by his successor, called for fifty-three evangelism seminars in North America with an attendance goal of 10,000 pastors and lay leaders.

The new vice-president of North American churches, Dr. Robert

T. Henry, carried out Project 10,000 with notable results. All told, 10,307 participants attended the regional seminars. Another five miniconferences covered all the Alliance college campuses.

The influence of this and other efforts became visible in conversions and extension churches that infused new life into the Alliance. Ninety-five new churches accounted for 59 percent of inclusive membership growth in 1984. The ratio of converts to members was one to five in the new congregations, and one to thirteen in churches organized before 1978. Nearly 66,000 inclusive members entered the Alliance within seven years.

Citing 1985 figures, Dr. King could report that since the launching of Centennial Advance, the denomination realized a net growth of 394 new churches—nearly one-quarter of all churches in the United States and Puerto Rico.[9]

Specialized Ministries

Ethnic churches played a significant part in that growth, just as minorities assumed an expanding importance in the general population of the United States.

The overall characteristics of racial and cultural minorities in the nation changed dramatically between the first decade of the century and the 1970s. While European immigration slipped from 91.6 to 18.4 percent of total immigration, the Asian influx climbed from 3.7 to 35.3 percent and the flow of South Americans rose from 4.1 to 43.5 percent.

The victory of Communism in Indo-China and deteriorating economic conditions in Latin America precipitated something of a stampede to American shores in the seventies. The arrival of Vietnamese, Cambodians and Laotians gradually dwindled to a trickle in the 1980s. The Hispanic population, however, grew to 23 million legal aliens, according to 1980 census figures, and was expected to surpass blacks as the nation's largest minority.

Arrival of Alliance church families by the thousands from Indo-China in 1975 and later years spurred administrative personnel at Nyack to set up an emergency center to help in the placement and care of war refugees. These humanitarian efforts eventually merged with other ethnic programs under the Office of Specialized Ministries.

Based on the recognized need of people to worship God in a way natural to their cultural and linguistic heritage, Specialized Ministries proved to be an operation in tune with the times. It grew in ten years to encompass eleven ethnic groups and an inclusive membership of over 21,000—almost one in every ten inclusive members of the Alliance by 1985. (Chinese, black and Haitian churches opted in 1985-86 to merge with the regular church districts.)

The growing ethnic population in the United States appeared to Rev. E. A. Cline, director of Specialized Ministries, as an opportunity for missions-minded Alliance churches to have a cross-cultural ministry of their own. The "Love Your Neighbor" program started in 1986 promoted this unique opportunity.

Arlington (Virginia) Memorial Church dramatized just what that ministry could be. By 1985 it was giving shelter and support to five ethnic congregations: Chinese, Hispanics, Vietnamese, Cambodians and Ethiopians. Church deacons coordinated activities of the different groups to avoid program conflicts. Various groups occasionally met together for services, such as one baptismal service that required three interpreters so all could understand.

"The preoccupation with reaching out to different communities has rejuvenated our congregation," said Pastor H. Bruce Leastman. "One unexpected blessing of this ministry is seeing young people from the ethnic groups become active in our Alliance Youth Fellowship as they make the transition to American culture."[10]

Urban Focus

While the Centennial Advance moved ahead by steps in the United States, it bounded forward overseas.

An 11.7 percent increase in inclusive members meant over 192,000 persons added to the local congregations in 1984—some 64,600 inclusive members ahead of schedule for the centennial goal of 1,771,610 that year. Although established churches fell 764 short of the year's goal, 411 new churches were started—better than one per day.[11]

Much of this growth took place in burgeoning cities of the developing countries. This fact suggested that history was repeating itself: The Alliance had begun in cities of North America, and now it was moving to cities of the world.

Dr. Simpson and his associates launched their missionary movement with a rallying cry, "Mobilize the neglected forces at home to reach the neglected masses abroad." But more often than not, as Alliance missionaries went overseas, they found other missions already established in population centers.

In a spirit of comity—not duplicating in an area what another mission had already started—Alliance missionaries moved into more primitive, even dangerous, interior regions to proclaim the Gospel to scattered and unreached tribes. In other undeveloped areas and countries, Alliance missionaries were truly pioneers—preceding not only other missions, but governments as well. As a result, Alliance fields in numerous countries were removed from population centers.

Then came the social phenomenon of urban migration. Cities like Lima in Peru, Kinshasa in Zaire, and Bangkok in Thailand, doubled in size every five to ten years.

A report in *National Geographic* noted that in 1950 only seven urban centers held more than five million people. By 1985, thirty-four cities had that distinction. In the year 2025, an estimated ninety-three cities would belong to the five-million club—eighty of them in developing nations.[12]

Alliance missionaries increasingly found themselves ministering to shrinking populations as people moved to the cities. The population shift called for a basic change in strategy, and the Division of Overseas Ministries, under Dr. King's leadership, did just that.

Lima, Peru, stood out as a showcase of evangelism and church growth strategy. The Lince Church in Lima's central district had organized in 1958 with twenty-four members. The congregation slowly grew to 120 members in nine years. Then the pastor moved and stagnation set in.

A nucleus of believers grew concerned about the church's paltry witness in a city of five million Peruvians. They began praying and events started to move. The most significant event was the arrival of Rev. Alfredo Smith, an Argentinian pastor who assumed spiritual leadership of the Lince Church in 1973.

Under the banner, "Lima to an Encounter with God," he began fifteen consecutive months of two-week evangelistic campaigns alternating with two-week discipling classes for new believers. It was the longest, most intensive evangelistic effort ever undertaken to date in the Alliance. The congregation followed their pastor in a spirit of unity that spared neither time, talent nor resources.

Financial help from numerous sources helped the Lince pastor and congregation bring their vision to reality.[13]

A low-interest loan from the LeTourneau Foundation to the Alliance made possible a modern, attractive church seating 1,000 people. The foundation also helped the project with outright grants to bring some of South America's outstanding evangelists for the two-week series of meetings. Additional grants from the same source enabled the church to mount a multimedia campaign to draw the city's attention to the salvation readily available in Christ.

The fifteen months of continuous evangelism and discipling programs resulted in over 2,000 conversions. Sunday service attendance increased to 700, and that was just the beginning.

Lince Church's membership swelled to 2,000 in ten years. The congregation also sponsored thirteen daughter churches with a total community exceeding 5,200 baptized members. Missiologists and national church leaders came from everywhere to study the dynamics of growth in the Lince project. Lessons learned found fertile ground elsewhere in South America, Africa—even North America.

Kinshasa, Zaire, used another formula for extension, but with equally gratifying results. In 1965 the capital city had not one Alliance congregation. By 1985, over 100 churches dotted the city and its suburbs. Additional scores of prayer groups, some numbering 250 people, held the potential for even more organized congregations.

Most Kinshasa churches in fact began in the small, undramatic manner of a prayer group, often crowding into one side of a two-room, cement-block house. It seemed that once a prayer group, through sacrificial giving and donated labor, could erect a building, they were then able to fill it with people.

Outsiders had first to be convinced the Christians were serious about church, not just another fickle cult group that would be gone before the next rain. The church building provided that proof, so the outsiders came, and came, and came.

Dr. McGavran visited Kinshasa and estimated that Alliance churches totalling 20,000 members by 1990 would not be an unrealistic goal.[14]

Refocusing missionary resources on Third World cities was an expensive shift, but extra funds became available from several sources.

The Women's Missionary Prayer Fellowship enthusiastically backed the move with prayer and funds. In 1981, WMPF groups gave nearly $187,000 for churches in four key cities. The following year they set aside $20,000 to train urban church planters through special seminars in Lima, Peru. Again in 1982-83 prayer fellowships raised over $200,000 to purchase properties for churches in many large cities.

Over a period of four years the Alliance produced colorful "Good News for Great Cities" calendars. This special focus on a different strategic city each month generated $465,490 in funds and countless hours of an even more valuable asset: prayer.

General Council in 1981 expressed its support of focus on cities by giving over $35,600 for an intensive evangelism and extension effort in Quito, Ecuador.

Alliance Men supported the focus on cities by their own unique contribution: the construction missionaries. One project involved ten men from churches in Ohio. The team of builders went to Mali in January of 1986 to help the Mali Alliance mission and national church expand their work in Bamako, the nation's capital and largest city.

Like numerous other teams of laymen builders since 1975, the men had to pay their own way to and from the work area, and their in-country expenses as well. Some men used their own resources, while others received help in raising the needed $1,500 for the month ahead.

Using tools they had brought along, the men built a parsonage for a Malian pastor and put a roof on a church in the city. They also completed smaller projects on outlying stations. Neighborhood children in Bamako watched with fascination as the men worked in high spirits under an oppressive tropical sun. Although the men did not know the local language, they taught the children to sing gospel choruses in English.

This dramatic shift of attention to cities stirred legitimate concern for remote areas and unreached peoples that historically laid claim to the hearts of Alliance people. The tumbled mountains of interior Irian Jaya, clogged jungles of interior Peru, and wastelands of interior Mali would never see modern cities rise in their regions, but their scattered and isolated villages had still to be reached.

The overwhelming need of mega-cities and their exciting potential for evangelism and church growth had become the wave of the future for Alliance missions. Yet a thin cry of need from solitary clusters of people in backward regions would not let mission strategists quite forget them.

Canadian Autonomy

It perhaps seemed strange to other national churches in the Alliance World Fellowship that C&MA churches in Canada and the United States worked as one organization for ninety-three years. They would have had to understand the unique relationship between the two English-speaking democracies for many years.

In addition to trade links that topped the list in each country's economy, the nearly 5,000-mile border is the world's longest undefended dividing line between two nations. Almost the entire Canadian population lives within 200 miles of that border.

Relaxed attitudes between the two countries enabled pastors to serve on either side of the border with few restrictions. Canadian missionaries could serve under a sending agency in the States.

Close church ties were rooted in the very beginnings of the Alliance. Some of the most illustrious Alliance leaders were Canadian born. In addition to the founder, A. B. Simpson, leaders like Henry Wilson, May Agnew Stephens, John Salmon, William Howland, R. J. Zimmerman, R. A. Jaffray, A. W. Roffe, A. E. Thompson, R. H. Glover, Walter and John Turnbull, P. W. Philpott and David LeLacheur were Canadian born.

But as surely as north is north and south is south, the two countries were different, and so were their churches.

Canadian and American Alliance leaders sometimes differed in church matters, and the time came when Canadians thought it better to direct the work in their country according to their own perceived needs and convictions, and let Americans do the same in theirs.

Therefore, in 1978, a Canadian tridistrict conference voted for autonomy by an 87.6 percent majority.

General Council appointed a committee on organization. It was empowered to convene an all-Canadian assembly no later than June of 1980. The assembly would then determine the details that would give form and substance to an autonomous Canadian Alliance: organizational and administrative structure, constitution and bylaws and the first officers. The new organization was to be in place and approved by January, 1981.

The founding assembly met in Winnipeg, Manitoba, in 1980. With few exceptions, all went as planned. The new constitution generally followed the one used in the United States, with a president and Board of Directors. General Assembly would meet every two years and be chaired by a moderator appointed by the Board of Directors.

Canadian churches would continue their overseas ministry in close cooperation with the Alliance in the United States through a director of personnel and missions.

The first officers were: Melvin P. Sylvester, president; Gerald L. Fowler, executive vice-president; Arnold P. Reimer, secretary; G. Lloyd Matheson, treasurer; and Arnold L. Cook, director of personnel and missions.

Nationalizing the Canadian Alliance had the desired effect on growth. Between 1980 and 1985, the churches gained nearly 4,000 members and adherents a year, a 42 percent jump from 38,000 to 56,768. In the same period, churches increased 18 percent, from 241 to 287.

New Directions

Growth of the Alliance in North America—increase in churches and membership, expansion of colleges and graduate schools, push for extension programs, commitment to minority ministries—generated a whole new set of obligations. All of these heightened emphases necessarily belonged in the agenda of a denomination wanting to serve God effectively in its own generation and culture.

But how were these legitimate ministries to be supported when the Alliance was founded as a fellowship of deeper life beliefs and a missionary movement designed to give priority in funds and personnel to secure followers for Christ in other cultures and nations?

Rev. David H. Moore, later elected vice-president for overseas ministries, spoke of these tensions in a 1982 conference of district superintendents, pastors and administrators of the Alliance. "Historically, the C&MA has developed from a missionary society into a missionary denomination," he said. "Objectives, programs and concerns have broadened accordingly. Missions emphasis has shifted, almost imperceptibly at first, until now it is evident in our giving, our involvement, our priorities.

"The issue is not only what priority missions should have in the Alliance, but what priority should be given to evangelism, church planting in North America, education and other vital concerns."[15]

Balancing these priorities would not be easy in the Alliance, whose founder maintained: "There is no desire on the part of anyone connected with our work to build up a new sect or separate people from the churches where the Lord has called them to work and worship." [16]

Dr. Simpson's objective was to stir Christians within existing churches to a deeper walk of faith in the Spirit and to a greater commitment to world evangelism.

Holding to that original, uncluttered vision, while slowly, even reluctantly adjusting to the complexities of changing times and needs, the Alliance altered in form. By 1980, it was truly a missionary denomination. Giving for missions (including Canada) averaged $7,500 per church, or $54 per inclusive member. The churches averaged one missionary for about every 230 inclusive members.[17]

By 1980, inclusive membership in the overseas churches was five times larger than the Alliance in North America and supported three times as many organized churches.[18]

Would the Alliance continue to maintain its essential character as a missionary denomination? "The weight of history is against the C&MA maintaining missions priority,"[19] warned Moore, but he also pointed out that it was breaking new ground. The Alliance had no other denomination with which to compare itself, except perhaps the Moravian Church at its peak.[20]

The future of the Alliance as a missionary denomination therefore depended on how long and to what degree priority would be given to overseas outreach in local church giving, personnel and program. It would require an attitude such as the Apostle Paul expressed, "This one thing I do."

The Divine Pattern

Dr. Simpson would have weighed such questions and choices in comparison to the divine pattern he believed God had given for the New Testament church: "Just as the Tabernacle of old was to be constructed according to the pattern that was shown to Moses on the Mount, so the church of Christ has a divine plan, and should be in every particular constructed accordingly."[21]

In that divine pattern he envisioned certain objectives for the church. "First, she must worship God and glorify her Father in heaven," he wrote. "Second, she must bear witness to the truth."

He then elaborated: "Therefore her heavenly object is propagation, evangelization, to gather to her bosom the sinful world, to instruct and to build them up in the life of Jesus, to be a training school for heaven, and to give the Gospel to all mankind. This is her heavenly calling." [22]

Dr. Simpson's moving description of "the divine pattern" prophetically described an overseas church as it would appear a century later in the country to which he once felt called: China.

By 1949, China represented sixty-two years of Alliance investment in money and prayer, and by a total of 576 missionaries. Then the church in China was lost from view behind a bamboo curtain drawn by hostile hands. The Communist government declared war on Christians. Arrests, trials and summary executions or imprisonment followed.

The worst was yet to come.

After a brief and disastrous attempt to liberalize control in 1957, Chairman Mao unleashed the Red Guards against intellectual, cultural and religious communities. Millions were killed or crippled for life from beatings, churches and schools ransacked and destroyed, Bibles and literature of every kind burned.

Religious analysts assumed that the church was obliterated or reduced to an insignificant secret remnant by such attacks. But when the bamboo curtain began to part after President Richard Nixon's visit to China in 1972, an amazing story unfolded.

Purged in the white heat of persecution, the church emerged not only refined, but revived. Estimates of the number of Christians varied between twenty-five and thirty million, many of them members of house churches, groups that met in secret at great risk to worship. Remarkable stories circulated about the conversion of ardent Marxists and high government leaders.

Although Alliance missionaries had been gone from China for decades, the results of their work remained and grew. Dr. Janet Fowler glimpsed evidence of this in 1983 when she visited Minhsien, West China, where Rev. William N. Ruhl had lived and worked until he died in 1943.

While visiting Ruhl's gravesite, she met Miss Bao, a former Bible woman of the mission. "Then came one of the most dramatic and emotional experiences of my life, my visit to Miss Bao's home," wrote Dr. Fowler. "The former Bible woman had spread the word and the courtyard was filled with Christians as well as all the city's curious onlookers who could push their way in."[23]

A pastor in the group told her that now more than 1,000 Christians lived in Minhsien and its suburbs. The former Alliance pastor and four of his preacher sons had died during the turbulent years, but a family member was still serving the Lord in another region.

The investment of lives and funds and prayers by Alliance people was still paying off in Minhsien. Not even decades of repression by one of history's most ruthless regimes could undo that work.

Dr. Simpson's words concerning the church of Jesus Christ never seemed more timely: "She is the only divine society on earth, the only institution that is essential, eternal and will survive the wreck of time and the dissolution of the present age." [24]

Essential and Eternal

The essential and eternal character of the church of Jesus Christ explains why an impassioned appeal surged from the heart of Dr. Simpson: "Let us understand her high calling, and oh, let her be true to it." [25]

How well has The Christian and Missionary Alliance in succeeding generations of twice-born members responded to that high calling?

Its day never ends.

Alliance churches in fifty-one nations and in every state of the Union during the 1980s formed links that traversed the world from Alaska in the north to Argentina in the south, from California in the west to China in the east. Those marvelous links ranged from snowy Andean highlands of Ecuador to emerald valleys of the Philippines, from wind-scorched deserts of Mali to the cacophony of Hong Kong thoroughfares.

Its witness never ceases.

Somewhere, any time of day or night, inclusive members of the 2,120,000 Alliance community were in some active service of witness during the mid-eighties. The 231 languages they spoke would have sounded like babel to the human ear, but to God they were the familiar and universal language of truth.

Its work never stops.

When the Alliance radio studio in Hong Kong fell silent at the close of day, the radio staff in Guinea was still at work and "Alianza en Marcha" prepared to go on the air. Each week during 1985, 412 broadcasts raced across the airwaves to blanket nations. As the psalmist wrote, "Their voice goes out into all the earth, their words to the end of the world."

Other voices swelled and faded in daily cadence as 3,463 full-term and 11,600 short-term Bible school students in thirty nations prepared for ministry.

Alliance printing presses in Indonesia and Hong Kong poured out annually more than 20,000,000 pages of Christian literature in the mid-eighties. And as their workday wound down, smaller literature centers scattered through Africa and South America were beginning theirs, raising the total to 66,500,000 pages.

These and other ministries proliferated as the work of Dr. Simpson grew from a handful of people to multiplied tens of thousands, and two Alliances changed from the simplicity of deeper life and missionary movements to the complexity of a missionary denomination.

Yet through all the diversity and expansion of The Christian and Missionary Alliance during its first century of service ran that distinctive high calling of the church as envisioned by the founder: Experience the deep truths of God's Word and proclaim His Gospel in all the world.

Epilogue

We Are Specialists

By Louis L. King

"This is an age of specialists," observed Dr. Simpson.

"Modern science and all our secular and industrial lines of activity are running more and more into particular departments and men are becoming experts not in some general branch of knowledge or industry, but in some particular detail....

"And so in Christian work the Lord gives 'to every man his work' and each of us has some divine calling if we have but the discernment of the Spirit to recognize it and the faithfulness to fulfill it."

Dr. Simpson then identified two imperative reasons for the formation of a new religious movement: "The Alliance has its place and calling to lead the people of God farther on into all the heights and depths of the life of Christ and farther out into all the aggressive work which the children of God have so long neglected....

"And so we learn to recognize Christ in all His members and see the good in all the movements of His providence and grace without becoming bigoted or narrow in our exclusive attachment to any single one.

"At the same time along with this larger charity," admonished the Alliance founder, "we need to know the standard under which we fight, recognize 'our own company,' and be true to the spiritual trust which God has assigned us."

ALLIANCE HISTORY illustrates in detail the nature of "the special trust" cited above by our founder. The Alliance is a unique missionary denomination—a maverick movement into whose soul the Head of the Church breathed "Go!" from the very start.

The passage of a century has served to prove that the Alliance sense of being sent was not a mere stage of development or an enthusiasm that peaked early and faded fast. That century has been characterized among denominations in general by religious inertness, spiritual coldness, ever-widening rationalism and secular humanism. Yet the spirit of "Go!" remains at the center of Alliance thought and conduct.

It all began with a man and a few followers. A century later, their numbers have grown to over two million adherents. In 1985 alone, inclusive membership increased by nearly a quarter-million. Even larger numbers will follow, because the Alliance believes that no province or region or country should be exempted from the opportunity to hear the Gospel—witnessing that intends to convert.

This is our special trust, and we will specialize in it.

However, limiting our reason for existence to missionary endeavor would not only distort Alliance history, it would threaten the dynamic of Alliance missions at the very source.

The record makes clear that Dr. Simpson and his associates first organized the Evangelical Christian Alliance. This fellowship of Christians united in their devotion to Jesus Christ and to the truths of Scripture that pointed to Him as the all-sufficient Lord. Afterward, they formed the Evangelical Missionary Alliance as the missions arm of that fellowship in faith.

They followed this sequence not because the Great Commission was of secondary importance, but because its fulfillment depended on Holy Spirit-filled individuals who supremely loved Jesus.

Our special trust to evangelize at home and abroad therefore finds its source and strength in a very personal imperative: to experience the truth we proclaim, truth that finds its complete expression and fulfillment in Jesus Christ.

Dr. Simpson himself set for us that standard: "I felt I dare not hold any truth in God's Word as a mere theory or to teach others what I had not personally proved."

God has graciously given the Alliance a century marked by growth as a movement and by usefulness in extending His Kingdom.

We cannot take for granted that further increase and blessing will characterize the Alliance in its second century. These distinctions are earned, not inherited.

Let us therefore:

• Be certain that our message and ministry overflow from the reality of personal commitment to Jesus Christ.

• Be careful to reject the natural tendencies to put personal comfort and security first, or to serve primarily the people of our own country and culture.

• Be diligent to preach and teach those essential doctrines of God's Word that inspire deep thinking, strong faith and bold action in service to God.

• Be alert in promoting evangelism as necessary for our local community as well as for people overseas.

• Be convinced that by fulfilling the missionary assignment of the church we bring closer the Second Coming of Christ, for "this gospel of the Kingdom shall be preached in all the world for a witness unto all nations, and then shall the end come."

In sum, as we in The Christian and Missionary Alliance advance into our second century of service, let us purpose, by His grace, to be all for Jesus.

APPENDICES

The Founder's Team

DR. A. B. SIMPSON had a gift for attracting high-caliber men and women as his associates in ministry. The following compilation of brief biographical notes on some—but not all—of his co-workers explains why the movement grew strong and fast in the early years, and also why it earned the name "Alliance."

Dr. J. Hudson Ballard

Through family members, Dr. Ballard was introduced to the Alliance early in life. He came to the Missionary Training Institute while still in his teens and graduated in 1898 with the first class to finish on the Nyack campus.

Upon graduation he received an appointment to serve the Alliance branch in Corning, New York. He was asked in 1902 to become superintendent of the Alliance work in Los Angeles. In spite of heavy responsibilities as superintendent, Ballard completed the necessary college credits for bachelor's and master's degrees.

In July of 1909, the Board of Managers invited him back to Nyack as principal of Wilson Academy, an Alliance-sponsored high school. During his tenure, the academy received accreditation from the New York State Board of Regents.

Also during his years at the academy, Ballard earned a Ph.D. at Columbia University, preached regularly at the Gospel Tabernacle and at summer conferences, became assistant editor of the Alliance's magazine, taught at the Missionary Training Institute, and gave lectures at the (Alliance) Home School in New York City. He served on the Board of Managers from 1912 to 1915, and became the first education secretary during the reorganization of 1912.

Dr. Ballard resigned from his responsibilities at Nyack in 1915 and took a Presbyterian pastorate in Hornell, New York. He continued some limited ministries in the Alliance until he moved to the West Coast, where he taught for many years at the San Francisco Theological Seminary.

Emma F. Beere

Emma Beere began her association with the Simpsons in 1895 as secretary to Dr. Simpson's son, Albert, who was a publisher. A shorthand expert, she recorded Dr. Simpson's sermons at the Gospel Tabernacle. He then hired her as his personal secretary and she worked devotedly with him on his twelve-hour days.

Most of Dr. Simpson's books grew out of sermons delivered at the New York Gospel Tabernacle, transcribed and prepared for publication by Miss Beere. She assisted A. E. Thompson in preparing *The Life of A. B. Simpson,* the official biography of the Alliance founder.

She was a charter member of Simpson Memorial Church in Nyack. After forty-seven years, one of the longest periods of service at the C&MA headquarters, she retired from the publication department.

William E. Blackstone

William E. Blackstone (1841-1935) was an early and influential associate of Dr. Simpson. Their friendship remained warm and unbroken throughout life. It was Blackstone's sermon at the first Old Orchard convention that played a major role in the decision to organize the movement.

He achieved phenomenal success as a businessman in property and investments. He consistently gave of his wealth and accepted no payment for his ministry to the Lord. He was a friend of the nation's leading statesmen and military leaders, including generals Grant and Meade and President Abraham Lincoln. He served with the United States Christian Commission, now called the chaplaincy.

Blackstone authored a document entitled "Memorial," procured the signatures of 413 religious leaders and published it in newspapers across the nation. It was an appeal for the return of Palestine to the Jews. President Benjamin Harrison approved the idea and sent the "Memorial" to leaders in principal nations of the world. On the seventy-fifth anniversary of the publication of "Memorial," the

State of Israel planted a grove of trees to honor Blackstone's memory.

His book, *Jesus Is Coming,* sold over a million copies in thirty-six languages. R. A. Torrey and J. Wilbur Chapman testified that the book transformed their ministries.

Blackstone founded the Chicago Hebrew Mission, now the American Messianic Mission. As an ardent supporter of both Jewish and foreign mission work, it was appropriate that he should live to see four generations of his children become missionaries to China.

Dr. Robert Roger Brown

Robert Roger Brown (1885-1964) related to Dr. Simpson as student to mentor. After graduation from Nyack in 1910, he received his first assignment from Dr. Simpson himself. Dr. Brown seemed to have imbibed his mentor's passion for souls, and he adhered to the methods and teachings of the early Alliance throughout his fifty-three years of ministry.

Dr. Brown was born in Western Pennsylvania and became a Christian at age eighteen. Following his first pastorate in Beaver Falls, Pennsylvania, he moved to Chicago, where he founded the first Alliance branch in the city. In 1920 he was appointed superintendent of the Western District. He served in that position until 1943, while simultaneously carrying on a number of other ministries.

In 1922, radio station WOW in Omaha began broadcasting. Dr. Brown was invited to prepare a religious broadcast for the station's first Sunday on the air. His program was so well received that WOW offered him free radio time. The program, "World Radio Chapel," continued for more than forty years—even beyond his death in 1964.

Radio formed only part of Dr. Brown's ministry. He founded the Omaha Gospel Tabernacle and pastored there for forty-one years and, with the Old Orchard Convention as a model, he launched an annual Bible and Missionary Conference Center for all ages at Okoboji Lakes, Iowa.

Dr. Brown was elected to the Board of Managers while still a young man. It was he who developed the first Preachers' Chorus at General Council, a ministry he continued for forty years. His genius also inspired the first missionary rallies at General Council.

L. K. Brubaker

"Daddy" Brubaker (d. 1940) was a Pennyslvania Dutch layman characterized by astute business abilities, faithfulness and a warm personality. His first association with Dr. Simpson dated back to his student days at the New York Missionary Training College in 1896.

He later served as business manager of the Missionary Training Institute at Nyack from 1903 to 1919 and as manager of the Alliance Home until 1932. When the school needed an independent source of water, he dreamed of a subterranean lake in the Nyack hillside when no one else knew of its existence. Subsequent drilling tapped the water reservoir.

When Dr. Simpson's health declined, "Daddy" Brubaker became his constant attendant.

Dr. R. Kelso Carter

R. Kelso Carter, a mathematics and science teacher in a nearby military academy, spoke frequently at early Alliance conventions. He lectured at the New York Missionary Training College in 1891-1892.

As an author, he published fourteen books, including two novels. As a hymn writer, he wrote both words and music to "Breathe Upon Us" and "Standing on the Promises." He was the primary compiler of the first edition of *Hymns of the Christian Life.* His name was associated with the words, music or both for 101 of the 455 hymns and gospel songs included in its index.

R. Kelso Carter was a man of diverse gifts. In mid-life he studied medicine at John Hopkins University and became a practicing physician.

Rev. William Christie

William Christie, a Scot who came to America at age nineteen, became a skilled craftsman in five building trades. Influenced by Dr. Simpson during a missionary convention in 1881, he offered himself to the Lord for work overseas. He immediately quit his job and enrolled in the New York Missionary Training College.

His fifty-eight years of ministry began with pioneer missionary work in Tibet. His exploits made him something of a hero and the missionaries characterized him as "the Livingstone of Northeast Tibet."

Christie was a devoted student of Chinese culture and wisdom. Loved by the Chinese, Christie's selflessness and generosity were proverbial. According to David Fant, Christie was a "tireless worker; he never drove but led."

In North America, Christie served as superintendent of the North-western District, principal of St. Paul Bible Institute, treasurer (1930-1946) and vice-president (1932-1946) of the Alliance. He was also a member of the Board of Managers. For one year he was responsible for both the foreign and publication departments.

The Missionary Training Institute, his alma mater, was always very important to Christie, and he devoted much time to its development. In later years, he procured property and raised funds for a dormitory later named for him—Christie Hall.

Dr. John E. Cookman

John E. Cookman (d. 1891) was born into a family of four generations of Wesleyan and Methodist Episcopal ministers. His father, Rev. George G. Cookman, served for a time as Chaplain of the United States Senate.

Dr. Cookman became a Christian while still a boy. Early in his Christian life he embraced the Wesleyan doctrine of sanctification and made plans to enter the ministry. Except for three years, his entire ministry—spanning more than a quarter-century—was spent in and near New York City.

In 1883, after suffering intensely from insomnia, depression and heart disease, Dr. Cookman discovered that Christ could also be his Healer. From that time until his death in 1891, he was known as a "veritable dynamo of spiritual energy."

Soon after his healing, while pastoring the Bedford Street Methodist Church in New York City, Dr. Cookman came into contact with Dr. Simpson. He traveled widely with Dr. Simpson, speaking in deeper life and missions conventions. He remained a Methodist minister until shortly before his death, when he entered the ministry of the Protestant Episcopal Church.

David Crear

David Crear was an outstanding example of the talented laymen surrounding Dr. Simpson. In Chicago he had earned an enviable reputation as a master builder. In New York he erected the New York Life and the Metropolitan Insurance buildings, and also the New York Gospel Tabernacle. Business associates called him "Honest David."

He devoted his wealth to missions, and when the church was low on funds, he quietly paid the bills. Oldest member of the Board of Managers, Crear served as the first treasurer and a vice-president. He was also an elder in the Gospel Tabernacle.

Crear was made chairman of the prayer committee of the Evangelical Missionary Alliance in 1887. The appointment was well deserved because prayer formed an integral part of his life.

Dr. Frederic W. Farr

After graduating from Newton Theological Seminary in 1885 and pastoring two churches in Massachusetts, Frederic Farr (1860-1930) was called to serve as an associate pastor with Dr. Simpson in New York City. His next pastorate was the Bethlehem Baptist Church in Philadelphia, where he worked for twenty years. In 1915, he accepted a call to Calvary Baptist Church in Los Angeles, where he had a fruitful ministry for another fifteen years until failing health forced him into retirement.

Dr. Farr's interest in the Alliance continued throughout his ministry, part of which time he spent on the Board of Managers. He served as dean of the Missionary Training College in New York City. After the school moved to Nyack, he continued to lecture on homiletics and Bible topics.

William John Fenton

Irish by birth, William John Fenton (d. 1917) grew up in Hamilton, Ontario, where his family was known for strong evangelical Presbyterianism. Fenton, however, decided to go his own way and became known as the "father" of Brethrenism in Hamilton. In 1883, he moved to Toronto in connection with his business, a real estate agency.

In November of 1886, he was diagnosed as having epilepsy. Unable to work, Fenton went to New York in search of divine healing through the ministry of Dr. Simpson. After attending meetings for a week, he was anointed, prayed for by Dr. Simpson, and completely healed. Returning to Toronto, Fenton became the energetic and devoted assistant of Rev. John Salmon, who was involved in laying the groundwork for the Christian Alliance in Canada.

Along with Salmon, Fenton attended the founding convention of the two Alliances, where he gave his testimony of divine healing. He was among five Canadians elected to the first General Committee, and was also a founding vice-president of the Evangelical Missionary Alliance.

Fenton was part of the leadership team for the Canadian Alliance. More often than not, he was the one who followed through, making sure that plans were carried out. He was elected secretary of the newly organized Canadian Alliance. Of the Canadian leaders, it was

Fenton who became the chief advocate for Alliance missions, perhaps because Plymouth Brethren assemblies had no strong foreign missions program.

Though Fenton totally embraced the Fourfold Gospel, he was unable to support the Alliance's move toward a denomination. When a convention voted in favor of organized churches and ordination of pastors, he resigned from the movement. For him, the issue was one of organization, not faith. He always identified with Alliance teachings and admired its missionary program.

Dr. R. A. Forrest

Born in the North, R. A. Forrest was sent by Dr. Simpson to live and work in the South, where he literally lived "hand to mouth" by faith. But, as Dr. Forrest explained, "It was a glowing experience, for it was God's hand and my mouth. I never missed a meal, but did postpone a few."

Soon after arriving in the South, Dr. Forrest was appointed as the area's first district superintendent. His territory stretched from the District of Columbia to Dallas. At the time there were no Alliance branches established in the district.

Dr. Forrest was a versatile man. A supersalesman, he was full of confidence in his mission. He was a remarkable preacher, educator and leader. He was also an accomplished vocal and instrumental musician.

Mrs. Forrest, an excellent Bible teacher and expositor, started weeknight classes in Atlanta, Asheville and Greenville, with audiences as high as 500 men and women. Though they had no children of their own, the Forrests took five children into their home and saw to their education.

Due to Mrs. Forrest's poor health, they were not accepted for foreign service. However, they convenanted to send substitutes, and their ministry produced workers on mission stations around the world. Their most enduring memorial is Toccoa Falls College, which Dr. Forrest founded in 1906.

Rev. Albert E. Funk

Albert Funk (1852-1927) had been a minister with the Mennonite General Conference for nine years when he heard of the Alliance in 1885. He enrolled as a student in the New York Missionary Training College.

A year later he became associated with Dr. Simpson in the pastorate of the Gospel Tabernacle. He was present at Old Orchard in 1887, when the Evangelical Christian Alliance was formed.

At the time of reorganization in 1912, Funk was given charge of the foreign department and served as the first foreign secretary. He was remembered for his service to missionaries in preparing them for the field, and then keeping in touch with them after they went abroad.

Funk taught at the training college in New York, and when the school moved to Nyack in 1897, he became the superintendent. He was still active in the Alliance as a teacher and member of the Board of Managers when he died.

Dr. Robert Hall Glover

Robert Hall Glover (1871-1947), native of Toronto, received his Doctor of Medicine degree from New York University (1893) and his Bible training at the New York Missionary Training College under A. B. Simpson. He graduated with honors from both schools. At the University he was awarded the Carnegie Medal for Surgery.

According to Dr. Glover, the most important impact on his early life was made by Dr. Simpson. While in New York, Dr. Glover studied with Robert A. Jaffray, with whom he later pioneered in Kwangsi Province, China (1895). They held their ground against antiforeign sentiments, eventually winning the respect of the Chinese. Jaffray and Glover were known as "the two Robs of South China."

Dr. Glover's service in the Alliance spanned twenty-six years, and in the greater evangelical community totaled fifty years. He founded two Bible schools in China: the Wuchow Bible Institute in Kwangsi Province, and the Blackstone Institute in Wuchang. The alumni of these schools became the spiritual leaders of the China Alliance church. He was chairman of the Alliance Central China Mission for several years.

He became foreign secretary of the Alliance (1913-1921), taught at Wilson Academy and Missionary Training Institute (1945-1947), and spoke frequently at missionary conventions.

Dr. Glover's larger role in other evangelical groups included being chairman of the missions department at Moody Bible Institute in Chicago (1921), director of the China Inland Mission organization in North America (1930), and president of the Interdenominational Foreign Mission Association.

His textbook, *The Progress of Worldwide Missions,* became a major text in 90 percent of the Bible institutes and colleges of North America.

Ellen A. Griffin

"Nellie" Griffin (d. 1887), as she was affectionately called, was born in Binghamton, New York. Left a half-orphan in her early years, she developed qualities of self-reliance and responsibility that later characterized her ministry.

Raised a Roman Catholic, Miss Griffin was born again during the Moody/Sankey meetings in New York City in 1876. She quickly became involved in city mission work and was an early member of the Gospel Tabernacle. When the training college was opened in 1883, she enrolled and graduated with the first class a year later.

Miss Griffin volunteered to serve as a deaconess in the Berachah Home and ministered to the needs of people who came to the home in search of divine healing.

Hon. William Holmes Howland

William Howland (d. 1893) was among the greatest Christian lay leaders ever known to the city of Toronto. Son of the first Lieutenant Governor of Ontario, he seemed marked for success from the start. At age twenty-five, Howland had become director of a trust company, president of two insurance companies, a bank and the Toronto Board of Underwriters. He was vice-president of four other companies.

Howland was converted at age thirty-two through the witness of Rev. Dr. W. S. Rainsford, an Anglican rector who also influenced Dr. Henry Wilson. William Howland then devoted much of his time and energy to a succession of Christian enterprises, often at considerable cost to his business and social standing.

The poor, sick and neglected people of Toronto became Howland's greatest concern. He organized the Toronto Coffee House Association, Ltd., and the Toronto Mission Union. Noticing that most of the people in St. John's Ward, Toronto's worst slum, attended no church—and would have been unwelcome in most churches—he had a church of their own built for them. Night after night he walked the streets in search of broken men and women who needed help. It was in this work that he became acquainted with Rev. John Salmon, father of the Canadian Alliance.

A popular demand emerged in Toronto during 1885 for a man of high moral character and outstanding executive ability to run the city. Howland was elected mayor with an unprecedented majority.

He again directed his vast energies to Christian work after retiring from public office in 1891. A year later he became president of the Dominion Auxiliary Branch of the Christian Alliance. His home,

"Blythe Cottage," became the first administrative headquarters of the Canadian Alliance. More and more of his time was devoted to Alliance matters in Toronto and New York, where he served as a vice-president and member of the Board of Managers until his death.

Rev. John E. Jaderquist

John Jaderquist (1866-1946) went to Africa as a young man with the Gospel Missionary Union. Enroute to the field, he and six companions stayed at Berachah Home while awaiting passage on a ship. He returned from the field in 1892 and joined the Alliance. A graduate of Knox College in Galesburg, Illinois, he entered the Missionary Training Institute in 1897. After graduation, he became superintendent of a local Alliance branch. He then served for six years as district superintendent in New York State.

In May of 1912, at Dr. Simpson's request, Jaderquist was elected publication secretary. He served concurrently as an associate editor of *The Alliance Weekly* and as a member of the Board of Managers. He continued active in ministry until 1920, when he withdrew from the Alliance and continued in ministry elsewhere. One of his daughters married Merrill C. Tenney, a respected New Testament scholar and professor at Wheaton College, Illinois.

Sophie Lichtenfels

Sophie Lichtenfels (d. 1919), a German immigrant living in New York City, became famous as "Sophie, the Scrubwoman." She was a rare character, effective as a public speaker despite her heavily accented English, and made famous through a widely distributed tract entitled "Sophie's Sermon, or, Called to Scrub and Preach."

Sophie was an ardent mission worker, and her life left a marked impression on the work among fallen men and women. Superintendents from almost all the rescue works in New York City and from missions in Philadelphia attended her funeral service as a homage to her support of their work.

In her middle fifties, Sophie went to Rev. A. E. Funk, the foreign secretary, and told him the Lord was calling her to be a missionary. Funk explained that she was past the age limit for foreign service. Later she said the Lord had appeared to her, saying, "Sophie, who is your next door neighbor?" "A family of Switzers," she replied. And in the rear of her building were Italians and Chinese. The Lord showed Sophie she could be a foreign "missioner" at home.

Throughout her life, Sophie was a creative and forceful witness, and gave liberally of her hard-earned income as a scrubwoman. *The Alliance Weekly's* announcement concerning Sophie's death stated, "It is quite remarkable that there was a difference of only four days in her age and that of Dr. Simpson, and that she followed him four days after his transition from earth to heaven. How she loved and prayed for him, her pastor; and how her inimitable 'Hallelujah!' gave point and power to many a sermon by him and others in the Gospel Tabernacle."

Rev. David W. LeLacheur

David W. LeLacheur (1841-1901) was a native of Prince Edward Island in Canada, Dr. Simpson's birthplace. Ordained a Wesleyan minister, he pastored several Methodist churches. While in Portland, Maine, he learned about the Alliance and was drawn to Dr. Simpson.

LeLacheur received his first assignment in 1893: Singapore, the base for Alliance advance in the South Sea islands. Later he was mission superintendent during the Boxer War crisis. Dr. Simpson sent him on extensive travels to Japan, Philippines, China, Tibet, India, the Holy Land and Africa to scout for areas needing a gospel witness. He died in Africa while conducting such a survey trip.

Ulysses Lewis

Ulysses Lewis, a cultured and courteous southern gentleman, was an attorney for forty years in Atlanta, Georgia. A devout Methodist, he was elected one of the first vice-presidents of the Alliance and was the architect of the 1912 constitution. Along with Dr. Forrest, he founded Toccoa Falls Bible Institute.

Lewis was known professionally as a man of strict integrity. He would not accept a criminal case unless he was convinced of its merits. At his death he was honored for elevating the ethical standards of the legal profession in Atlanta.

William T. MacArthur

William T. MacArthur (1861-1949) was born to Scottish immigrant parents in New York. He began his early ministry preaching in Baptist churches in eastern Pennsylvania. During this time he came in contact with Alliance workers and the writings of Dr. Simpson. Through Dr. Simpson's prayers, he witnessed the instantaneous healing of one of his sons who was suffering from diphtheria.

When MacArthur joined the Alliance, Dr. Simpson said of him,

"I have caught a rare bird." The two men had a close relationship with an open and frank understanding of each other. They often shared the platform at Old Orchard conventions.

MacArthur pastored Alliance branches in Pennsylvania, Illinois and Massachusetts. He was district superintendent of the Northwest, a member of the Board of Managers, an evangelist and speaker at many conventions, and both trustee and teacher at the Missionary Training Institute.

Known for his ability to present truth with unique clarity, MacArthur was sought after as a speaker by churches of many denominations. His keen mind and natural sense of humor were accompanied by an intense love for God and people. The Alliance requested him to visit mission fields and minister to missionaries.

All of MacArthur's children achieved successful careers, including his daughter-in-law Helen Hayes, the acclaimed "First Lady of the American Theater." He often referred to their generosity in his later years, which included a trip around the world to visit mission stations.

Dr. Kenneth MacKenzie

As a youth, Kenneth MacKenzie fought a running battle with sickness. At one point, he weighed no more than seventy-five pounds. After hearing of divine healing, he became convinced it was God's will to heal him. The restoration he experienced was total, and served as a prelude to his call to serve the Lord.

MacKenzie began his ministry in rescue missions of New York City. After three years, he became private secretary to an Episcopalian rector, who arranged private tutoring for him at General Theological Seminary, New York, in preparation for pastoral ministry. After ordination by the Episcopal Church, he became assistant pastor in one of the denomination's largest churches in the city.

In 1883, he began a friendship with Dr. Simpson that lasted until his death. Though he never left the Episcopal Church, he participated in Alliance conventions, taught at the Missionary Training Institute, and contributed articles to the Alliance magazine.

Dr. MacKenzie pastored Holy Trinity Parish in New York City for thirteen years, then St. Thomas Church in New Windsor, New York, for three years. From there he moved to the Episcopal church in Westport, Connecticut, for the next fifty-three years. While he proved of immense value to the Alliance, the movement also greatly contributed to his ministry. A fellow clergyman noted, "How immeasurably the Christian Alliance has influenced his mind would be impossible to calculate."

Dr. J. Gregory Mantle

As a Wesleyan minister, J. Gregory Mantle (1853-1925) traveled circuits in England. He also worked in the West London Mission. In Deptford from 1903 to 1908 he organized and built up a large mission work, calling it "Central Hall," a model of mission work repeated in other cities.

Dr. Mantle had other interests as well. His skills as a writer and publisher resulted in *The Illustrated Missionary News.* Pictorial publications were considered as innovative in England as they were in North America at the time. Mantle's magazine attracted support for a large number of evangelists and Bible women in India, China and elsewhere.

He may have been the first to use cinematography as an aid to missionary effort. During extended tours in India, China and Japan, he carried cameras and came away with some remarkable pictures.

Dr. Mantle spent the last twelve years of his life in the United States. He authored several books, including *The Way of the Cross.* During those years he affiliated with the Alliance and took an active part in conventions and taught at the Missionary Training Institute. Taylor University in Upland, Indiana, conferred the honorary Doctor of Divinity on him.

Rev. Stephen Merritt

Stephen Merritt was one of the earliest associates of Dr. Simpson. At age twenty, he entered Armenia Seminary in Duchess County, New York. After inheriting his father's undertaking business, he developed it into one of the largest of its kind. He directed funeral services for many of New York's distinguished citizens, including General Ulysses Grant, eighteenth President of the United States. In contrast, Merritt was also a friend of the various rescue missions of New York City and took care of indigent burials free of charge.

Merritt was a clergyman for forty years, during which time he pastored fifteen churches. He served as vice-chairman of the Board of Managers and is listed in the first annual report of the Christian Alliance.

Merritt's reputation as a supporter of missionary work was widespread. He was the instructor and benefactor of Sammy Morris, the Kru boy from Liberia, who came from Africa to Manhattan in search of a fuller understanding of the Holy Spirit.

Carrie Judd-Montgomery

The year after Carrie Judd (1859-1946) opened Faith Rest Cottage in Buffalo, New York, she began publishing the periodical,

Triumphs of Faith. It continued in publication until near the time of her death.

In 1890, she married George Simpson Montgomery of Oakland, California, where they established a shelter for those who sought healing. They named it "Home of Peace," and in later years it served as a furlough center for missionaries.

Mrs. Montgomery's testimony of healing had a profound influence on Dr. Simpson, and he kept in contact with her after his own miraculous experience. She spoke at the October Convention of 1885 and was present at many subsequent conventions until her marriage in 1890 took her to California. Among the women appointed to key leadership positions in the early days of the Alliance, she served as recording secretary on the Board of Managers.

Dr. George P. Pardington

George P. Pardington (1866-1915) was born in St. Clair, Michigan. At the age of ten, he received a thrashing from a schoolteacher that caused a physical disability from which he suffered most of his life. He appeared for a period of time to have been healed, but later the problem returned. Despite his handicap, he lived a victorious and productive life.

He began his ministry, as did his father, as pastor of a small Methodist church. His higher education at New York University and Drew University culminiated in a Ph.D. in 1898. He attributed the deepening of his spiritual life during his years of graduate studies to Dr. Simpson. He began his teaching career at the Missionary Training Institute in 1897. His classes in biblical and theological studies were demanding, yet full of humor.

His publications included several books very significant in Alliance schools: *Outline Studies in Christian Doctrine* and *The Crisis of the Deeper Life.* He also prepared *Twenty-five Wonderful Years,* official history of the Alliance after its first quarter-century of ministry. Apart from Dr. Simpson, perhaps no other person was as influential as Dr. Pardington in the development of Alliance doctrine, especially the subject of sanctification.

Dr. Peter W. Philpott

Peter W. Philpott, born in Canada and a blacksmith in his early life, spent his first nine years of Christian service with the Salvation Army. Later, he served as a national evangelist and then pastored two of America's largest evangelical churches: Moody Memorial Church in Chicago and Church of the Open Door in Los Angeles.

At the age of eighty-eight and the celebration of his seventieth year of ministry, he received a congratulatory cable from Queen Elizabeth.

Born with a hereditary condition that claimed the lives of both his father and brother, Dr. Philpott was healed completely at age twenty-seven. He had a strong voice and constitution that enabled him to have an effective ministry in open-air meetings and outdoor amphitheaters. For fifteen years he was one of the great preachers at the Carnegie Hall Bible Conference.

Dr. Philpott actively supported the Canadian Alliance and served on the Board of Managers. On numerous occasions he was invited to speak at the New York Gospel Tabernacle.

Josephus L. Pulis

According to George P. Pardington, Pulis was one of the most impressive trophies of grace in the early years of the Alliance. He was the subject of the only biography written by Dr. Simpson, *From the Uttermost to the Uttermost.*

Pulis was transformed from a life of street living, dissipation, filth and prison to a life of assurance and power. One of the original seven who started the Gospel Tabernacle with Dr. Simpson, he became an elder in the church and conducted the four o'clock afternoon services at the tabernacle's Berachah Chapel. Pulis served on the Board of Managers for many years. His connection with Dr. Simpson spanned more than thirty years.

Pulis experienced a miraculous healing of a faulty heart and affected vital organs. His personal testimony inspired the faith of many others to seek and find divine healing. Simplicity characterized his ministry to the many people who came to the four o'clock service for prayer and counsel. Often these people were of the highest culture.

Dr. Paul Rader

Born in 1879, Paul Rader was one of ten children in the home of a Methodist minister serving at the time in Denver, Colorado. He was converted at age nine and by age sixteen was leading the singing for his father's revival campaigns throughout the state of Colorado.

Rader attended universities in Colorado, Missouri and Minnesota and was active in the sports programs. For two years he was athletic instructor at the University of Puget Sound, Washington, then went east to attend Harvard. He became pastor of a Congregational church in Boston.

Rader returned to the West in 1906, married and became pastor of a church in Portland, Oregon. By 1910, however, he was so disillusioned by the liberalism he had embraced that he left the ministry. Returning to New York, he sank to the level of participating in prizefighting exhibitions. Eventually he drifted into the oil business and worked in a New York office.

During this time, Rader received news of his father's death. Deeply moved by the passing of his father, and his own aimless existence, Rader confined himself to his room on Forty-fourth Street for three days and finally surrendered himself totally to God. Unknown to him, he was within a few doors of the Gospel Tabernacle and Dr. Simpson.

Rader began immediately to preach in the streets of New York. Through a Methodist publisher in the city, he was led to F. H. Rossiter, superintendent of the Alliance branch in Harrisburg, Pennsylvania, and the beginning of a significant role in the Alliance, eventually succeeding Dr. Simpson as its president.

Rev. E. J. Richards

E. J. Richards (1869-1939) was ordained to the ministry of the Alliance in 1900 in Lancaster, Pennsylvania. One of his early pastorates was in New Castle, where he served for five years, strengthening the foundations of what would become one of the Alliance's stronger churches in later years. From New Castle he moved to the work of field evangelist before his appointment as superintendent of Alliance work in New York and later of the Eastern District.

Richards served as home secretary for eighteen years, and the work grew under his administrative skill. He was called in 1929 to become pastor of the Gospel Tabernacle. After six years he returned to the field of evangelism.

E. G. Selchow

E. G. Selchow (d. 1915) was a prominent and respected New York businessman of the Selchow and Richter Company, a diversified company that imported, manufactured, published and distributed. Still in operation, the company manufactures and distributes the well-known game of "Scrabble."

Home amusements may have seemed strange for someone as dedicated to the cause of Christ as Selchow was, but he gave generously of his time and money for the Lord's work. Not only was he a charter member of the Gospel Tabernacle and instrumental in establishing the Berachah Home, he also served as a member of the Board of Managers in the early years.

Louise Shepard

Little is known of Miss Shepard's early life. Records indicate that she was raised in a non-Christian home. In 1890, Louise and her mother stayed in the home of a friend who was attending Dr. Simpson's Friday meetings. She persuaded Mrs. Shepard to attend, but Louise refused at first to go. She finally relented and was soundly converted in late December of 1890.

Miss Shepard, a gifted and trained musician, soon began to travel with Dr. Simpson's convention team. In June, 1891, she became managing editor of *The Christian Alliance* magazine. She taught at the New York Missionary Training College, wrote articles for the magazine and authored several books. In 1900, Miss Shepard left New York to marry Rev. C. H. Pridgeon, a Presbyterian pastor in Canonsburg, Pennsylvania.

May Agnew Stephens

May Agnew Stephens (d. 1935), a Canadian, met Dr. Simpson when she was a Salvation Army recruit in New York. She became his song leader and pianist, while she worked on the editorial staff of the Salvationist magazine, *The War Cry.* She not only participated in the services of the Gospel Tabernacle, but also in some of Dr. Simpson's major conventions. Along with Dr. Simpson, his daughter Margaret, and R. Kelso Carter, she worked on *Hymns of the Christian Life* (numbers 1, 2, and 3 combined). The hymnal contained twenty-two of her hymns.

Her evangelistic enthusiasm was as ardent as her musical ability. In 1899, she opened the Eighth Avenue Mission.

She later married Harold L. Stephens, who pastored the Parkdale Alliance Tabernacle in Toronto. He became an international evangelist and she traveled with him for twenty-five years in his campaigns. Although from infancy she suffered from a foot deformity and walked with a cane, she did not allow the handicap to keep her from a full and active public ministry.

Rev. William Coit Stevens

W. C. Stevens followed his father's example and became a Presbyterian minister. After meeting Dr. Simpson, however, he became an enthusiastic supporter of the Alliance.

To his college training, he added studies at Union Seminary in New York and two years of graduate work in Germany. A gifted linguist, he acquired fluency in Greek, Hebrew, Latin, German, and French. Though he earned numerous degrees and scholastic honors, he disavowed them all, preferred to be called "Pastor Stevens."

Stevens organized the Gospel Tabernacle in Los Angeles and also served as superintendent of Alliance efforts along the Pacific Coast from Mexico to British Columbia. He then moved to Nyack to become dean and instructor in the Missionary Training Institute. He also left his mark as an educator on Kansas Bible School, St. Paul Bible Institute, Simpson Bible Institute, and Seattle Bible Institute, where he was principal his last five years of ministry.

One of the many men influenced by Stevens was L. E. Maxwell, president of Prairie Bible Institute at Three Hills, Alberta, Canada. Another educator he encouraged was Harold Freligh, who taught at St. Paul Bible Institute, and then at Nyack from 1933 to 1956.

Rev. Albert E. Thompson

Albert E. Thompson (1870-1927) was born in Ontario, Canada. While studying at the University of Toronto, he became very ill, but was healed through the ministry of Rev. John Salmon, the Alliance leader in Toronto. The course of Thompson's life was changed when he heard Dr. Simpson speak in a missionary convention. He then enrolled in the Missionary Training Institute.

Thompson began his missionary service in Palestine in 1903. Though the territory was under Turkish control and the population was largely Muslim and hostile to Christianity, Thompson laid the foundation for an aggressive work. The American Free Church was organized, a corregated metal tabernacle was erected and, finally, a church built in 1913.

Thompson authored *The Life of A. B. Simpson,* the official biography of the founder.

Dr. Walter A. Turnbull

As a young Canadian attending the Missionary Training Institute, Turnbull was drawn to Dr. Simpson. In 1903, he sailed for India as an Alliance missionary, but subsequently found a larger ministry in North America as a vice-president, both education and foreign secretaries, treasurer of the Alliance, and editor of *The Alliance Weekly.*

Harriet A. Waterbury

Harriet Waterbury (d. 1891) was by birth and early training a Quaker. An exceptional teacher, she was promoted to principal of a public school. Little is known as to how she first came into the Alliance, but she answered the call of God by enrolling in the Missionary Training College when it first opened in New York City. She was a member of the first graduating class in 1884.

After graduation, Miss Waterbury was encouraged to remain in New York to assist in the work. Her skills soon led her to a teaching position at the training school. Dr. Pardington said that her courses in Bible doctrine and church history were among the strongest ever given at the institute.

Rev. E. D. Whiteside

E. D. "Daddy" Whiteside (d. 1927) was born in Canada, where he was first licensed to preach in the New Brunswick Conference of the Methodist Church. Due to poor health, he was unable to carry on a regular ministry.

Hoping to regain his health and to enter business, he moved to Pittsburgh, Pennsylvania. Soon after arriving, he felt called to do slum work, but was greatly hindered by his weak physical condition.

He described his miraculous healing in these words, "Years were consumed in the search for health. But I finally threw up my hands. That was what was needed. To my utter amazement, when I finally threw up my hands I was instantly touched by Jesus. Divine life flowed through my body." From that hour, God became very real to him and he entered into a rare fellowship with God.

When Dr. Simpson came to Pittsburgh to establish an Alliance branch, he appointed Whiteside to be superintendent. The growth that occurred in the city and in the entire district was a result of his ministry. His influence extended and multiplied through the workers he trained. These pastors and missionaries were often referred to as "Whiteside's boys."

Known as "the praying man of Pittsburgh," Whiteside's answer to problems was, "Brethren, let us pray." Prayer was perhaps the outstanding force in his life. He taught people to pray and he himself spent many entire nights in prayer. Dr. Shuman said of him, "There was about him an atmosphere that made one conscious of the presence of the Lord."

For twenty-five years, Whiteside ministered to prisoners in Allegheny County Prison. He testified that his earlier work in the slums with "thieves, murderers and vagabonds" was helpful in the preparation for service that came later. It was said that he had more friends among the bums of Pittsburgh than any other man.

Mr. Whiteside served on the Board of Managers of the Alliance, and he also worked with the South African General Mission, the Central American Mission, the Board of Mission to the Jews and Peter Robinson's mission to black people. His annual conventions in Carnegie Music Hall, Pittsburgh, generated thousands of dollars for missions.

A year before his death, Whiteside stated his desire for the remainder of his life: "I desire to live that I may pray. I do not want to go to heaven yet. I want to stay a while longer to pray."

Dr. Henry Wilson

Henry Wilson (1841-1908), a Canadian, was educated at Trinity College, Toronto. An honor student, he earned several degrees and received an honorary Doctor of Divinity degree. His conversion in a Salvation Army service and an open approval of them caused tensions with his Anglican Church superiors and his eventual move to New York City, where he joined the pastoral staff of St. George's Episcopal Church.

In 1889 he became associate pastor of the New York Gospel Tabernacle, where he served for nineteen years. Dr. Simpson leaned heavily upon him and it was said there was no one closer to the founder. They often participated in a joint ministry, with Dr. Simpson preaching and Dr. Wilson serving communion.

On tours, Dr. Wilson often doubled as a preacher and a children's worker. His simplicity of character made him a natural friend to children, and he called himself "B.B.B." (Big Baby Brother). For many years he published a weekly children's section in *The Alliance Weekly*. He gladly served as president of the Junior Missionary Society, consisting of 5,000 Alliance children praying for 5,000 children in other lands.

Having always taken a great interest in the educational work of the Alliance, he was a leader in founding a high school at Nyack, which was later named Wilson Memorial Academy in his honor. He was an accomplished scholar, being well versed in Greek and Latin, the classics of literature. A Greek New Testament was his pocket companion at all times.

While maintaining his connections with the Episcopal Church and acting with the full consent of his bishop, Dr. Wilson became one of the incorporators and officers of the Alliance. After ten years at the Gospel Tabernacle, he was asked to become field superintendent of the Alliance, a responsibility which involved extensive travels and often difficult situations.

It was while attending an Alliance missionary convention in Atlanta, Georgia, that he died after speaking in a children's meeting.

Notes

Chapter One: The Louisville Experience

1. A. E. Thompson, *The Life of A. B. Simpson* (New York: The Christian Alliance Publishing Co., 1920), p. 43.
2. Albert Benjamin Simpson, *The Alliance Weekly* (June, 1914): p. 210.
3. Albert Benjamin Simpson, "A Personal Testimony," *The Alliance Weekly* (October, 1915): p. 11.
4. Albert Benjamin Simpson, *The Fulness of Jesus* (New York: The Christian Alliance Publishing Co., 1890), p. 81.
5. Thompson, *Life of A. B. Simpson,* p. 66.
6. Ibid., p. 68.
7. A. W. Tozer, *Wingspread* (Harrisburg: Christian Publications, Inc., 1943), p. 45.
8. Simpson, "A Personal Testimony," p. 11.

   The early Keswick meetings were generated through W. E. Boardman and R. Pearsall Smith, who together visited England in 1873 in the interest of D. L. Moody's mass evangelistic meetings. In their thirty years of friendship (*Signs of Our Times,* June 9, 1975, p. 360) Boardman and Smith had forged an emphasis on "the higher Christian life" that became the backbone to the Keswick movement. Boardman authored a book titled *The Higher Christian Life* in 1858, which was revised in 1871. Smith's wife, Hannah Whitall Smith, authored *The Christian's Secret of a Happy Life* in 1870. Both books went through numerous editions and became widely known. Breakfast meetings on "the higher Christian life" were sponsored by Samuel Morely, a member of Parliament for Bristol, and an estimated 2,400 ministers were exposed from England and the continent. A conference was organized by an Anglican bishop of Keswick, Rev. Canon Battersby which multiplied and became known as Keswick conferences.

9. Simpson, "A Personal Testimony," p. 11.

10. Simpson, *The Fulness of Jesus,* p. 66.
11. Thompson, *Life of A. B. Simpson,* p. 68.
12. Ibid., p. 71.
13. *Louisville Courier Journal,* February 26, 1875, p. 4.
14. Ibid., March 1, 1875, p. 4.
15. Ibid., March 15, 1875, p. 4.
16. Ibid.
17. Ibid., March 14, 1875, p. 3.
18. Ibid.
19. Thompson, *Life of A. B. Simpson,* p. 44.
20. Albert Benjamin Simpson, "A Story of Providence," *Living Truths* (March, 1907): p. 150.
21. Tozer, *Wingspread,* p. 63.
22. Thompson, *Life of A. B. Simpson,* p. 120.
23. Ibid., p. 121.
24. Ibid., p. 122.
25. Ibid., p. 57.

Chapter Two: Foundation Years

1. A. E. Thompson, *The Life of A. B. Simpson* (New York: The Christian Alliance Publishing Co., 1920), p.10.
2. Ibid., p. 5.
3. Ibid., p. 7.
4. Ibid., p. 9.
5. Ibid., p. 10.
6. Ibid., p. 8.
7. Ibid., p. 14.
8. Ibid., p. 12.
9. Ibid., p. 15.
10. Ibid.
11. Ibid., p. 16.
12. Ibid., p. 18.
13. Ibid., p. 21.
14. Ibid., p. 36.
15. Ibid., p. 22.
16. Ibid., p. 35.
17. Ibid., p. 33.
18. *Hamilton* (Ontario) *Spectator,* July 27, 1805, p. 2.
19. *Hamilton Evening Times,* September 13, 1805, p. 3.
20. *Hamilton Spectator,* December 15, 1875, p. 4.

Chapter Three: The New York Pastorate

1. Diary of Albert Benjamin Simpson, November 25, 1879, p. 152 (Simpson Historical Library, Nyack, New York).

   Mr. Simpson's difficulties with his wife continued for some time. The diary shows that he continually prayed for her and for himself as well, that he would be "kept in compassion, love and holy forgiveness." (Tues., Nov. 25, 1879, p. 152.)

   Three days later he wrote: "Tonight from 9:30 to 12:00 led to stay with Maggie and pray and talk with her. Aid given so quietly and gently and she came fully and sweetly...with many tears to the Shepherd. I leave her with Him and pray for grace to be wise, faithful and loving." (Fri., Nov. 28, p. 155.)

But her displeasure flared up again a few days later. He wrote: "To come to my home is like coming out of light and peace into the dark and fiery pit. My children were in tears when I returned tonight and in strife." (Thurs., Dec. 4, p. 156.)

In contrast, two days later: "much tenderness given me today for my wife and much quietness to her." (Sat., Dec. 6, p. 157.)

On his thirty-seventh birthday he wrote: "blessed fellowship and prayer all day. Maggie so peacefully blessed." (Mon., Dec. 15, p. 159) And the next day: "praise for my wife's kind and loving and altered spirit. God seems so to bless her as he leads me in the peculiar path he has of late so clearly shown." (Tues., Dec. 16, p. 159.)

At the end of the month she was quite sick, but her husband wrote that it "brought [her] so near to Christ." (Tues., Dec. 30, p. 163.) On New Year's day, this entry: "my wife is very ill the past three days. Much conflict, but now great rest. She has much peace and comfort and simple trust in God." (Thurs., Jan. 1, 1880, p. 164.)

She apparently continued to improve in health, and Simpson does not mention her again until Feb. 17th. He simply writes: "much anxiety and prayer for Maggie last night." (p. 175.) And then in March he records "Maggie very ill since Sabbath." (Wed., Mar. 3, p. 178.) His wife was probably pregnant with Howard Home. The previous pregnancy with Margaret May nearly cost Maggie her life. Her pregnancy with Howard may well account for her behavior during the move from Louisville to New York. The dairy contains considerably more descriptions of the family strife than is written here.

2. A. E. Thompson, *The Life of A. B. Simpson* (New York: The Christian Alliance Publishing Co., 1920), pp. 47,48.
3. Katherine Alberta Brennen, *Love Stands* (published privately), p. 13.
4. Simpson diary, p. 149.
5. Ibid., p. 151.
6. Ibid., p. 152.
7. Ibid.
8. Ibid., p. 153.
9. Ibid., p. 158.
10. Ibid., p. 160.
11. Ibid.
12. Ibid., p. 163.
13. Ibid., p. 165.
14. Ibid., p. 167.
15. A. B. Simpson, "A Story of Providence," *Living Truths* (March, 1907): p. 150.
16. Simpson diary, p. 152.
17. A. B. Simpson, "Editorial," *The Gospel in All Lands* (February, 1880): p. 60.
18. Simpson diary, p. 167.
19. Ibid., p. 168.
20. Ibid., p. 171.

21. Simpson, *The Gospel in All Lands* (July, 1880): p. 42.
22. Ibid., p. 42.
23. Ibid., inside back cover.
24. *The Gospel in All Lands* (August, 1880): inside back cover.
25. *The Gospel in All Lands* (September, 1881): inside back cover.
26. *The Gospel in All Lands* (July, 1881): inside back cover.
27. A. B. Simpson, "My Medicine Chest," *The Alliance Witness* (October, 1913): p. 18.
28. Thompson, *The Life of A. B. Simpson,* p. 74.
29. Old Orchard Beach is located about twelve miles south of Portland, Maine. The last quarter of the 19th century and the first part of the 20th century, it was the major summer resort on the east coast. There were train connections to Old Orchard from New York, Boston and Montreal. Fifty-four trains a day during the season stopped at Old Orchard. Passenger ships also came from New York and Boston.

    In July of 1873 an association comprised mostly of Methodists purchased about 50 acres of land within a half-mile of the beach. They needed a larger camp meeting site than the one already used at West Kennebunk, Maine, a few miles from Old Orchard. Much of the land was a forest of oak, maple and pine, in the midst of which was located a natural amphitheatre. It would accommodate about 7,000 persons.

    Much of the land was cleared and benches were erected throughout the amphitheatre to provide seats. The acoustics were so remarkable throughout the vast outside auditorium that an ordinary speaker could be heard distinctly. Around the perimeter the campers pitched their tents and eventually built cottages. Those who desired could rent rooms in the hotels on the beach.

    Throughout the summer months various Christian groups and organizations rented the grounds to conduct spiritual conventions. It seemed as if the Lord designed this place especially for camp meetings. It was on these grounds that the Alliance was first organized and Mr. Simpson conducted his largest summer conventions.

    J. Staples Locke, *Historical Sketches of Old Orchard* (Boston), p. 48,49.

30. "Old Orchard Convention Supplement," *The Word, the Work and the World* (July/August, 1887). See also: Thompson, *The Life of A. B. Simpson,* p. 75.
31. William T. MacArthur, *Twenty Sermonettes* (published privately): p. 47.
32. Ibid.
33. Thompson, *Life of A. B. Simpson,* p. 75.
34. Ibid., pp. 75, 76.

    1. As I shall meet Thee in that day, I solemnly accept this truth as part of Thy Word, and of the gospel of Christ, and God helping me, I shall never question it until I meet Thee there.

    2. As I shall meet Thee in that day, I take the Lord Jesus as my physical life for all the needs of my body until all my life work is done; and God helping me, I shall never doubt that He does so become my life and strength from this moment, and will keep me under all circumstances until His blessed coming, and until all His will for me is perfectly fulfilled.

    3. As I shall meet Thee in that day, I solemnly agree to use this blessing for

the glory of God, and the good of others, and to speak of it or minister in connection with it in any way which God may call me or others may need me in the future.

35. Ibid.
36. Ibid.
37. Ibid., p. 78.
38. A. B. Simpson, *The Gospel of Healing* (New York: The Alliance Press Co., 1888), pp. 258-259.
39. A. W. Tozer, *Wingspread* (Harrisburg: Christian Publications, Inc., 1943), p. 81.
40. A. B. Simpson, "What God Is Doing in Our Age," *The Word, the Work and the World* (July/August, 1885): p. 209.

    In June of 1885 at the Bethshan International Convention on Divine Healing and True Holiness in London, Mr. Simpson bore testimony to his dual experiences of receiving the Lord Jesus as his Sanctifier and as his Healer. In regard to the latter experience he said:

    "From that hour I have been permitted by God to work (I say this to His honor and thousands could bear witness to it) about four times as hard as I ever did in my life. I have had the entire charge of a large magazine for these four years and for which I have done half the writing and all the editing and supervision. I have been pastor of a church where we have had services every night in the week and three on Sunday. I have had charge of a home—Berachah, which is open for those who come for healing and where hundreds have called in the past year. And for these four years I can truly say that, with the exception of two nights, I have never been tired, and on those two nights I just felt the Lord wanted me to rest on His bosom a little. I thank God I have not had one hour away from work and have not had one single summer vacation. I have not done this to glory in it, but because I could not help it."

    He omitted one major enterprise. In October of 1883 he opened a Missionary Training College in New York. Even while he was at Bethshan and speaking the words just quoted, five of the first graduates of the college were in Africa.

41. Ibid., p. 209.
42. A. B. Simpson, *Baptism and the Baptism of the Holy Spirit* (New York: The Christian and Missionary Alliance, May, 1902), p. 286.
43. Thompson, *Life of A. B. Simpson,* p. 86.
44. Ibid., p. 84.
45. A. B. Simpson, "A Story of Providence," *Living Truths* (March, 1907): p. 151.
46. Ibid.
47. Thompson, *Life of A. B. Simpson,* p. 258.
48. Ibid., p. 87.

Chapter Four: The Gospel Tabernacle

1. A. B. Simpson, *Missionary Messages* (New York: The Christian Alliance Publishing Co., 1925), p. 19.
2. A. B. Simpson, *The King's Business* (New York: The Word, Work and World Publishing Co., 1886), pp. 103,104.
3. A. E. Thompson, *The Life of A. B. Simpson* (New York: The Christian Alliance Publishing Co., 1920), p. 94.

4. Ibid. Also *The Word, the Work and the World* (June, 1882): p. 215.

   Part of the article reads:

   "It is proposed by the Divine blessing to build up a Free Gospel Church here on simple Scriptural and voluntary principles in the name of Jesus, [and to pursue] evangelistic and missionary work among the neglected and non-church-going population, especially the middle classes who are the most neglected in our great cities."

5. Thompson, *Life of A. B. Simpson,* p. 93.
6. A. B. Simpson, "The Story of Providence," *Living Truths* (March, 1907): p. 152.
7. Thompson, *Life of A. B. Simpson,* p. 88.
8. A. B. Simpson, *The Word, the Work and the World* (November, 1882): p. 263.
9. "Gathering in the Sinners" (newspaper clipping, November 5, 1883).
10. Thompson, *Life of A. B. Simpson,* p. 200.
11. Ibid., p. 198.
12. Ibid., p. 202.
13. A. B. Simpson, *The Word, the Work and the World* (August, 1882): p. 64; (November, 1882): p. 203.

    Simpson held a special Divine healing service at the Grand Opera Hall on Thursday evening, May 25, 1882. There was a large attendance. It is the first account in Simpson's periodical of such a meeting. It may have been the harbinger of the Friday meetings. "The meeting was called for the purpose of presenting the teaching of the Word of God" regarding Divine Healing. It had been "a familiar subject of teaching and testimony in all the meetings," and "in a few days a house was to be formally dedicated to God for the work of Divine Healing." (A House of Healing, 980 DeKalb Ave., Brooklyn. J.C. Young, formerly with Dr. Charles Cullis, would be in charge. This home was not directly connnected with the Gospel Tabernacle.)

14. Thompson, *Life of A. B. Simpson,* p. 139.
15. Ibid., p. 139.
16. Ibid., p. 140.
17. A. W. Tozer, *Wingspread* (Harrisburg: Christian Publications, Inc., 1943), p. 107.
18. Thompson, *Life of A. B. Simpson,* p. 123.
19. "Annual Report of the Gospel Tabernacle," *The Word, the Work and the World* (March, 1883): p. 46.
20. Tozer, *Wingspread,* p. 94.
21. A. B. Simpson, *The Word, the Work and the World* (March, 1883): p. 46, 47.
22. A. B. Simpson, *The Word, the Work and the World* (April, 1883): p. 68.
23. A. B. Simpson, *The Word, the Work and the World* (July, 1883): p. 113.
24. A. B. Simpson, *The Word, the Work and the World* (October, 1883): p. 154.

    The article begins, "With devout thanksgiving to God we record the opening of the Missionary Training College on Monday, October 1 in this City. The opening services were held in the building which has been temporarily fitted up for the College at 446 8th Ave."

    In March, 1890, at the dedication of the buildings on 8th Ave. and 44th St., Harriet Waterbury gave a report of the history of the school. She was a member of the graduating class in 1884 and then taught at the college. She also was an assistant editor of *The Word, the Work and the World.* She had been a Quaker and also principal of a public school.

In her report she said, "The Training College opened on the first Monday in October, 1883, on the first floor of a building on 8th Ave. just above 32nd St., where for a time it seemed as though the whole work would be permanently located. After a few weeks it was removed to the second floor of the same building. Before Christmas another change was made which transferred the College to the Grand Opera Hall." (*Christian Alliance and Missionary Weekly,* March 1890, p. 204.)

Nyack College's position that the school was founded in 1882 is based on documentation dating back to the late 1890s, including statements by Dr. Simpson, Walter Turnbull and A. E. Funk. Even the institute manuals in 1897 cite 1882 as the year of beginning.

The confusion in dates is no doubt related to the fact that Dr. Simpson began conducting Bible classes as part of the Gospel Tabernacle program in 1882—actually in the closing days of 1881—and may have considered those classes as the forerunner of the New York Missionary Training College.

Nyack College may lay claim to those Bible classes as the actual beginnings of the school, just as the C&MA lays claim to the first missionary band sent out in 1884 by the Gospel Tabernacle before the two Alliances were formed.

The distinction of Nyack College being the first Bible school in North America is not in jeopardy, since the later date of 1883 is still earlier than either Moody Bible Institute (1887) or Gordon College (1889). However, the word "continuing" must be added to the distinction of "first," because Dr. Charles Cullis opened his school on Beacon Street in Boston in 1875. By 1892 it disappeared.

25. Thompson, *Life of A. B. Simpson,* p. 216.
26. Ibid.
27. A. B. Simpson, *The Word, the Work and the World* (July, 1884): p. 160.
28. Thompson, *Life of A. B. Simpson,* p. 91.
29. A. B. Simpson, "Editorial," *The Word, the Work and the World* (July, 1883): p. 113.
30. Lindsay Reynolds, *Footprints* (Toronto: The Christian and Missionary Alliance in Canada, 1981), pp. 77,78.
31. A. B. Simpson, "Editorial," *The Word, the Work and the World* (October, 1885): p. 280.
32. Thompson, *Life of A. B. Simpson,* p. 108.
33. Tozer, *Wingspread,* p. 98.
34. Ibid., p. 129.
35. A. B. Simpson, *Wholly Sanctified* (Harrisburg: Christian Publications, Inc., 1982 edition), p. 58.
36. Tozer, *Wingspread,* p. 54.
37. Eugene Rivard, "Alliance History of Music" (Unpublished study, Canadian Bible College, November, 1984).
38. Margaret Simpson Buckman, "The Hymns of Dr. Simpson," *Nyack Missionarian* (Nyack, N.Y.: Nyack College, 1945), p. 17.
39. May Agnew Stephens, "Dr. Simpson's Ministry in Song," *The Alliance Weekly* (December 20, 1919): p. 206.
40. Tozer, *Wingspread,* p. 119.

Chapter Five: The Two Alliances

1. Mary Gray Tinkham, "Recollections," Simpson Historical Library, International Headquarters, Nyack, New York.
2. Ibid.
3. *The Word, the Work and the World* (May, 1887): p. 317.
4. *The Word, the Work and the World* (June, 1887): p. 367.
5. *The Word, the Work and the World* (June, 1887): p. 365.
6. *The Word, the Work and the World* (June, 1887): pp. 365,366.
7. Ibid., p. 366.
8. Ibid.
9. Walter Turnbull, "Editorial," *The Alliance Weekly* (November 8, 1919): p. 99.
10. A. E. Thompson, *The Life of A. B. Simpson* (New York: The Christian Publishing Co., 1920), p. 111.
11. *The Word, the Work and the World* (September, 1887): p. 66.
12. A. B. Simpson, "Reasons for the Alliance" (Pamphlet, April, 1888).

    A copy of the pamphlet was placed in the cornerstone of the Gospel Tabernacle, New York, in January, 1889, and is in the Simpson Historical Library, International Headquarters, Nyack, New York.

13. A. B. Simpson, "Editorial," *The Word, the Work and the World* (September, 1887): p. 110.
14. A. W. Tozer, *Wingspread* (Harrisburg: Christian Publishing, Inc., 1943), p. 103.
15. Thompson, *Life of A. B. Simpson,* p. 134.
16. *The Christian Alliance* (January, 1888): p. 14.
17. *The Word, the Work and the World* (July-August, 1887): p. 108.
18. Lindsay Reynolds, *Footprints* (Toronto: The Christian & Missionary Alliance in Canada, 1981), p. 96.
19. Thompson, *Life of A. B. Simpson,* p. 104.
20. Ibid., p. 105.
21. "Editorial," *The Word, the Work and the World* (August, 1887): p. 112.

Chapter Six: The Missionary Explosion

1. A. W. Tozer, *Wingspread* (Harrisburg: Christian Publishing, Inc., 1943), p. 96.
2. Ibid., p. 97.
3. A. B. Simpson, *The Word, the Work and the World* (August, 1887): p. 111.
4. *The Christian Alliance and Missionary Weekly* (June, 1890): p. 426.
5. George P. Pardington, *Twenty-five Wonderful Years* (New York: Christian Alliance Publishing Co., 1914), p. 104.
6. Lindsay Reynolds, *Footprints* (Toronto: The Christian & Missionary Alliance in Canada, 1981), p. 110.
7. Ibid., p. 129.
8. Ibid.
9. A. B. Simpson, "Editorial," *The Christian Alliance and Missionary Weekly* (May, 1890): p. 321.
10. A. B. Simpson, "Editorial," *The Christian Alliance and Missionary Weekly* (August, 1890): p. 35.

    The prayer pledge card read: "Relying upon the Holy Spirit to bring it to my remembrance, I promise to pray daily for the evangelization of the world within the present century and for the speedy coming of the Lord Jesus." By October 2,000 had signed the pledge card.

11. Ibid., p. 40.
12. Ibid., p. 35.
13. Ibid.
14. A. B. Simpson, "Editorial," *The Christian Alliance and Missionary Weekly* (November, 1890): p. 274.
15. A. B. Simpson, *The Christian Alliance and Missionary Weekly* (July 17, 1891): p. 33.
16. Ibid.
17. A. B. Simpson, "Editorial," *The Christian Alliance and Missionary Weekly* (August 21, 1891): p. 98.
18. Ibid.
19. A. B. Simpson, "Why Our People Give so Much for Missions," *Living Truths* (November, 1905): p. 644.
20. "Dr. Simpson Gets $70,000," *Baltimore Sun,* August 8, 1897.
21. A. B. Simpson, "Editorial," *The Christian Alliance and Missionary Weekly* (September 18, 1891): p. 178.
22. A. B. Simpson, "Editorial," *The Christian Alliance and Missionary Weekly* (October 16, 1891): pp. 227,228.
23. Tozer, *Wingspread,* p. 94.
24. Thompson, *Life of A. B. Simpson,* p. 229.

Chapter Seven: Changes, Crises and Convictions

1. A. W. Tozer, *Wingspread* (Harrisburg: Christian Publishing, Inc., 1943), p. 101.
2. Lindsay Reynolds, *Footprints* (Toronto: The Christian & Missionary Alliance in Canada, 1981), p. 268.
3. George P. Pardington, *Twenty-five Wonderful Years* (New York: Christian Alliance Publishing Co., 1914), p. 79.
4. Dr. Simpson's periodicals assumed various formats, partly in an attempt to coordinate the periodicals with the changing names and activities of the Alliance, as the following list attests:

Dates	*Title*	*Frequency*
1880 Feb - 1881 Oct	*The Gospel in All Lands* 50-80 pages	monthly
1882 Jan - 1887 Dec	*The Word, the Work and the World* 48 pages	monthly
1882 Feb - 1882 Dec	*The Work and the World* 32-64 pages	monthly
1888 Jan - 1889 June	*The Christian Alliance* 16 pages	weekly
1889 Aug - 1893 Dec	*The Christian Alliance and Missionary Weekly* 16 pages	weekly
1894 Jan - 1896 Dec	*The Christian Alliance and Foreign Missionary Weekly* 24-28 pages	weekly

1897 Jan - 1898 Nov	*The Christian & Missionary Alliance Weekly* 24 pages	weekly
1898 Dec - 1899 May	*The Christian & Missionary Alliance Weekly* 32 pages	monthly
1899 June - 1911 Sept	*The Christian & Missionary Alliance Weekly* 16 pages	weekly
1902 July - 1907 Sept	*Living Truths* 64 pages	monthly
1911 Oct - 1958	*The Alliance Weekly* 16 pages	weekly
1958 1967	*The Alliance Witness* 20 pages	biweekly
1967 1973	*The Alliance Witness* 24 pages	biweekly
1973	*The Alliance Witness* 32 pages	biweekly

5. Tozer, *Wingspread,* p. 127.
6. Harry M. Shuman, "A God-Touched Man," *The Alliance Weekly* (May 1, 1957): pp. 3,4.
7. Ibid.
8. "The Missionary Institute," *The Christian and Missionary Alliance Weekly* (April 6, 1897): p. 362.
9. Robert L. Niklaus, *The School that Vision Built* (Nyack, N.Y.: Nyack College, 1982), p. 13.
10. A. E. Thompson, *Life of A. B. Simpson* (New York: The Christian Alliance Publishing Co., 1920), p. 221.
11. Pardington, *Twenty-five Wonderful Years,* p. 59.
12. Thompson, *Life of A. B. Simpson,* p. 169.
13. Madele Wilson, *Henry Wilson, One of God's Best* (New York: The Alliance Press, 1908), p. 124.
14. Ibid., p. 125.
15. "The Last Message from Our Swedish Missionaries," *The Christian and Missionary Alliance Weekly* (January 19, 1901): p. 30.
16. Thompson, *Life of A. B. Simpson,* p. 231.
17. Thomas Moseley, "William Christie—The Livingstone of Northeast Tibet," *The Alliance Weekly* (February 16, 1955): pp. 5,6.
18. Niklaus, *The School that Vision Built,* p. 13.
19. Reynolds, *Footprints,* p. 252.
20. David J. Fant, "Robert A. Jaffray," *The Alliance Witness* (December 5, 1973): p. 7.
21. Ibid., p. 8.
22. *The Christian and Missionary Alliance Weekly* (June, 1905): p. 353.
23. *The Christian and Missionary Alliance Weekly* (November, 1906): p. 289.
24. A. B. Simpson, "Editorial," *The Christian and Missionary Alliance Weekly* (November 17, 1906): p. 305.
25. *The Christian and Missionary Alliance Weekly* (March 31, 1906): p. 185; (April 21, 1906): p. 233; (May 19, 1906): p. 297.
26. *The Alliance Weekly* (December, 1917).

27. *The Christian and Missionary Alliance Weekly* (January, 1907): p. 40; (February, 1907): pp. 64,65; (July, 1907): p. 44.
28. "Notes from the Home Field," *The Christian and Missionary Alliance Weekly* (April 27, 1907): p. 201.
29. Ibid.
30. Tozer, *Wingspread,* p. 133.
31. A. B. Simpson, "Editorial," *The Christian and Missionary Alliance Weekly* (April 6, 1907): p. 157.
32. A. B. Simpson, *Living Truths* (April, 1907): p. 191.
33. A. B. Simpson, "Editorial," *The Christian and Missionary Alliance Weekly* (March, 1907): p. 121.
34. Thompson, *Life of A. B. Simpson,* p. 75.
35. Diary of Albert Benjamin Simpson, May, 1907 (Simpson Historical Library, Nyack, New York).
36. Ibid.
37. Simpson diary, August 9, 1907.
38. Simpson diary, September 12, 1907.
39. Simpson diary, September 13, 1907.
40. Ibid.
41. A. B. Simpson, "Farther On," *The Christian and Missionary Alliance Weekly* (September, 1907): p. 134.
42. Simpson diary, October 6, 1912.
43. "Editorial," *The Christian and Missionary Alliance Weekly* (April, 1910): p. 78.
44. "Where We Stand," *The Alliance Witness* (May 1, 1963): p. 19.
45. William W. Menzies, *Anointed to Serve* (Springfield, Missouri: Gospel Publishing House, 1971), pp. 70, 71.
46. Thompson, *Life of A. B. Simpson,* p. 253.

Chapter Eight: Question of Succession

1. A. W. Tozer, *Wingspread* (Harrisburg: Christian Publishing, Inc., 1943), p. 138.
2. Katherine A. Brennen, *Love Stands* (published privately), p. 20.
3. A. E. Thompson, *The Life of A. B. Simpson* (New York: The Christian Alliance Publishing Co., 1920), p. 265.
4. "Annual Report, 1914/1915," The Christian & Missionary Alliance (Nyack, N.Y.: Simpson Historical Library), pp. 21, 22.
5. Lindsay Reynolds, *Footprints* (Toronto: The Christian & Missionary Alliance in Canada, 1981), p. 367.
6. "Minutes of Board of Managers," The Christian & Missionary Alliance, May 30, 1914 (Nyack, N.Y.: Simpson Historical Library).
7. Robert L. Niklaus, *The School that Vision Built* (Nyack, N.Y.: Nyack College, 1982), p. 17.
8. Ibid.
9. Howard Van Dyck, *William Christie, Apostle to Tibet* (Harrisburg: Christian Publishing, Inc., 1956), p. 83.
10. George P. Pardington, "The Crooked Made Straight" (published privately).
11. Ibid.
12. David J. Fant, "Early Associates of Dr. Simpson," *Southeastern District Report* (May, 1972), p. 4.
13. "Annual Report, 1919/1920," pp. 64-66.

14. "Annual Report, 1916/1917," p. 24.
15. Thompson, *Life of A. B. Simpson,* p. 168.
16. "Annual Report, 1916/1917," p. 5.
17. "Annual Report, 1917/1918," p. 45.
18. Thompson, *Life of A. B. Simpson,* p. 136.
19. Ibid., p. 167.
20. Ibid., p. 190.
21. Ibid., p. 166.
22. Ibid.
23. Ibid., pp. 278, 279.
24. Reynolds, *Footprints,* p. 296.
25. Ibid., p. 306.
26. Robert B. Ekvall, ed., *After Fifty Years* (Harrisburg: Christian Publications, Inc., 1939), p. 32.
27. "Minutes of the Board of Managers," May 15, 1918.
28. John E. Jaderquist, personal correspondence, November 29, 1920.
29. Thompson, *Life of A. B. Simpson,* p. 280.
30. Jaderquist, personal correspondence, November 20, 1920.
31. Paul Rader, letter to the Board of Managers, April 3, 1919.
32. Ibid.
33. Ibid.
34. "Annual Report, 1918/1919," p. 3.
35. Thompson, *Life of A. B. Simpson,* p. 284.
36. Ibid., p. 286.
37. Jaderquist, personal correspondence, November 29, 1920.

Chapter Nine: Troubled Transition

1. *The Moody Church Story* (published privately), p. 12.
2. A. E. Thompson, *The Life of A. B. Simpson* (New York: The Christian Alliance Publishing Co., 1920), p. 292.
3. Leon Tucker, *The Redemption of Paul Rader* (New York: The Book Stall, 1918 second edition), p. 127.
4. "Annual Report, 1920/1921," The Christian and Missionary Alliance (Nyack, N.Y.: Simpson Historical Library), p. 18.
5. "Annual Report, 1913/1914," p. 51.
6. "Annual Report, 1920/1921," p. 117.
7. "Editorial," *The Alliance Weekly* (July 2, 1921): p. 245.
8. Louis L. King, "Dr. Alfred Cookman Snead," *The Alliance Witness* (April 5, 1961): p. 5.
9. Ibid.
10. Thompson, *Life of A. B. Simpson,* p. 293.
11. Independent or unattached congregations were first reported in the United States census of 1890. There were then 156 independent congregations, besides 231 independent Lutheran organizations. *The New Schaff-Herzog Encyclopedia of Religious Knowledge* (Grand Rapids: Baker Book House, reprinted 1977, VII), p. 392.
12. The International Prophecy Conference of 1878 became a model for similar conferences on prophetic study, attracting conservative leaders and scholars from England, Europe and America. This interest was sparked largely by John Nelson Darby, who introduced a new historical scheme for prophecy of the Bible. One of the main keys of this interpretation, that the church age is a

parenthetic period of grace, was popularized by C. I. Scofield in his reference Bible. By the turn of the century, interest in these conferences waned as conflict over this interpretation broke out into the open. But dispensational influence in the fundamentalist "come-out" movement (from mainline churches) and in the Keswick movement, which began in 1875 during D. L. Moody's evangelistic meetings in England, had a large part in the shaping of the conservative evangelical image.

13. "Annual Report, 1923/1924," p. 101.
14. E. J. Richards described the development of the home work in four categories: branches supplying the need of a church; rescue missions; gospel centers for Bible and missionary conferences, evangelistic campaigns, youth rallies; independent churches affiliated with the Alliance. *The Alliance Weekly* (December 20, 1919): pp. 215, 224.
15. "Annual Report, 1918/1919," p. 37.
16. According to the biography of Oswald Smith's wife by her daughter, "Daisy's two greatest contributions to [Oswald's] ministry came within the first year of their marriage." These were the doctrine of the Spirit-filled life and her perspective on foreign missions, both emphases from her background in an Alliance church and at the Missionary Training Institute. Hope Evangeline, *Daisy* (Grand Rapids: Baker Book House, 1978), pp. 97,98.
17. Oswald Smith wrote in his own publication, *The Prophet,* an itemized article titled "Our Home Policy": "1. Not the multiplying of churches. There are already far too many. Some might well be abandoned. How often do we find a mere handful of people overfed and underworked, made up for the most part of women, self-satisfied and even anti-evangelistic! There is no vision of enlargement and no sense of obligation to get the Message to the masses. A dried-up, stagnant pool with no outlet. And yet each such little company demands the administrations of a pastor, who might be used somewhere among the unevangelized on the far-flung battle line. As an Alliance of believers, allied for the purpose of world evangelism, emphasis should be placed on the fact that our mission is to train workers for the foreign field, the unoccupied areas of the world rather than for the homeland, the watchword being, 'Forward into the regions beyond.' 2. The establishment of a number of large tabernacle centers in the big cities, to broadcast the truth at home and to form the basis of our foreign work from the standpoint of prayer, money, and missionaries. Such centers will commend the Alliance as a worth-while movement. And with strong executive heads in charge of each place mighty things will be accomplished in the short time that remains before our Lord returns." As quoted in *The Alliance Weekly* (February 9, 1924): p. 804.
18. "God is raising up a great nationwide Tabernacle work, specifically for Evangelism. And in these Tabernacles the fires of Evangelism are kept burning. Necessarily, they are outside and apart from the churches. Their work is the salvation of souls at home and abroad. The originator was probably the Rev. A. B. Simpson, D.D. At least, God gave him the vision. And as long as a Tabernacle remains true to the original God-given vision, it prospers. As soon, however, as it seeks to become a church, it fails and the people leave. Ichabod is then its name." Oswald J. Smith, *Can Organized Religion Survive?* (Toronto: Toronto Tabernacle Publishers, 1932), p. 27.
19. W. H. Chandler left the College Church at Wheaton, Illinois, in 1903 to serve as field evangelist or as chief liaison between evangelical churches and the C&MA. He promoted the convention system for more than two decades.
20. "Annual Report, 1921/1922," pp. 67,68.

21. For years dispensational teaching largely dominated the fundamentalist movement. W. E. Blackstone in *Jesus Is Coming,* which became exceptionally popular with its stress on the demise and ruin of the church, wrote: "There is truly a Church, and it is THE BODY OF CHRIST, one and indivisible, composed of all true believers in Him. It may be called a church within, or among the churches—the wheat among the chaff." *Jesus Is Coming* (New York: Fleming H. Revell, 1908), p. 95.

    George M. Marsden explains, "[American dispensationalists] thought of religion primarily in terms of individuals rather than institutions. The important spiritual unit was the individual. The church existed as a body of sanctified individuals united by commitment to Christ and secondarily as a network of ad hoc spiritual organizations. The institutional church hence had no particular status." *Fundamentalism and American Culture* (New York: Oxford University Press, 1980), p. 71.

    There is no doubt that both Rader and Smith had this mentality.
22. Smith was appointed director of The Christian World Couriers in Canada as founded by Paul Rader. Rader assisted Smith to raise $25,000 in his second missionary convention in Toronto. Oswald J. Smith, *The Story of My Life* (London: Marshall, Morgan and Scott, 1961), pp. 82-88.
23. "The Dawn of an Eternal New Year," *The Alliance Weekly* (February 9, 1924): p. 807.
24. A. W. Tozer, *Wingspread* (Harrisburg: Christian Publications, Inc., 1943), p. 143.
25. David J. Fant, "Early Associates of Dr. Simpson," Southeastern District Report (January, February, 1974): p. 4.
26. Robert L. Niklaus, *The School that Vision Built* (Nyack, N.Y.: Nyack College, 1982), p. 21.
27. Ibid., p. 23.
28. "Annual Report, 1923/1924," p. 23.
29. "The Home-Going of Rev. F. H. Senft," *The Alliance Weekly* (December 12, 1925): p. 856.
30. Ibid.

Chapter Ten: Mixed Signals

1. In 1939 Asbury College conferred the honorary Doctor of Divinity degree on Mr. Shuman.
2. Nathan Bailey, "God Shaped His Life," *The Alliance Weekly* (March 29, 1967): p. 9.
3. Ibid., p. 10.
4. H. M. Shuman, "God Shaped My Life," *The Alliance Weekly* (September 1, 1965): p. 7.
5. Ibid.
6. Ibid.
7. Ibid.
8. H. M. Shuman, "The Modern 'Deeper Life' Is Not Deep Enough," *The Alliance Weekly* (May 16, 1956): p. 6.
9. Bailey, "God Shaped His Life," p. 9.
10. "Annual Report, 1922/23," The Christian and Missionary Alliance (Nyack, N.Y.: Simpson Historical Library), p. 126.
11. *The Cleveland Coloured Gospel Quintette* (Kilmarnock, Scotland: John Ritchie, Ltd., 1937), p. 3.

12. Ibid., p. 5.
13. Ibid., p. 8.
14. The country between Toronto and Winnipeg was mostly wilderness, a distance of 1,300 miles. At that time, a person traveling by car would have driven by way of Chicago.
15. "The Household of Faith," *The Alliance Weekly* (December 2, 1922): p. 606.
16. *The Alliance Weekly* (December 30, 1922): p. 652.
17. Lindsay Reynolds' history of the Alliance in Canada, *Footprints,* (Toronto: The Christian and Missionary Alliance, 1981) provides valuable information on the early days of the movement.
18. A. B. Simpson, *The Christian and Missionary Alliance Weekly* (October 27, 1906): p. 241.
19. Charles S. Morris, "Boydton Institute, Va.," *The Alliance Weekly* (January 10, 1920): p. 274.
20. The expectation that American blacks would be more effective than whites as missionaries proved disappointing for various reasons. Both black and white Americans were unable to overcome their prior prejudices and promote harmony based on equality and mutual trust.

    The situation was further complicated by colonial officials who feared that the example of black missionaries in leadership roles could give Africans troublesome ideas about running their own country.

    In some areas, Africans did not accept black American missionaries on the assumption that, being black, they lacked the educational advantages and resources available to whites.

    The 1952 General Council appointed a special committee to study the question of black missionaries. The committee's report concluded that the ban on black missionaries could "be traced directly to social customs rather than a spiritual defection" (Board of Managers Minutes, December 9, 1952). In 1955, the Board of Managers approved the foreign department's recommendation to send black missionaries to fields that would receive them. By then, however, black candidates were no longer available within Alliance ranks.
21. "Annual Report, 1928/1929," pp. 8,9.
22. William Christie, "Fuel for the Flame of Prayer and Giving," *The Alliance Weekly* (November 8, 1930): p. 727.
23. Robert B. Ekvall, ed., *After Fifty Years* (Harrisburg: Christian Publications, Inc., 1939), p. 99.
24. Lindsay Reynolds, *Footprints* (Toronto: The Christian and Missionary Alliance, 1981), p. 412.
25. "The Missionary Spirit," *The Toronto Globe* (May 11, 1931), as reported in *The Alliance Weekly* (May 30, 1931): p. 352.
26. R. Pierce Beaver, "Missionary Motivation," *Reinterpretation in American Church History,* J. C. Brauer, ed. (Chicago: University of Chicago Press, 1968), pp. 115,116.
27. Richard H. Harvey, *70 Years of Miracles* (Beaverlodge, Alberta: The Horizon House, 1975), p. 79.
28. "Annual Report, 1930/31," p. 113.
29. Ibid., p. 25.
30. In 1955 a stringent, mandatory policy of indigenous church planting was applied. Until then, there was virtually no progress. When the indigenous policy was to be enforced in 1955, it was strenuously opposed by many missionaries, including some outstanding mission leaders.

31. "Annual Report, 1928/1929," p. 24.
32. Maximum allowances excluded the housing costs which were provided, but included basic costs of living, such as electricity, water, purchase and preparation of food. This constituted 65 percent of the allowance; 35 percent covered all other needs. The mission also provided transportation to and from the field, and on the field when necessary.
33. A. W. Tozer, *Let My People Go* (Harrisburg: Christian Publications, Inc., 1947), p. 86.
34. Ibid., p. 91.
35. Ibid., p. 92.
36. Ibid., p. 106.
37. Ekvall, *After Fifty Years,* p. 24.

Chapter Eleven: Crucible of Conflict

1. Robert G. LeTourneau was a generous contributor to the Alliance. Head of a sizable industrial empire engaged in building earth-moving machines and movable oil-rig platforms, he testified to keeping only 10 percent of company profits for himself, while giving 90 percent to the Lord. He and his wife founded LeTourneau College, an engineering and technical institution that later included liberal arts, in Longview, Texas.
2. G. Verner Brown, "At the Home Base," *The Alliance Weekly* (January 2, 1937): p. 3.
3. "Twin Cities Crusade," *The Alliance Weekly* (June 5, 1937): p. 355.
4. "Annual Report, 1939/1940," The Christian and Missionary Alliance (Nyack, N.Y.: Simpson Historical Library), p. 13.
5. "Our Foreign Secretary," *The Alliance Weekly* (October 30, 1937): p. 691.
6. Since 1937, Japanese occupation of Manchuria and parts of China had disrupted particularly the Central China Mission of the Alliance. The danger increased when Japan invaded French Indo-China (now Vietnam, Laos and Cambodia) and signed a tripartite pact with Germany and Italy in 1940.
7. A. W. Tozer, *Let My People Go* (Harrisburg: Christian Publications, Inc., 1947), p. 119.
8. "Annual Report, 1941/1942," p. 96.
9. "Professions of faith" in home department annual statistical reports first appeared after Nelson left office. Baptisms were not reported. Membership, including adherents, reflected average attendances in Sunday morning services. The emphasis in General Council reports on home work expansion was in terms of extension progress and the amount raised for missions. In contrast, foreign work reports stressed conversions, churches planted, and baptized members.
10. "The Blood of the Martyrs" (New York: The Christian and Missionary Alliance, 1946), p. 13.
11. Lorna B. Grobb, "Internment in French Indo-China," *The Alliance Weekly* (January 12, 1946): p. 24.
12. *Liberated!* (New York: The Christian and Missionary Alliance, 1945), p. 7.
13. E. F. Gulbranson, "When Thou Passest Through the Waters," *The Alliance Weekly* (March 2, 1946): p. 136.
14. Tozer, *Let My People Go,* p. 121.
15. R. Mabel Francis, "When Christ Took Over My Life," *The Alliance Witness* (May 15, 1963): p. 10.
16. Mabel Francis, *One Shall Chase a Thousand* (Harrisburg: Christian Publications, Inc., 1968), p. 24.

17. Ibid., p. 71.
18. J. H. Hunter, *Adrift* (New York: Evangelical Publishers, 1943), p. 115.
19. Tozer, *Let My People Go,* p. 125.
20. Ibid., p. 119.
21. H. M. Shuman, "Our Missionary Program," *The Alliance Weekly* (May 1, 1943): p. 279.
22. A. C. Snead, "Missionary Reoccupation and Advance in 1946," *The Alliance Weekly* (March 8, 1947): p. 152.
23. Gulbranson, "When Thou Passest Through the Waters," p. 136.
24. W. H. Oldfield, "Distributing Relief in War-torn Areas," *The Alliance Weekly* (August 17, 1946): p. 520.
25. Dorothy C. Haskin, "Fifty-one Glorious Years in Japan," *The Alliance Witness* (April 19, 1961): p. 13.
26. Anita M. Bailey, "A Legend in Her Time," *The Alliance Witness* (July 30, 1975): p. 28.
27. French Indo-China became three sovereign states: Vietnam, Cambodia and Laos. The Netherlands East Indies became known as the Republic of Indonesia in 1950. This new nation included 13,000 islands eventually grouped under the Sulawesi, Java, Kalimantan, Moluccas, Bali, Sumatra, Timor and Irian Jaya.
28. Walter H. Post, "Sifted as Wheat," *The Alliance Weekly* (June 21, 1947): p. 394.
29. Some policies regarding the indigenous church:

I. Objective
"The winning of adults to Christ and establishing of churches in all places where converts are won is regarded as the primary objective of all missions."

II. The Indigenous Church

1. "We recognize the Church as God's agency through which the Holy Spirit works for the building up of believers and evangelizing of surrounding areas.
2. "We further recognize that the teaching of the New Testament indicates there should be local indigenous churches with powers of self-government and when these increase in number they should be organized into a larger body, the Conference, which should exercise authority over the local church.
3. "The spiritual leadership in the local church is not necessarily a paid pastorate, and where there is no pastor, leadership may be exercised by elders and deacons who are self-supporting.
4. "We emphasize the value of an itinerant ministry where one pastor has the oversight of several churches, all of which should contribute to his support.
5. "Every local church should be a training center for instruction in the Word of God and in spiritual ministry.
6. "In the future every church established shall be self-supporting from the beginning, but in large cities, such as provincial capitals or trading ports where property is expensive and preaching places can only be secured at considerable expenditure, this principle may have to be modified for a time.

7. "Where the policy of self-support and self-government has been neglected the Mission, although giving assistance in the meantime, shall take effective steps to change this state of affairs." Other policies of church/mission relations were also outlined in *The Alliance Weekly* (June 23, 1928): p. 403.

30. A partial report of the special committee stated: "The indigenous church will never be developed until we as a Society insist that it must be. It can never be developed until we send out missionaries who are willing to take the hard way and insist on the development of the church rather than the easy way of begging for money from America in order to pay more workers to do more preaching, to open more stations.

"Until we can clearly work together as a unit in all our fields, advanced and retarded, poor and rich, areas of much result and areas of little result, and work consistently and unitedly toward the advancement of the church, we are failing. Success of our work as an organization cannot be based on the number of foreign missionaries or the number of American dollars spent.

"We are not successful until we have baptisms, people brought from degradation into sanctification, united as a body, the Church of Christ going forward to help others into that same glorious spiritual experience. That alone is the criterion of successful missionary activity." "Annual Report, 1954/1955," pp. 264,266.

31. "Conscription and God," *Newsweek* (July 7, 1945): p. 76.
32. In 1943, the recognized schools in the Alliance were assigned specific regions to provide a firmer base of financial support and student recruitment. Western Canadian Bible Institute, established in 1941 at Regina, Saskatchewan, was recognized by the Alliance in 1945, and all the schools were organized with their own boards of directors and presidents.

In 1954, General Council recognized these schools as having equal status. Missionary candidates were no longer required to attend the Missionary Training Institute.

In 1955, the Alliance colleges included a total student enrollment of 1,226: 609 at the Missionary Training Institute, 351 at St. Paul Bible Institute, 156 at Simpson Bible College and 110 at Western Canadian Bible Institute.

Beginning with Simpson Bible College in December of 1954, all four official institutes became known as colleges by 1957.

33. A. W. Tozer, "Union or Unity," *The Alliance Weekly* (June 17, 1950): p. 371.
34. Walter Turnbull, an Alliance veteran of Dr. Simpson's day, was asked where he would put missionary radio stations. His reply was prophetic: "At least three places suggest themselves to me as possible locations. First, there is the Philippines for the masses in the Orient; then some place in South America for the millions of Spanish- and Portuguese-speaking souls; and then perhaps Palestine for the Moslem and African world." Clarence Jones, *Radio, the New Missionary* (Chicago: Moody Press, 1946), p. 19.
35. Clarence W. Hall, "The White Man Comes to Shangri-La," *Reader's Digest* (February, 1957): p. 35.

Chapter Twelve: Converging Lines

1. "Annual Report, 1959/1960," The Christian and Missionary Alliance, (Nyack, N.Y.: Simpson Historical Library), pp 27, 29, 30.
2. "Harry L. Turner," *The Alliance Witness* (August 11, 1976): p. 10.
3. Tim Stafford, "The Father of Church Growth," *Christianity Today* (February 21, 1986): p. 23.
4. Ibid., p. 21.
5. Louis L. King, "Remembrance: One Motive for Missions" (Nyack, N.Y.: Office of the President, May 10, 1978), p. 5.
6. Ibid., p. 7.
7. Louis L. King, "The Second Asia Conference" (Nyack, N.Y.: Office of the President, April 11, 1958), p. 5.
8. King, "Remembrance," p. 7.
9. Louis L. King, "The Third Asia Conference" (Nyack, N.Y.: Office of the President, September 8, 1961), p. 2.
10. Bernard S. King, "Leslie Wayne Pippert," *The Alliance Witness* (September 12, 1973): p. 6.
11. Ibid.
12. "Annual Report, 1962/1963," p. 226.
13. "Annual Report, 1965/1966," p. 14.
14. King, "Leslie Wayne Pippert," p. 6.
15. Walter O. Meloon, *Men Alive!* (Harrisburg: Christian Publications, Inc., 1982), p. 39.
16. "Annual Report, 1963/1964," p. 19.
17. A 1960 survey, with nearly 50 percent of Alliance churches responding, revealed that 1,270 Alliance young people were attending non-Alliance colleges and graduate schools. A survey of ministerial students the same year indicated they were attending eight different seminaries, but by 1968 another study revealed they were attending twenty-five such institutions. With such proliferation, the loss to the society was obviously heavy, and the development of graduate schools became a necessary investment in both the heritage and future of the Alliance. The Christian and Missionary Alliance Office of Education (Nyack, N.Y.).
18. "A World-wide Ministry," *The Alliance Witness* (July 24, 1963): p. 6.
19. Ibid.
20. Raymond McAfee, "He Fell Down to Worship," *The Alliance Witness* (July 24, 1963): p. 9.
21. Louis L. King, "First and Foremost a Preacher" (Nyack, N.Y.: The President's Office, May 30, 1986), p. 2.
22. Ibid.
23. "A World-wide Ministry," p. 6.
24. A. W. Tozer, "The Vital Place of the Church," *The Alliance Witness* (March 19, 1952): p. 178.
25. McAfee, "He Fell Down to Worship," p. 9.
26. Ibid.
27. "A World-wide Ministry," p. 6.
28. Donald A. McGavran, *Understanding Church Growth* (Grand Rapids, Mich.: William B. Eerdmans, rev. ed., 1980), p. 26.
29. "Key 73, the carefully planned national evangelistic campaign to be launched in the coming year, is supported by 140 denominations and will directly or indirectly involve 100 million Christians and nearly 250,000 parishes and congregations. It has received the official approbation of Roman Catholic bish-

ops...." Donald G. Blosch, "Key 73: Pathway to Renewal?" *Christian Century* (January 3, 1973): p. 9.

30. Barry Doyle, "Key 73: More in '74?" *Christianity Today* (November 9, 1973): p. 66.
31. "C&M Alliance Converts to Denominational Status," *Eternity* (August, 1974): p. 8.

Chapter Thirteen: This One Thing

1. In 1921 at Lake Mohonk, New York, the International Missionary Council was formed as an all-inclusive, ecumenical Protestant movement. In 1928, it sponsored its first world missionary conference in Jerusalem, where it recognized non-Christian religions as collaborating forces for the betterment of society. At the same time, it charged that in the past Christianity had allied itself with forces guilty of oppression.

   This was reinforced in 1932 by a study commission financed by the Rockefeller Foundation. The commission's report, a volume titled *Rethinking Missions,* claimed a transition from the old-school theology and traditional missionary policy to one compatible with a modern world in which God was seen as a part of different religions fulfilling divine possibilities of personal, social and cultural life. In 1958, the International Missionary Council merged with the World Council of Churches. Their programs and objectives set out in militant fashion to subvert traditional doctrines and missionary policies of the evangelical churches.

2. Nathan Bailey, "Toward an Alliance World Fellowship," *The Alliance Witness* (February 26, 1975): p. 16.
3. Article II—PURPOSE of the constitution stated the reasons for the Alliance World Fellowship:

   (1) To affirm our commitment to the Bible, God's Word, as His complete and authoritative written revelation to man.

   (2) To bear testimony to the particular truths of the Fourfold Gospel: Christ our Saviour, Sanctifier, Healer and Coming King.

   (3) To support and encourage one another in the task of Mission and Evangelism which we understand to be the special calling of the Church.

   (4) To provide opportunity and encourage expression of fellowship among members of The Alliance World Fellowship.

   (5) To provide a non-legislative means of consultation and cooperation among the world community of the member churches.

   (6) To share our mutual concerns and insights relating to the various crucial spiritual and temporal issues of the Church.

   (7) To promote ministerial and missionary education.

   (8) To uphold one another in prayer and administer relief in times of crisis.

   (9) To advance unity of theological and moral standards among the members of The Alliance World Fellowship.

   (10) To promote the exchange of personnel in special areas of ministry.

4. H. Robert Cowles, "Of One Blood All Nations," *The Alliance Witness* (July 2, 1975): p. 6.

5. Harvey Boese, "Missions Come Full Circle," *The Alliance Witness* (May 11, 1983): p. 20.
6. "Annual Report, 1977/1978," The Christian and Missionary Alliance (Nyack, N.Y.: Simpson Historical Library), pp. 249, 250.
7. "Centennial Principles and Objectives"

   We believe that the glory of God and the highest good of Alliance churches are best served by a structure in which there is a place for local churches, districts, and Headquarters to cooperate at every stage.

   We believe that a cooperative effort at all levels provides the greatest assurance of spiritual freedom and success.

   We believe there is true ingenuity in each church and district to devise the best, the most economical, the most efficient way to achieve the goals. We believe that the Headquarter's responsibility is to make sure that the people's desire as expressed in Council action is properly understood—that the necessary options are thoroughly evaluated before a plan is promulgated.

   We believe that Headquarter's role is to set the criteria, give suggestions, and help provide resources in personnel and finances to assist churches and districts to achieve the goals.

   Centennial Principles and Objectives, The Christian and Missionary Alliance (Nyack, N.Y.: Division of Church Ministries).
8. Tim Stafford, "The Father of Church Growth," *Christianity Today* (February 21, 1986): p. 23.
9. "Annual Report, 1985/1986," p. 9.
10. Louis L. King, ed., "Ministry Openings," *Open Line* (May - June, 1985): p. 2.
11. "Annual Report, 1985/1986," p 9.
12. Robert L. Niklaus, "Global Report," *Evangelical Missions Quarterly* (April, 1985): p. 173.
13. Outside help for this pilot project came from: the Division of Overseas Ministry, the LeTourneau Foundation, Bible Literature International, and the Kinderwerk Lima German Mission, as well as from churches and individuals in Peru and other nations.
14. M. Fred Polding, "Good News for Kinshasa," *The Alliance Witness* (January 21, 1981): p. 18.
15. David H. Moore, "Growing Tensions in the Alliance Concerning Missions Priority" (Nyack, N.Y.: Division of Overseas Ministries, 1982), p. 1.
16. A. B. Simpson, "Editorial," *The Christian Alliance* (October, 1889): p. 194.
17. Moore, "Growing Tensions," p. 8.
18. "Annual Report, 1980/1981," pp. 7, 16.
19. Moore, "Growing Tensions," p. 16.
20. Albert B. Simpson, *The Word, the Work and the World* (January, 1883): p. 33.
21. Albert B. Simpson, *Missionary Messages* (New York: The Christian Alliance Publishing Co., 1926), p. 19.
22. Albert B. Simpson, *Present Truth or the Supernatural* (New York: The Christian Alliance Publishing Co., 1897), pp. 72, 73.
23. Janet Fowler, "Minhsien Revisited...After 34 Years," *The Alliance Witness* (December 7, 1983): p. 10.
24. Simpson, *Present Truth,* p. 73.
25. Ibid.

Bibliography

Context of the Times

Aberly, John. *An Outline of Missions.* Philadelphia: Muhlenberg Press, 1945.

Ahlstrom, Sydney E. *A Religious History of the American People.* New Haven: Yale University Press, 1973.

Askew, Thomas A., and Peter W. Spellman. *The Churches and the American Experience.* Grand Rapids: Baker Book House, 1984.

Bruun, Geoffrey. *Nineteenth-Century European Civilization.* New York: Oxford University Press, 1960.

Cross, F. L., ed. *The Oxford Dictionary of the Christian Church.* New York: Oxford University Press, 1974.

Douglas, J. D., general ed. *The New International Dictionary of the Christian Church.* Grand Rapids: Zondervan Publishing House, 1979.

Elwell, Walter A., ed. *Evangelical Dictionary of Theology.* Grand Rapids: Baker Book House, 1984.

Haley, William, ed. *Encyclopaedia Britannica.* Chicago: William Benton, 1969.

Handy, Robert T. *A Christian America.* New York: Oxford University Press, 1981.

______. *A History of the Churches in the United States and Canada.* New York: Oxford University Press, 1977.

Hudson, Winthrop S. *Religion in America.* New York: Charles Scribner's Sons, 1973.

Hunter, James Davison. *American Evangelicalism.* New Brunswick, N.J.: Rutgers University Press, 1982.

Kane, J. Herbert. *A Concise History of the Christian World Mission.* Grand Rapids: Baker Book House, 1985.
Kincheloe, Samuel C. *Research Memorandum on Religion in the Depression.* Westport, Conn.: Greenwood Press, 1970.
Langer, William L., ed. *An Encyclopedia of World History.* Boston: Houghton Mifflin Company, 1968.
Marsden, George M. *Fundamentalism and American Culture.* New York: Oxford University Press, 1980.
Mason, Alfred DeWitt. *Outlines of Missionary History.* New York: Hodder and Stoughton, 1916.
Mulder, John M., and John F. Wilson, eds. *Religion in American History.* Englewood Cliffs, N.J.: Prentice-Hall, Inc., 1978.
Noll, Mark A., ed. et al. *Eerdmans' Handbook to Christianity in America.* Grand Rapids: William B. Eerdmans Publishing Co., 1983.
Phillips, Cabell. *The New York Times Chronicle of American Life.* London: The Macmillan Co., 1969.
Shelley, Bruce. *Church History in Plain Language.* Waco, Tex.: Word Books, 1982.
Smith, Timothy L. *Revivalism and Social Reform.* New York: Abingdon Press, 1957.
Sweet, William Warren. *The Story of Religion in America.* New York: Harper and Brothers, 1950.
Vos, Howard F. *An Introduction to Church History.* Chicago: Moody Press, 1984.

Main Text

ARTICLES

The Alliance Weekly. Articles taken from December 30, 1922; February 9, 1924.
Annual Reports. The Christian and Missionary Alliance, 1913/14;1914/15; 1916/17;1917/18;1918/19;1919/20;1920/21;1922/23;1923/24;1927/28;1928 /29;1930/31;1939/40;1941/42;1954/55;1959/60;1962/63;1963/64;1965/66; 1977/78;1980/81;1985/86.
Bailey, Anita M. "A Legend in Her Time." *The Alliance Witness* (July 30, 1975).
Bailey, Nathan. "God Shaped His Life." *The Alliance Weekly* (March 29, 1967).
______. "Toward an Alliance World Fellowship." *The Alliance Witness* (February 26, 1975).

Blosch, Donald G. "Key 73: Pathway to Renewal?" *Christian Century* (January 3, 1973).

Boese, Harvey. "Missions Come Full Circle." *The Alliance Witness* (May 11, 1983).

Brown, G. Verner. "At the Home Base." *The Alliance Weekly* (January 2, 1937).

Buckman, Margaret Simpson. "The Hymns of Dr. Simpson." *Nyack Missionarian* (1945).

"C & M Alliance Converts to Denominational Status." *Eternity* (August 1974).

Christian and Missionary Alliance, Division of Church Ministries. "Centennial Principles and Objectives."

Christian and Missionary Alliance Weekly. Articles taken from June 1905; March 31, 1906; April 21, 1906; May 19, 1906; November 1906; January 1907; February 1907; July 1907.

Christie, William. "Fuel for the Flame of Prayer and Giving." *The Alliance Weekly* (November 8, 1930).

Cowles, H. Robert. "Of One Blood All Nations." *The Alliance Witness* (July 2, 1975).

Doyle, Barry. "Key 73: More in '74?" *Christianity Today* (November 9, 1973).

"Dr. Simpson Gets $70,000." *Baltimore Sun* (August 8, 1897).

Editorial Committee. "Editorial." *The Alliance Weekly* (July 2, 1921).

Fant, David J. "Early Associates of Dr. Simpson." *Southeastern District Report* (January/February 1974; May 1977).

______. "Robert A. Jaffray." *The Alliance Witness* (December 5, 1973).

Fowler, Janet. "Minhsien Revisited . . . After 34 Years." *The Alliance Witness* (December 7, 1983).

Francis, R. Mabel. "When Christ Took Over My Life." *The Alliance Witness* (May 15, 1963).

Grobb, Lorna B. "Internment in French Indo-China." *The Alliance Weekly* (January 12, 1946).

Gulbranson, E. F. "When Thou Passest Through the Waters." *The Alliance Weekly* (March 2, 1946).

Hall, Clarence W. "The White Man Comes to Shangra-La." *The Reader's Digest* (February 1957).

Hamilton Evening Times (September 13, 1805).

Hamilton Spectator (July 27, 1805; December 15, 1875).

"Harry L. Turner." *The Alliance Witness* (August 11, 1976).

Haskin, Dorothy C. "Fifty-one Glorious Years in Japan." *The Alliance Witness* (April 19, 1961).

"The Home-Going of Rev. F. H. Senft." *The Alliance Weekly* (December 12, 1925).
"The Household of Faith." *The Alliance Weekly* (December 2, 1922).
Jaderquist, John E. Personal Correspondence (November 1920).
King, Bernard S. "Leslie Wayne Pippert." *The Alliance Witness* (September 12, 1973).
King, Louis L. "The Second Asia Conference." President's Office (April 11, 1958).
______. "Dr. Alfred Cookman Snead." *The Alliance Witness* (April 5, 1961).
______. "The Third Asia Conference." President's Office (September 8, 1961).
______. "Remembrance: One Motive for Missions." President's Office (May 10, 1978).
______. "Ministry Openings." *Open Line* (May/June 1985).
______. "First and Foremost a Preacher." President's Office (May 30, 1986).
Louisville Courier Journal (February 1875; March 1875).
McAfee, Raymond. "He Fell Down to Worship." *The Alliance Witness* (July 24, 1963).
"Minutes of Board of Managers." The Christian and Missionary Alliance, May 30, 1914; May 15, 1918.
"The Missionary Spirit." *The Alliance Weekly* (May 30, 1931).
Moore, David H. "Growing Tensions in the Alliance Concerning Missions Priority." C&MA Division of Overseas Ministries, 1982.
Morris, Charles S. "Boydton Institute, Va." *The Alliance Weekly* (January 10, 1920).
Moseley, Thomas. "William Christie-the Livingstone of Northeast Tibet." *The Alliance Weekly* (February 16, 1955).
Newsweek (July 7, 1945).
Niklaus, Robert L. "Global Report." *Evangelical Missions Quarterly* (April 1985).
"Notes from the Home Field." *The Christian and Missionary Alliance Weekly* (April 27, 1907).
Oldfield, W. H. "Distributing Relief in War-torn Areas." *The Alliance Weekly* (August 17, 1946).
"Old Orchard Convention Supplement." *The Word, the Work and the World* (July/August 1887).
"Our Foreign Secretary." *The Alliance Weekly* (October 30, 1937).
The Pioneer. C&MA Indonesia Mission (January 1946).
Polding, M. Fred. "Good News for Kinshasa." *The Alliance Witness* (January 21, 1981).

Post, Walter H. "Sifted as Wheat." *The Alliance Weekly* (June 21, 1947).

Rader, Paul. Letter to Board of Managers (April 3, 1919).

Richards, E. J. "Development of the Home Work." *The Alliance Weekly* (December 20, 1919).

Shuman, Harry M. "Our Missionary Program." *The Alliance Weekly* (May 1, 1943).

______. "The Modern 'Deeper Life' Is Not Deep Enough." *The Alliance Weekly* (May 16, 1956).

______. "A God-Touched Man." *The Alliance Weekly* (May 1, 1957).

______. "God Shaped My Life." *The Alliance Weekly* (September 1, 1965).

Simpson, A. B. "Editorial." *The Gospel in All Lands* (February, July, and August 1880).

______. "Editorial." *The Gospel in All Lands* (July and September 1881).

______. *The Word, the Work and the World* (August and November 1882).

______. *The Word, the Work and the World* (March, April, July, and October 1883).

______. "What God Is Doing in Our Age." *The Word, the Work and the World* (August 1885).

______. "Editorial." *The Word, the Work and the World* (May, June, August, and September 1887).

______. "Report of Old Orchard Beach, Me." (July 31-August 9, 1887).

______. *The Word, the Work and the World* (May, June, August, September 1887).

______. *Christian Alliance* (January 1888).

______. "Editorial." *The Christian and Missionary Alliance Weekly* (October 1889).

______. *Christian Alliance and Missionary Weekly* (March, May, June, August and November 1890).

______. *Christian Alliance and Missionary Weekly* (July and August 1891; September 18, 1891; October 16, 1891).

______. "The Missionary Institute." *The Christian and Missionary Alliance Weekly* (April 6, 1897).

______. "The Last Message from Our Swedish Missionaries." *The Christian and Missionary Alliance Weekly* (January 19, 1901).

______. "Baptism and the Baptism of the Holy Spirit." *The Christian and Missionary Alliance* (May 1902).

______. "Why Our People Give So Much for Missions." *Living Truths* (November 1905).

______. "Editorial." *The Christian and Missionary Alliance Weekly* (October 27, 1906; November 17, 1906).
______. "Editorial." *The Christian and Missionary Alliance Weekly* (March 1907).
______. "Farther On." *The Christian and Missionary Alliance Weekly* (September 1907).
______. "A Story of Providence." *Living Truths* (March 1907).
______. "Editorial." *The Christian and Missionary Alliance Weekly* (April 1910).
______. "My Medicine Chest." *The Alliance Weekly* (October 1913).
______. *The Alliance Weekly* (June 1914).
______. "A Personal Testimony." *The Alliance Weekly* (October 1915).
Smith, Oswald. *The Prophet.* Quoted in *The Alliance Weekly* (February 9, 1924).
Snead, A. C. "Missionary Reoccupation and Advance in 1946." *The Alliance Weekly* (March 8, 1947).
Stafford, Tim. "The Father of Church Growth." *Christianity Today* (February 21, 1986).
Stephens, May Agnew. "Dr. Simpson's Ministry in Song." *The Alliance Weekly* (December 20, 1919).
Tozer, A. W. "Union or Unity." *The Alliance Weekly* (June 17, 1950).
______. "The Vital Place of the Church." *The Alliance Witness* (March 19, 1952).
Turnbull, Walter. "Editorial." *The Alliance Weekly* (November 8, 1919).
"Twin Cities Crusade." *The Alliance Weekly* (June 5, 1937).
"Where We Stand." *The Alliance Witness* (May 1, 1963).
"A World-wide Ministry." *The Alliance Witness* (July 24, 1963).

BOOKS

Beaver, R. Pierce. "Missionary Motivation." *Reinterpretation in American Church History.* Chicago: University of Chicago Press, 1968.
Blackstone, W. E. *Jesus Is Coming.* New York: Fleming H. Revell Co., 1908.
Brennen, Katherine Alberta. *Love Stands.* N.p., n.d.
The Cleveland Coloured Gospel Quintette. Kilmarnock, Scotland: John Ritchie, Ltd., 1937.
Ekvall, Robert B., ed. *After Fifty Years.* Harrisburg: Christian Publications, Inc., 1939.

Evangeline, Hope. *Daisy.* Grand Rapids: Baker Book House, 1978.
Francis, Mabel, with Gerald B. Smith. *One Shall Chase a Thousand.* Harrisburg: Christian Publications, Inc., 1968.
Harvey, Richard H. *70 Years of Miracles.* Beaverlodge, Alta.: Horizon House, 1975.
Hunter, J. H. *Adrift.* Toronto: Evangelical Publishers, 1943.
______. *Beside All Waters.* Harrisburg: Christian Publications, Inc., 1964
Jones, Clarence. *Radio, the New Missionary.* Chicago: Moody Press, 1946.
Locke, J. Staples. *Historical Sketches of Old Orchard.* Boston: n.p., n.d.
MacArthur, William T. *Twenty Sermonettes.* N.p., n.d.
McGavran, Donald A. *Understanding Church Growth.* Grand Rapids: Wm. B. Eerdmans Publishing Co., revised edition, 1980.
Marsden, George M. *Fundamentalism and American Culture.* New York: Oxford University Press, 1980.
Meloon, Walter O. *Men Alive!* Harrisburg: Christian Publications, Inc., 1982.
Menzies, William W. *Anointed to Serve.* Springfield: Gospel Publishing House, 1971.
______. *Moody Church Story.* N.p., n.d.
The New Schaff-Herzog Encyclopedia of Religious Knowledge, Vol. 7. Grand Rapids: Baker Book House, reprinted, 1977.
Niklaus, Robert L. *The School That Vision Built.* Nyack, N.Y.: Nyack College, 1982.
Pardington, George P. *The Crooked Made Straight.* N.p., n.d.
______. *Twenty-five Wonderful Years.* New York: Christian Alliance Publishing Co., 1914.
Reynolds, Lindsay. *Footprints.* Toronto: The Christian and Missionary Alliance in Canada, 1981.
Rivard, Eugene. *Alliance History of Music.* N.p., n.d.
Simpson, A. B. *Diary.* N.p., n.d.
______. *The Fulness of Jesus.* New York: The Christian Alliance Publishing Co., 1890.
______. *The Gospel of Healing.* New York: The Alliance Press Co., 1890.
______. *The King's Business.* The Word, the Work and the World Publishing Co., 1886.
______. *A Larger Christian Life.* New York: Christian Alliance Publishing Co., 1890.
______. *Missionary Messages.* New York: The Christian Alliance Publishing Co., 1925.

______. *Present Truth or the Supernatural.* New York: The Christian Alliance Publishing Co., 1897.
______. *Wholly Sanctified.* Harrisburg: Christian Publications, Inc., 1982 edition.
Smith, Oswald. *Can Organized Religion Survive?* Toronto: Toronto Publishers, 1932.
______. *The Story of My Life.* London: Marshall, Morgan and Scott, 1961.
Thompson, A. E. *The Life of A. B. Simpson.* New York: The Christian Alliance Publishing Co., 1920.
Tinkham, Mary Gray. "Recollections." N.p., n.d.
Tozer, A. W. *Let My People Go.* Harrisburg: Christian Publications, Inc., 1947.
______. *Wingspread.* Harrisburg: Christian Publications, Inc., 1943.
Tucker, Leon. *The Redemption of Paul Rader.* New York: The Book Stall, second edition, 1918.
Van Dyck, Howard. *William Christie, Apostle to Tibet.* Harrisburg: Christian Publications, Inc., 1956.
Wilson, Madele, and A. B. Simpson. *Henry Wilson, One of God's Best.* New York: The Alliance Press, 1908.

PAMPHLETS

"The Blood of the Martyrs." New York: C&MA, 1946.
"For Courage and Fortitude." New York: C&MA, 1945.
"Liberated!" New York: C&MA, 1945.
Simpson, A. B. "Decision for Christ." New York: C&MA, 1911.
Simpson, A. B. "Reasons for the Alliance." April 1888.

Index